The Reality of my Life

(Help I'm not me)

By
Carol Royce

authorHOUSE®

AuthorHouse™ UK Ltd.
500 Avebury Boulevard
Central Milton Keynes, MK9 2BE
www.authorhouse.co.uk
Phone: 08001974150

© 2010 Carol Royce. All rights reserved.

No part of this book may be reproduced, stored in a retrieval system, or transmitted by any means without the written permission of the author.

First published by AuthorHouse 3/1/2010

ISBN: 978-1-4490-8602-2 (sc)

This book is printed on acid-free paper.

Contents

Introduction	vii
Chapter One	1
Chapter two	8
Chapter three	17
Chapter 4	23
Chapter Five	54
Chapter Six	66
Chapter Seven	75
Chapter Eight	81
Chapter-Nine	88
Chapter-Ten	95
Chapter Eleven	99
Chapter Twelve	110
Chapter Thirteen	121
Chapter Fourteen	128
Chapter fifteen	135
Chapter Sixteen	143
Chapter Seventeen	152
Chapter Seventeen	158
Chapter Eighteen	183

Chapter Nineteen	202
Chapter Twenty	212
Chapter Twenty-one	221
Chapter Twenty-two	234
Chapter Twenty-three	249
Chapter Twenty-four	255
Chapter Twenty-five	266
Chapter Twenty-six	272
Chapter Twenty- seven	283
Chapter twenty - eight	287
Bibliography	290
About the Author	295

Introduction

The names used in this book have been changed to protect their identity.

What do you do when you know you're different from other people in a way that causes some of them to avoid or even hurt you? You want to fit in with everyone else, but your body shape, a birth mark, some lines or spots on your face, how you look by the way you walk, talk, and do everyday things, stands out. The fact about you that stands out is generally seen as weird, awkward, not the norm - leading many to think that, at best, you're something to be pitied, at worst, a freak to be avoided or got rid of in case your weirdness rubs off on them. I was one of those who stood out. My difference began on the inside.

I had always felt uncomfortable with my male body. As far back as I can remember, I had thought of myself as female. Before becoming my true self I was labelled 'gender dysphoric' or 'transsexual'. Transsexual is a term we can make simpler by breaking it down into two parts: 'trans' means 'cross'; 'sexual' means 'gender'; 'gender' means 'the state of being male or female.' So, transsexuals are people, male or female, who are convinced they're trapped in the wrong sex. They have bodies that don't fit the sex they feel they are.

I hate the word 'transsexual'. For me, it's an ugly, male word that sounds like a juggernaut rolling across the Australian outback. I prefer 'gender dysphoric' which is the psychiatrists' term for my former condition and, 'Trans-male/female' and 'transgendered' are also used to describe it - all better than 'transsexual'. Another term, 'trans-person' refers to something a little more complicated.

As a sufferer of gender dysphoria, I lived its contradictions.I was born male: at least, that's what the delivery team who helped bring me into the world decided. Looking back, I believe I knew as early as three or four years old there was something wrong with me: the way I was made and the way I felt just didn't go together. My feelings of unhappiness followed, made worse by the grief I got from people. Although there were positive influences around me such as my loving family, life worked against me moulding me into an angry young person. I was on a setting to self-destruct.

There are people all over the world now as I used to be, probably represented by someone of every profession. This condition isn't limited to people who were once very active and competitive who are now professionally burnt-out and unsuccessful, as some critics would have you believe. Transsexuals are still not seen in the right light by many of the rule makers and judges of human behaviour in our society, but who have power over us. There are always those moralists who come from different backgrounds, including some religious people who won't even listen to my point of view, and sometimes, I'm sorry to say, neighbours and so-called friends who reject anyone who is different.

With this book, I want to encourage acceptance of those who are suffering because they're different. We can accept these sufferers as they are and try to step into their shoes emotionally, to get a sense of the pain they're feeling.

I'm telling the story of my search for my ***real self*** in the hope that it helps other people. To begin with, I wouldn't admit to anyone I had a problem. Who I was in those dark, early days was this confused person swinging between doubt and certainty. At a conscious level, I was hiding what I saw then as the social stigma that went with my condition. I didn't want to be different from anyone else. I tried to be who I thought the world wanted me to be. It didn't work. The cracks began to show. To survive I destroyed the love of those closest to me and to my partner and children most of all, I was deceitful. I didn't care about anyone but myself. Everything I did was selfish and irresponsible. It reached a stage where my one and only goal was to be female and anything that got in the way of this was kicked to one side.

You'll see I was angry with everything. Even today, the thought of how I hurt people, particularly my partner and children, shocks me. If there is one thing this story shows, it is how easy it was for me to mess up my life and my family's as well. Within the framework of my life story I want to explain to you why I lived the way I did. I expect many of you will find my experiences hard to understand. They're here inside me now and always will be; they will never leave me. I want to share them with you so that I may help as many people as possible to understand.

People who are unhappy with their biological gender should feel they can see a doctor who, if need be will arrange an appointment for them to attend a gender clinic. It is important that when a person's difference from others could lead them to be socially rejected they are at least treated with compassion and if possible, empathy, their difference seen as something that happens to some people which shouldn't take anything away from their value to the world and is what makes them unique as human beings. Only recently, I've heard these terms used to describe people who are stuck with a body that doesn't fit how they see themselves. 'Trans-man' or 'trans-woman' and 'trans-person' at least hint at transsexualism being more human and acceptable than it is portrayed. I can't say I like them a lot but I am more comfortable with being called a 'trans-woman' than a 'transsexual'. Of course I want to be called a woman, full-stop.

An umbrella term for 'transsexualism' or 'gender dysphoria' is 'gender identity disorder'.

'Trans-person' is an odd term. As I understand it, a trans-person is someone who lives their life gender free. They don't recognise the distinction of male and female. I can't see how anyone can escape being conditioned into our society's bi-polarised gender system. Surely there has to be something like a gendered society to help us make sense of our lives? It's hard to imagine how we'd survive as a species without that starting point of the difference between male and female to form the basis of our identities and to shape and guide our behaviour.

Why do I think people should read this book? To start with, it brings the debate on gender dysphoria into the present. It also describes the reality of the condition in detail. Finally, it shows how important it is to value the uniqueness of every human being.

This condition is now being seen as a real problem

for the sufferer. Hospitals now treat individuals with compassion, from the psychiatric doctors to hospital consultant doctors. The help that can be offered today is huge to what it was when I was young. All the people concerned today at least have some knowledge of the condition and deal with it in the proper manner. The days of being called a pervert have gone at least by most of the people. How we are seen by the public is still a mystery you don't see so much in the media like you used to, say a decade ago. We still have to deal with the deluded person who are seeking money for being messed up by the medical help they receive from those that are trying to help them. The trouble is it is easy to say what you want in a convincing way to psychiatrists, then blaming them when you find you have made a mistake. The grass is not greener on the other side despite what you might think.

This book is only about me it's not how things are done correctly in to-days world. The medical help is very good.

Chapter One

My fate was, as some would say set, it was going to happen no matter what I had decided to do that day. It was late afternoon and I was thinking of going out that evening with some friends.I had nearly got through the day when the event that set the course for the rest of my life happened ......B .... ang!!!!!!!

All hell broke loose. The flashing lights of ambulances, fire engines and police cars became part of the chaos. Loud sirens sounded together like a bad orchestra, gate - crashing my confused thoughts. I was not sure whether the strobing was coming from - emergency vehicles or had I started hallucinating?My instinct was to put out the fire but in my semi- conscious state the blaze of light and noise blocked my mind.

At the time I was running a business refurbishing petrol service stations across the country. One of my responsibilities in this role was to supervise the cleaning out of the petrol tanks. This often required me to go down into these tanks and check they had been cleaned out properly.On that defining day in the summer of 1984, I was inspecting the inside of one at a garage in Pin Green, Stevenage, and Hertfordshire.Eight feet down, in a dark, claustrophobic space, I was talking to one of my men.He was standing above me on the surface looking into the manhole through which I had entered the tank.Somehow, the man accidentally kicked my stilsons which were laying at the edge of the manhole down into the petrol tank, they hit the strike plate which is welded on the floor of the tank which is located directly beneath the manhole. Sparks shot off the strike plate igniting the vapour in the tank. An explosion knocked my employee away from the manhole and miraculously blew me out of it. There was a vivid flash and extreme heat. A massive rush of hot, pressurised air propelled me to the surface. The whole of Stevenage was momentarily lit with an intense, orange glow. The explosion had set off all the other manholes igniting the residue left in the tank tops. With most of my clothes burnt off, I staggered back to the manhole instinctively going through the motions of my usual "I can cope". I was aware of the smell of my flesh and hair burning … then I collapsed. My appearance was as if somebody had put a polythene bag over my head and set light to it. All the sounds around me had become sub-aural. I had stepped out of real time into a world operating in slow motion.

The heat flash had penetrated the hard shell that had formed around me. Its effects spread over the rest of my body leaving a pain that would not let go, making me struggle for breath. Even my throat had been caught. The tender, scalded flesh of my arms cried out to be swabbed gently by caring hands.

On my arrival at the burns unit of Billericay hospital in Essex, staff had to cut off my overalls which had melted on to me. A watery fluid leaked from my burns. Compulsory salt baths chafed my sensitive skin and every time I moved it was agony.

I had to spend about eight weeks in hospital doing very little. This gave me the chance to think about my life. Realising that I had been close to death, I asked myself why in the past I had not been concerned for my own safety. Before having the accident I had always been reckless. Often doing dangerous things like driving over the speed limit and/or under the influence of alcohol, it never occurred to me that if I did not learn to control these impulses I could end up being responsible for someone's death. In that hospital bed, l saw that I had had many chances. There had to be a better way for me to live.I cared now.

I was thirty-three when the accident happened. It brought me to the conclusion that I had wasted those thirty-three years and hurt so many people along the way.The person I felt I had hurt the most was my partner, Jackie. By that time, we had a child.My daughter Sophie was very upset over what I looked like as a result of the accident.The terrible sight and sound of my own child screaming at me was repeated each time I came home from hospital after having had my bandages changed.There were days when she wouldn't come near me. I desperately wanted to pick her up to reassure her that the bandages were there to help me get better. I tried to cuddle her even that was painful due to my weak physical condition.My injuries upset my partner and my daughter more than they did me. It was their response to my condition which had such an emotional effect on me.

Before the accident, I found it easy to make money. I had a good income that was not damaged by the recession gripping the country at that time. Although I ran a successful business, on my own admission it was primarily to finance *my* life, not my Partner's or our

Children's. My life was a long way from the cosy suburbia with which many people appear to be happy. Paying the household expenses was a token of my fulfilment of my responsibility to my family, but most of the money went on *my perversion*, as my partner put it. I did what I thought was right at the time. By continuing to support my family, I had a clearer conscience.

My partner, my children, and other's who had a strong influence in my life, and me, all played 'let's pretend'. I had been good at that game all my life. I was an expert at it and I carried on playing it into my late thirties. *Naive* is too kind a word to describe what I did. *Stupid* is the only way to describe it.

I used my male role to feed my female life. This carried on until 1993 when I managed to seek help for my gender dysphoria. In 1984, at the moment of the blast, I was partially shaken free of my unreal self which made me aware of what I could be - what I had to be - my real self. My mind said: "STOP THIS - BE YOU!" You have to accept and explore your real inner self to be able to find and express your real outer self. You can't spend a lifetime being unreal without trouble somewhere along the line. For me, my recovery in hospital and later, at home, was spent getting rid of an arrogant ego that one might think of as a snake shedding its outer skin.

Having survived the blast, perhaps hardened and tempered by it, I now had more than enough time during my convalescence, to reflect on my life. The shocking reality of my true gender identity hit me. My struggle began in my mother's womb. By all appearances, I was born a male in Central Middlesex Hospital, Park Royal, near Greenford, at 7.45 a.m. on 2nd November, 1950.

My life was almost like any other child's who grew

up in the fifties. I wanted for nothing. My mum and Dad didn't have much but they coped. Dad earned very little. Mum looked after me and my twin brother. It was hard for them both as Dad was in the army in the Tank Corps and in those early days we used to share with my Nan who was my Mum's Mum. Friction was common in the cramped conditions we lived in. My Nan was something else where my mum was concerned. The pair of them where always arguing. Nan seemed to pick on Mum a lot. At the same time, even at that stage, my problem was coming out in my behaviour. Being so young I didn't know how to deal with it.

I used to like visiting the canal near my Nan's home. It ran behind the whole length of the Bath works, including the Aladdin light bulb factory, spanning many miles to Greenford station.My Auntie Pat used to take me and my brother for walks along the canal path. She was always taking us for walks for the scenery and because she liked walking. We found our own route which began the same as Auntie Pat's then changed course as our built-in radar picked up and led us to whatever trouble was going on at the time.

If the sun was shining and it was hot, the water seemed clearer, purer, more real, and I wanted to touch it. Its cool, soothing surface invited me to jump in and be part of it, but I was worried that if I did I would catch something. Had I jumped in I probably wouldn't have drowned. I would have been the one who survived and caught Weil's disease or got poisoned by industrial waste

The canal was a health hazard. It flowed behind an iron foundry which was converted to an ammunitions factory during the war where my Nan used to do 'bogey picking', as she called it. Bogey picking was something to do with assembling munitions for the war effort, my Mum told me. The muck that came out of that factory over the years and found its way into the river was why the canal, which was a lifeline to all the factories in the area, should have had warning signs with skulls and crossbones painted on them, placed at regular intervals along the bank. Today, the horses with their mainly female riders, bounce gentle rhythms along the bridle path that runs parallel to the canal.

People often talk about how close they were to their Grandparents. I remembered my Grandfather Simmons with particular fondness, and how on one occasion whilst I was sitting on his knee he offered me simple but much needed words of comfort in a volatile household. "Everything will be all right. It will all sort itself out" he said to me, shortly before he died. It was as if he knew something about me that the others didn't. I remember carrying the large tin of Hack sweets we both liked over to him. He would give me one, take another for himself, and together we would enjoy that hot menthol rush. I think Granddad was addicted to them. From what I've been told, he nearly turned me into a Hack sweet addict.

Grandfather Simmons died in the year 1953 when I was two. He was seventy-three. My grandmother Simmons lived until she was ninety-two. My Mum knew what it meant to be part of a large, close family. Through wartime conditions Nan has acquired a habit of bartering.My Mum's stepbrother came out of a brief flirt Nan had that was long enough for her to conceive him. Her bartering instinct went too far that time. She often used me as a runner, frequently sending me off to the old corner shop to swap eggs from the chickens she kept that were often running round her house and garden, or sitting on her dining room table or in her pantry. She was a mistress of survival through bartering. In today's EU climate my Nan's poor hygiene would have had her put away for life as a danger to public health. Whenever she was cooking, she would lean over the stove with a fag that was more ash than cigarette in her mouth.

God knows where the ash ended up.
My dad's sister Midge married my Mum's brother, Pete. Everyone knew my Uncle Pete who I adored, was ill, except me. No one bothered to tell me and

Another thing that happened when I was older was my uncle Pete died without me knowing I was so hurt by that I have not seen certain members of my family since. When Pete died in 1995, he was one of the few people over whom I have ever cried. Breaking down at his funeral I realised my tough outer shell was very vulnerable.

As my Dad's sister married my Mum's brother, you might say there was no real Dad's or Mum's side of the family. In a church congregation, we'd all scramble together on the same side of the aisle then have to unscramble again and spread ourselves across both sides to make the church look fuller. We all thought of ourselves as one family Murphy and Simmons.

My Mum and Dad were both in their early twenties when my twin brother and I were born. They lived in Germany, first in Dusseldorf, then later in Hamburg. My Dad left the army in 1958 and the family found themselves entering a new phase.

Chapter two

From the age of four, this boy I thought I was, started to become this boy I was trying not to be. Somehow, being a boy began to feel uncomfortable. It was like I was left-handed but having to use my right hand all the time. My twin brother, Michael, who was fifteen minutes older than me, seemed comfortable being a boy. Although we were twins, I don't think my brother and I were very much alike. I'd even go as far as to say we were total opposites.

When I was seven, we moved from Nan's house to our own house in Essex. It was exciting moving from London to the country with all that open space.

In my childhood, the place was ideal for me. I can remember going for long walks that would last for hours. I'd often cut across these little streams in my Wellington boots. In a sense, I suppose I was finding myself. The house we moved into was new at the time. It was on a small housing estate surrounded by fields. Sadly, most of those fields were swallowed and digested by the London overspill. Mum and Dad still live in the same house.

The playing fields and allotments behind them barely remain, but from every other angle they're faced with an ever increasing sprawl of concrete and cars. Now, the estate has all but turned into a giant car park where finding a parking space is a common cause of grief.

In my childhood the place was ideal for me. I was always going missing, the hours eaten up walking to Epping and back on my own. Rambling through Epping Forest was pure freedom.My private adventures were untouched by fear. Time meant nothing to me in my comfortable world of innocent dreams. When I became aware of time again, I had to step out of my world and go home. I was always sad to leave what I had there. Being on my own lifted the pressure a little. Out there, I didn't have to prove myself to anyone. I would put off going home as long as I could. As soon as I got back, I had to slot into this role that I hated. My return was usually met by the words: "Where the hell have you been?" from Mum. I'd be rude to her, get a slap for it and be sent to bed.

Temporary confinement to my room was not an effective punishment and I soon got over its effects. The fields near our house were rich with nature and it was from this source I found my temporary soul mate who would keep me company whenever I was grounded. A shoe box under my bed was home to a friend I valued almost as much as my solitude. To me, he looked like a grass snake. Sometimes he would lie on my bed curled up, eyeballing me adoringly, showing me his sliver of a tongue darting in and out of his mouth, tasting the air. Occasionally, he would lie on my stomach. When he got fed up with me, he might go for a slither round my room. Reliable to the end, he always came back to me and the comfort of his shoebox.

Several months later we had a nature lesson at school. Our teacher asked us whether we had any unusual pets at home. By unusual pets, he meant ferrets, rats, and so on. Boring old ferrets and rats weren't the types of pet found in my possession. I had something that ate them. Putting my hand up I told our class that I had a grass snake and a feeling of extreme pride flushed through me when I was asked by our teacher to bring it to school.

Armed with the shoebox – 'armed' was the right word as it turned out. The next day I brought my pride and joy to show my class. Our teacher slowly removed the lid of the shoebox, then with a look of deep concern on his face, peered inside. Moby showed his head. To me, he was being friendly, that tongue of his going in and out at full throttle. The whole class fell silent through our teacher's shock at what was nestling in the box. Moby popped his head through a convenient hole between the slowly lifting lid and the box itself. Suddenly, our teacher broke the silence roaring: "This isn't a grass snake. It's a bloody adder!"

Having thought how cute my snake was with his distinctive markings, it did occur to me that he had a couple of fangs he might use during one of his more antisocial moments. Desperately pushing the lid of the box back down, our teacher secured it and removed it from the classroom. He then arranged for the RSPCA to come and pick it up.

As far as I know, Moby spent the rest of his days in the reptile house at the kid's pets corner zoo in Harlow Park. All the time I had him he never appeared nervous in my company or showed any hostility towards me. Adders are venomous snakes, yet I was never bitten by Moby. As I was the provider of his food and housing, maybe he let me off? I thought he was rather like me actually: unusual, and that's probably why in my naive, child-like mind, I saw us both as two pals that got on really well.

If I hadn't been grounded by Mum and Dad, I'd go out again the next day staying outer hours, and be late back. Lying to Mum about where I had been became a regular thing with me. To avoid punishment, I'd tell her I was at a friend's house.

Although I tried not to show it, my attitude was one of contempt for everyone except those I really cared for. Mum having two more boys didn't help and as time passed I vented my anger on all of my brothers. When I was out walking, deep in my own world, I used to think: "How dare my Mum have more boys. I want a sister."

It is easy for me to assume that the sister I wanted would have been someone I could have confided in. An understanding sister might have helped me. To be honest, I felt angry that I couldn't tell Mum and Dad how I felt inside. I remember looking at Mum and thinking: "If anyone should know what's wrong with me, you should."

I hid the real me from the eyes of the world. On the outside, I was a little boy. On the inside, I was my real self, who happened to be a little girl. People misread the signals I gave out, which were already wrong. I wanted everyone to see me as tough and street-wise. They saw me as this nasty, aggressive kid. My aim was to show them I was just a normal boy, which is what I thought they wanted me to be. This caused me to push the little "girl" who I believed to be my real inner self further down inside me, but she wouldn't be silenced and this complicated my life. I was an incomplete jigsaw, the remaining pieces of which I couldn't find anywhere.

Looking back I realise how extremely stressful my life had become.

My Dad would put boxing gloves on me and my brother and spar with us on the lawn in the back garden. Sometimes he would clobber me, probably because I was being a bit rough, and it really hurt. I'd take it, but I'd cry on the inside. I had to be seen as this tough young kid who never cried. As far as I was concerned, being sensitive was weak, so I didn't show my emotions. All mixed up and unable to talk to my Mum and Dad about it, whatever it was, the tension within me continued to build.

Now, I appreciate that my Mum was having problems of her own at that time. Having four children, all demanding her attention eventually made her ill. In those days depression was not dealt with properly. Today it's recognised as a genuine illness so there's less stigma attached to it. Poor mum had to get on with it. I remember thinking how tough she was.

Today, my Mum and I are very much alike. We're both a lot calmer than we were. Back then, it took a lot to make her angry, but God help anybody who pushed her too far. Like her, I'd explode. No matter who was on the receiving end of it I'd have to let my anger out, then it would be over.

As my brothers and I grew up, things must have got better for Mum. She came out the other side all right. As children, you don't understand what's happening to your parents. They are just there. Quoting her almost word for word, my Mum told me: "Once the children start growing up you get out of that cloud and appreciate your family".

I'm glad my Mum and Dad are my Mum and Dad. They're good parents who are still there for us today.

Although I believed I should try to be this boy, sometimes it felt right for me to go my own way, which amongst other things was to play with dolls. I loved the idea of dressing-up I would hang round mum's leg watching her put her make-up on. To me that was natural.

To the world, I was a boy, so Mum dressed me in boys' clothes. Once dressed, I'd take all these clothes off and walk round the house in my underpants.

Everything in my life was against what felt natural to me. As a child, picking up a toy car rather than a doll was part of my act. I had to be seen behaving like a normal boy. Inside I was saying: "I wish I could play with dolls".

Michael ended up with all my stuff. He'd happily lie on the sitting- room floor at home with the soldiers, forts, and boys' toys belonging to us, whilst I would be out on my own somewhere exploring. If I played with boys' toys, it would be because the boys in the playground were my friends and the only way I could play with them was to have a prop to hand like a Dinky truck.

As for Michael, he was just there. I don't mean that unkindly. I was his protector. When he was around me I looked out for him. He didn't look out for me. I know this sound's like a cliché but it's true that I almost always knew when he was in trouble:I spent a large part of my childhood helping him out of some sort of grief or another. ***Life is grief. I've lived it,*** and although the events I'm focusing on are in the past they feel so present; ***so now***.

People were always picking on Michael because he was quiet. The bullies of the school used to zoom in on him as if his bright orange tee-shirt had "Victim - walk all over me, please!" stamped across it.

The bullies were cowards in disguise, feeding off the weak and vulnerable. Their self-esteem was probably quite low too until they'd done over a few victims. "Don't get me wrong. Michael wasn't weak. He was sensitive. He would handle grief in his own quiet way which was all right for him but not for me. I'd have to jump in and take control. He was my brother. There was no way I'd let anybody hurt him. Any time I baled him out of trouble, he'd say: "What did you do that for?" meaning: "Why did you have to interfere? I was dealing with it".

I remember an incident that happened when I was about fourteen concerning someone who upset Michael. This boy pushed Michael while we were messing around in the cricket pavilion near our home. He was a clinically obese wind-up artist who tried to control others. His role was self-appointed leader of our gang. Most kids just let him get on with it because they didn't fancy colliding with him or ending up underneath him if they disobeyed. He didn't want Michael to have a say in what we should all do. I was standing at the back of this group listening to its so-called leader rant, blinked, and found myself at the front. He had pushed my brother. For that, I was going to block his next move and push him to the ground.I got him in a headlock which he soon found his way out of.We had a fist fight that wasn't really a fist fight because we spent the whole thirty seconds it lasted successfully dodging each other's punches; it looked more like we were dancing - very badly. Seeing his chance, he made for the big old oak tree that stood in the middle of the field where we used to play regularly.

I don't know about tie a yellow ribbon round the old oak tree:I wanted to tie him round it.During a recent visit home, I noticed the tree had been cut down. It must have been hundreds of years old.Those responsible have taken away a piece of my childhood.I think everyone I knew while I was growing up, and probably those of many generations before us, had climbed and carved their names on that tree.By leaving the signs of our lives on it, did we help to cause its death? Over the years, could all those people cutting into the bark of that poor tree, which was its protective layer, not only have interfered with its natural way of being but also shortened its life? I'd like to think that nature caused its end.Our own lives are a privilege allowed us by nature, and it could end them at any time.

We're gone for longer than we are here, which makes me think we are not that powerful and that we should respect natural laws.

The boy I was after managed to scale that tree but he had not reckoned on my determination to get him. Climbing a tree wasn't going to save him from justice. He was going to pay. About half way up, he stopped. Pleading with me to leave him alone, he clung to some branches. I caught hold of one of his legs and tightened my grip on it. Firmly in control of the situation, I yanked his leg, pulling him out of the tree. Next moment, he was lying on the ground. I had broken his arm. I did suggest to you that it was the 'aggressive male' bit of me that needed venting. That sounds as if I'm not taking responsibility for what I did. It's less an excuse for my actions, more a way of trying to explain the impulse that drove them. The emotion would burst out of me, but there'd always be a reason for this happening. I didn't look for trouble. Perhaps this was an important part of my process of becoming? I'd like to think that nowadays I only slammed the windows and doors of my rabbit hutch of a flat when 'drugs 'r' us' was pile-driving me out of it. Being able to deal with my anger in the right way only came through learning self-discipline.

As a child, I didn't have any. Later, after making many mistakes, I realised I couldn't get very far in this life without considering other people's feelings and points of view.

Mixing with boys in the school playground, in my street, and wherever else we played, often brought out my aggressive side. That kid got over his clash with me. Michael never had any grief from him again.

Chapter three

Michael became a butcher when he left school and came home from work every day stinking of meat. His emigration to Australia was an impressive leap of independence. That independence was to be snatched away from him almost as soon as he got there: he was called-up by the Australian government to do military service in Vietnam. Michael became a hero, of a sort - our very own veteran of the Vietnam War. Whilst traipsing through the jungle, he was hit in one of his legs by a stray bullet. The bullet shattered his kneecap. Michael still lives in Australia. Despite his disabling injury he can count himself lucky he got home from Vietnam and had a life afterwards. I hear he's doing all right.

Allen is Mum and Dad's third child - 'the middle one' as he's sometimes called. Always a big lad, you might say he was built for his destiny. I would not have thought it was possible for Mum to have a baby the size Allen was at birth; he was more than ten pounds and my mum was a size twelve. Before falling pregnant with him Mum was about eight stone. Whilst he grew in her womb Mum's dimensions were seriously stretched: Allen nearly split her sides. That wasn't the 'funny ha-ha' meaning of that phrase either, for I shouldn't think Mum would have thought it funny when she was in labour with him. Looking three months old when he was born, Allen's physical development was rapid. You couldn't pick him up easily when he was a baby and if you did manage to you soon put him down again. Having another male child in the house unsettled me. It felt like he was intruding on my territory. I spent most of his early years trying to sell him to anyone who called at the front door.

Allen is still big. He's twice my width and a lot taller. After leaving school, he went into the army and messed around with tanks a lot. Allen was in the REME, a section of the army that drove great transporters around to pick up damaged vehicles including tanks, low loaders and trucks, for repair. I've been told he and some of his mates nearly wiped-out part of a German village while taking a tank for a spin when they were all drunk. Ignoring the health and safety concerns of everyone in the area, they allegedly drove through a number of houses. If it ever happened, whatever hard feelings they had towards those Germans, they could have tried talking to them first! How reliable was Allen's memory of the alleged incident with the tank, given that he and his mates were drunk when they lived through it?

The story was told at every 'family do', either by Allen himself or one of his mates. To Allen's mates, I was just another bloke who they accepted into their company. I'd put up with listening to this tale time and time again, as I did with most of their incredible stories.

With no interest in their male pub talk, the feeling I had *never* been one of the boys was so strong I knew I had to stop looking as if I was going along with it. I forced myself to appear interested. To me they were like cartoon characters living in a cartoon world. I saw many things as cartoon-like:what was real to everyone else would often seem unreal to me. In trying to understand this stereotypically masculine place where my brother was, I was stepping out of my world into his and I didn't fit.

If I had joined the army, it would have been a waste of time and money. I could never have survived in that environment because I was too self-centred. Although I accept that women can join up and express what I call the masculine side of their femininity, I've always seen the defence services - particularly the army - as essentially masculine and therefore closed to the finer details of femininity as I understand them. There was no future for me in an institution that went in the opposite direction to where I wanted to go. For all my ability to look after myself, I reckon that even if I'd chosen to enlist, or in the event of a world war had been conscripted, there would still be no place for me in the army. Back then, I couldn't be told anything. I really thought I knew it all. In this sense Dad was the same as me at that age: he also thought he knew everything there was to know about life. Unlike me, he was able to adapt to the army regime and loved it.

I generally accept that discipline in the army is necessary for those who, with some knocking into shape, fit that lifestyle. Had I followed the pattern of my brothers and joined up, I would have seen it as hiding away. It would have made me even worse. I would have been stifled. I wouldn't be anything unless you counted what they moulded me into. I've put up with losing much of my personal freedom - that is, my freedom to be me - all my life without going near the army or anything like it. That's just how I feel about the army. It does help many people to make sense of the world though. It's an institution that offers excitement with structure and purpose to those who need it. The army wasn't made for male to female transsexuals like me; the army wasn't made for me, full stop.

I've got a lot of affection for Terry who's the youngest member of our family. One moment he was a baby, the next he'd left school. Certainly I remember having to look after him a lot and my childish resentment of this because I wasn't allowed to do what I wanted when I wanted. Lots of ideas flashed through my mind as I pushed him along the road in his pram. The pram itself - one of those big bouncy jobs with the large springs - is branded on my memory. Terry wanted to hang on to an easy life for as long as he could so it was in his best interests to put off learning to walk. As far as I was concerned, once he left his pram he was on his own.

Even though there was a ten year age gap between us, Terry and I are very close. Under my supervision, he nearly left his pram in spirit. One fond memory I have is of trying to float his pram across a pond with him still in it. Of course it sank more or less immediately I put him in. The mayhem and anguish of panicking adults running from the play scheme centre across the cycle track to the edge of the pond was one of the best laughs I've had. In those first confusing seconds, the play scheme staff tried to find out exactly what had happened. The leader was looking for facts that amounted to my nautical error. What I'd done out of curiosity or, more accurately, stupidity, was an experiment doomed to failure. The first priority was to try to get the pram out of the pond. I've introduced all my brothers to things that could have killed them. It's not funny, is it? But I could not help a little smile popping out as I write this bit.

Yes. I should be ashamed of myself, but I'm not. It wasn't funny. I wasn't cut out for childcare. I found it a burden. The floating pram project seemed like a good idea at the time, not from the point of view of seeing if Terry survived it, but to find out if the pram floated. I saw myself as a genius while everyone else saw me as stupid. Had it floated, with my mentality, I would have got in the pram with him and sailed round the pond till I became bored. Of course, it would have sunk and I would have probably drowned us both.

What was rescued from the pond, apart from Terry, his cherubic face beaming with smiles, was a messy gunged up heap of salvage that even failed as a pram till it was cleaned up. My mum's pride and joy, all covered in mud, was soon back to a kind of normal, although it still bore the scars of that day. Before it went in the pond, its rubber wheels were brilliant white.

After being cleaned, they were permanently stained grey. My mum still has what I call a misplaced affection for that pram even though she sold it as soon as she could.

Terry has forgiven me for nearly drowning him as a baby. My Mum and I often laugh over the affair of the sinking pram. Since everything's been brought out in the open, we have got on better than ever. When Terry's here, he brightens up my life. He's a very lovely man. He has a sense of humour that matches mine, I find him so understanding. He is the only one in my family who's never slipped up since learning about my choice to be 'me'. Without fail, he values and respects my feelings and understands my situation. He always calls me his big sister.

Chapter 4

I was brought up as a boy. How could I be maternal? In the role of adult male, I had children with my partner, Jackie, but it wasn't me who nurtured them. My partner brought them up while I followed my selfish lifestyle. That's different from me wanting children. When ours came along I loved them, but they weren't planned: I didn't choose to have them.

Had I had the luxury of gender realignment at an earlier stage of my life, I'm sure I would not have chosen to have children around me. I would have put me first. That doesn't mean I'd be totally selfish, I hope. Rather, I'd prefer to be a 'career woman', with a partner, but no children. On the evidence of my single-mindedness and physical drive - both well-exercised throughout my seemingly endless time playing male - I believe that is how I would be. Now I'm in a position to say that I still haven't got any maternal feelings, and that's after having hormone therapy for years and gender realignment surgery. I get on well with my brothers' and friends' kids. It's no secret I like them and enjoy playing with them, but I always want to hand them back at the end of the day. I can't see myself as ever being maternal. Perhaps I could be a nice auntie?

We already know how annoying I could be when I was a kid. I'm sure there were times when my Mum and Dad wished they could have handed me over to somebody else at the end of a long day.

Another feat of stupidity I was responsible for which again involved Michael began with us and some local lads meeting on a playing field to try out a bow and arrow Michael had made.Michael was reluctant to let anyone else touch his creation, let alone have a go of it, so I snatched it from him. I prepared the arrow for firing.As I pulled the bow back, my self-control went 'awol'. Aiming the weapon directly at Michael, I fired the arrow. Hitting Michael in the forehead the tip pierced his skin, drawing blood.He still carries the scars of that event.

Even at that age I needed help. Once I let go of my anger, I'd be still for a while, then the tension would start building up inside me again until the next explosive release, which could be weeks later or the next day.My single-mindedness didn't help. If I wanted to do something, I'd do it: I could not have cared less about the consequences.I've always demanded justice.I was aware of these two forces inside me competing with each other, one I wanted to be there, one I didn't.

Being reckless was my way of experimenting with life when I was young. One year, when I was about ten, I decided to see what would happen if I put a match to the Christmas decorations.Pleading with me not to do it, Michael, whose well-developed common sense could have saved our family a lot of grief if he'd had it his own way, found himself witness to my act of vandalism.I struck a match then held it against one of the paper decorations which soon caught light.Within seconds, a fireball rolled across the ceiling.Streamers going from the four corners of the living room to the middle, with bells and other seasonal shapes filling the gaps, provided the fuel and trail for the fire. Thirty seconds was all it took to wipe out these decorations.

Michael and I managed to stop the fire even though we were both walking hazards.By the time Mum and Dad returned, we'd cleared the worst of the debris. When dad saw a black ceiling with no decorations, out of the first hell I'd created, another one was let loose.

Eventually, Dad calmed down. He grounded us both for days. No punishment or restriction stopped me from following my instincts and acting on impulse. At secondary school, nicking a boy's bike because I had to have it was all part of an ordinary day for me. Having no conscience over stealing it, I kept the bike for several weeks before throwing it in the local pond.I even befriended the boy who owned it, having the audacity to help him look for it.I salvaged the bike from the pond the next day. The owner's dad rewarded me for finding it. My Mum remembers this.It was behaviour typical of me at the time.

Considering all the trouble I got into, I wonder how I ever made it through childhood without being put away. That drive to go out into the world and get what I wanted caused me to form a protective bubble around myself that was to remain for a large part of my life.

It seemed to me that girls in their teens would go into an attack of hysteria over almost anything and the odd attack of 'zits' would be a matter of life or death for them because this pimply skin disease threatened to leave permanent scars on their faces. How naive could I get? Whatever I believed, I certainly didn't slot comfortably into *my* teens. I suppose I was twelve when my confusion really hit me.

Today I can look back and say most of the things that interested boys bored me. Many of the lads in my class thought being in the school football team was the business. If I'd been picked for it, I would have found any way I could to get myself unpicked.

During the summer of 1963, Dad took us all to London to visit his sister Midge and Mum's brother Pete who were married to each other and lived in Camberwell. Exploring my new surroundings was urgent for me and I had to do this on my own.

I remember walking for a long time. I was 'gob smacked' by all those red buses. I'd never seen so many. They just kept coming. You had to wait an hour for a bus in Harlow, the place was so small. Sometimes it seemed as though there were about three a day for the whole of Essex.

Reaching the bus depot at Camberwell Green, I discovered a park or that's what the locals called it on the opposite side of the road, to me it was just a green with a bench at one end. I decided to sit on the end of a bench and watch these monsters come and go. A young lad, his face covered in zits, plonked himself down on the other end of the bench. This boy was to have a dramatic effect on my life.

About five minutes went by before he started talking while furiously writing down the numbers of the buses in a book. Route numbers appeared on the front of these symbols of London public transport - huge metal mammoths, lumbering their way along the often cluttered streets of the city suburbs. Shouting the bus route numbers at me as if I was a collector of such trivia and knew the destinations of these vehicles before

I'd even said a word to him, this boy set the pace. He forged the link between us on his terms. The first thing I had to do was enjoy his hobby. He knew which of the vehicles were late and which of them were on time. On his orders, I was learning to be an 'anorak'.

He knew where they were going. I didn't, nor was I interested. He looked atme and said: "My name's Dave Ingle. What's yours?"

Perhaps it was then I should have got up and walked away?

"Never talk to strangers," my Mum and Dad kept telling us. I thought 'strangers' were always adults. I never thought they could be my own age.

The boy had this refreshing liveliness about him which made him stand out. He spoke quickly, sometimes in a staccato way.

"Have you been to Tower Bridge?" he asked me, before I had time to ask him if it mattered what my name was. Even at that age I didn't want people to know much about me unless I was sure I could trust them. In the chaotic crossfire of words, he came straight back with: "Course it doesn't."

That was strange to me. Here was somebody who didn't mind who I was. I hated my name, his acceptance of me and his respect for my wanting to stay anonymous for the time being, made me feel more comfortable with him. There didn't seem to be any way to stop him talking though; a defensive, impatient, insecure, nervous talking where somebody just rambled on, which suggested to me he didn't want to answer any questions I might ask him.

Dave couldn't bear silence: he had to fill it. His favourite words were somethat up until then I'd never even heard of. "Sod" was the worst I'd come across. Saying that in front of the folks would have got me grounded for a week. Those words were, amongst others, f***, dink, and spam head. He was talking a whole new language called streetwise.

When I did manage to get a word into a space missed by Dave, I asked him where he lived. "Where I want," was his answer. "How can you live where you want?" I went on. I was so naive I thought everyone around my age lived at home. "Because I do," he replied sharply. I was impressed by Dave's resourcefulness at such a young age. I had to live with my Mum and Dad. Here was a guy who lived where he liked. At fourteen he'd cracked it. When I told him I lived in Harlow. "Where the f*** is 'arlow?!" He blasted at me in broad cockney.

After spending what seemed like hours talking to Dave that first day, I had to leave him sitting on the bench having promised Auntie Midge I'd be home at tea time, which was five o'clock. As I was leaving, Dave asked me if I'd meet him there the next day at the same time. Still having a conversation with him as I was walking away, I shouted to him that I had to go home that night with my Mum and Dad but he just yelled back: "I'll be here!"

When I got back to Midge and Pete's, I asked Mum if I could stay a couple more days as we were on holiday from school. After many "Please Mums" Mum said it was all right with her if it was all right with Midge and Pete. Pete said he'd make sure I caught the right bus home on Sunday which was a Green line from Aldgate station. That was the first of my many visits to London.

Excitement at the thought of meeting Dave

again drove me back to that park bench the next day. Already there, Dave looked at me saying: "I knew you'd come." "How did you know I'd be back?" I queried. "I just did," came the reply.

Immediately, I was catapulted into his dangerous world. Loath to take a breath except to stop himself from collapsing through lack of oxygen - although he was probably more in danger of hyperventilating - Dave treated me as if we'd known each other for years. After we had been sitting there for about an hour, he asked me if I would like something to eat as he was starving.

"There's a café just down by the kiosk," he said. The kiosk was a small lean-to shed up against a wall where somebody used to sell cigarettes and newspapers. "I go in there and see Fatso," he went on. "I like to spoil his day."

The café was about five minutes walk from the green where we were. Dave was in such a rush I had a job keeping up with him. We got to the café and went inside. As we passed through the entrance, we were met by this seriously large bloke who owned the place. While I don't want to slag this café owner off, he certainly needed a lot of room. Calling out to Dave as if he was a friend, but what I remember today as the café owner's creepy way of talking to kids - a mixture of patronising parent and sad comedian - there was an uneasiness about the atmosphere between them.

"Hello Davie boy," slithered the voice of the café owner, otherwise known as fatso to Dave. "My name is f****** Dave!" my friend emphasised, his voice louder, more resonant, startling his rival with its power. With the grievance of a cobra disturbed in its resting place,

Dave reared his head at Fatso, staring him out with eyes that showed only contempt.

"Whatever," Fatso backed down.

"Go and sit yourself down. Is it the usual breakfast?" asked Fatso in a spaghetti-English accent. From what I can remember I was told, he came from Italy, yet his brogue was more a mixture of Italian, Greek, Spanish, and English.

"What about your friend?" Fatso asked Dave, pointing at me."

"Just toast and a cup of tea, please," I replied, sitting down quickly. I wanted to get out of the way. Dave was still swearing to himself over being called Davie.

After about five minutes, Dave's breakfast turned up, so did my toast. "There you go, Davie," said Fatso, winding my new friend up even more. Surprised that Dave managed to eat his breakfast without choking, having ranted for half an hour, his restless, unstoppable energy made me want to be free and wild like him. Finishing his meal that he'd scooped into his mouth and swallowed with the swiftness of a top competitor in a speed-eating competition, he gathered himself together announcing: "We're getting out of here before he opens his gob again." Dave wanted to leave without Fatso seeing him. He failed. Fatso reappeared, the syrupy whining of his voice raising Dave's hackles. He'd been eyeballing us from a part of the shop hidden from our view, waiting to intercept us when we tried to escape.

"Going, Davie? Don't forget we have to pay," he patronised.

Dave felt inside his pockets for change. The first shock I had with him was his ability to get hold of large amounts of money. He pulled his hand out of one pocket clutching a fist full of crunched up banknotes. I'd never seen so much money in one go and it was being held by a fourteen year old kid. Pulling a ten-bob note from the wad, he threw it on to the counter.

"Don't forget the change, Davie," pressed Fatso. "Stuff it," spat Dave. Get your change, I told him. Dave just said: "His need is greater than mine....or it will be." This went straight over my head. It seemed a funny thing to say. Later on I realised what he meant. This sort of thing happened there every day yet Dave still kept going back.

Dave's dislike of being called Davie went back to his relationship with his Dad. He harboured a strong grudge towards authority figures and acted this out. By calling him that name several times a day in the most patronising way, Dave's Dad had created the conditions for his son's contempt for him. Dave hated anything to do with his Dad. In fact, both his parents rated zero on his scale of importance. If he'd heard they were dead he'd simply look at it as one problem out of the way for good.

A short distance from the café, Dave's mood changed again. He asked me if I'd go down the lane with him later. "What's the lane?" I asked him, with naive enthusiasm. "It's the market. It's near the Elephant," he answered. "What's the Elephant?" I pressed. "It's the Elephant and Castle," he explained in a tone suggesting I was stupid for not knowing where we were. Dave thought I should have been was a walking A-Z of London. The odd swear word from him followed as a further expression of irritation at my naiveté. "It's a f****** shopping centre.

It won't take long on the bus. I need to get there before it shuts."

Walking about aimlessly for too long caused our upbeat mood to drop. By deciding for both of us that it was time to go shopping, Dave had brought excitement back into our day.

"Come on, that's our 'bus!" he hollered, his eyes following one slowing down to stop. Sprinting towards it through fear of it going before I could get on it left me gasping - and that was *before* I'd started smoking twenty cigarettes a day. Dave had shot ahead of me when he first clocked the bus and was already waiting by it, restless and irritable. Once on board, we were greeted by another extra large person; our West Indian conductor, certainly bigger than Fatso who ran the café-another prime target for Dave's verbal abuse. Scathing with his insults about the conductor's size and body shape, Dave made heads turn and stay turned. His vile, what he called harmless banter, challenged the Conductor's and everyone belonging to his ethnic group's right to exist. For Dave, they should not only have not been living in this country; they simply should not have been living. This wasn't a view I shared then and certainly don't now. Then, I didn't know racism existed, let alone understood its twisted logic. Obscene words out of step with his friendliness towards me poured from his lips. Although only words, they were so bitter I started to feel tense and slightly paranoid. The impact of the way he spat those words out with such venom has stayed with me all these years. There was so much hatred in him, no emotional release however big, would have got rid of it all. Perhaps ill treatment early in life caused that hatred which became part of him. It's not my place to make a diagnosis of Dave's mental condition based on his behaviour then suggest what caused it. I can only describe the effect he had on me.

We had to sit on the top deck at the front of the bus so that whilst we were going along he could get a good view of the street below to see if anyone he knew was down there. All the way up the stairs Dave was going on about why they, the ethnic minorities, should not be here. He tossed me two shillings and said: "you ask for two threepences to the Lane."I did what he said.I didn't see Dave's problem with the conductor. Laughing all the time he spoke to me, so happy-go-lucky I could tell he loved life, as far as I could see there wasn't a trace of malice in him.Calling me 'Shorty' with an affection I didn't often get outside my family, he gave me the right change.After about ten minutes of an impromptu guided tour commentary on all the shops on the way, Dave rose from his seat insisting that this was where we had to get off.I'd no choice but to do the same otherwise I would have lost him.Done his way it had to be and done his way it was, or else…. On our getting to the bottom of the stairs and on to the platform, Dave jumped off the bus while it was still moving, which made the bus conductor lose his temper.He shouted at Dave, calling him a bloody fool.None of us there could hear what Dave was calling the Conductor due to the engine noise and brakes going into crisis as the bus seemingly went from a steady movement to dead-stop in the space of seconds.The conductor started talking to me very quickly, too fast for me to understand what he was saying.I don't think he was wishing Dave a nice day. Still not yet initiated into the world of the fast lane, I got off as soon I was sure the bus was stationary.

By the time the bus came to a screeching halt, Dave was about a hundred yards behind waving at me to get a move on. When I got to him seriously out of breath he didn't give me time to hang on to the little breath I had left. I felt a pressure on my left arm and realised that it was Dave's hand grabbing it with a roughness that surprised me. I found myself being pulled across the road. We started walking down the lane at his frantic pace. All the time he was looking along the stalls that lined both sides of the road like a small rodent scurrying in and out of the crowd. The market was packed with activity, vans strewn about parked awkwardly, creating minor annoyance to some, notably Dave. I had a job keeping an eye on him. Evidently I hadn't been watching him closely enough. Before I could make my next link, he was shouting at me to: "Run!" He yanked my arm with a force that was close to pulling it out of its socket. I noticed he was carrying some clothes and we were being chased by some very angry people. I didn't know I could run so fast! I had this sensation that I was a body just running and my real inner self had been left behind in the market place, still trying to register the link between one relatively ordinary experience and another strange and fantastically dangerous one.

From the age of about twelve to thirteen I realised there were easy ways to make money. The seeds of my entrepreneurial skills were beginning to germinate. Starting with a simple milk round that I shared with my younger cousin, who'd been doing it for quite a while at one pound and ten shillings for just Saturdays and

Sundays, I progressed to bigger and better things. For me, the milk round was at the lower end of the scale of what I was capable of. Seeing a good business in loading the milk floats, I set about making friends with the Milkmen, cutting bargains with them. Deals I organised gave them the chance to have a lie-in. Having enjoyed an extra hour in bed, they'd arrive ready for work at five a.m. instead of four a.m. without having to go to the cold room and load up their floats. Consistently up at the proverbial crack of dawn - without complaining about it - I soon got the reputation for being reliable. It didn't take me long to gain a good knowledge of all the milk rounds and the quotas required for each. I did most of the vehicles at two and sixpence a float for loading the milk and charged a supplementary fee for loading the groceries. That self-funding venture of mine helped me keep-up with Dave financially.

The car washing business came about through the co-operation of a friend in Harlow. Doing all the cars on the market car park and those of visitors to the shops as well, we could earn as much as fifteen pounds on those Saturdays I wasn't able to meet Dave.

Recalling that first visit to "the Elephant" with Dave has stimulated other memories of our later meetings there. It was no coincidence that some borderline to outright criminal activity took place wherever we turned up. On many Saturdays between 1963 and 1969, Dave and I had some great times together. In the mornings, we'd go swimming at the local baths known affectionately to its supporters as the Old Bathhouse on Camberwell Road, but to the cynics as the 'Verruca Farm'. It was my view that out of all the times you visited the Old Bathhouse, you could not escape adopting a Verruca or suffering a spell of Athlete's Foot - although there was nothing athletic about the way I got my Athlete's Foot. Many unhappy hours were spent having verrucas burnt out of my feet.

At lunchtime, we'd queue to get our pie and mash. Dave found ways of jumping the queues that used to build up.It was the same every week we never finished our dinner without him arguing with someone over something he'd done that he shouldn't.

I remember seeing on the menu in the café 'Jellied Eels' and asking Dave about them.He said that lots of Londoners love them.I wouldn't be surprised if my Granddad spent time at the canal catching eels, taking them home to boil ready to eat.

Once they were killed I suppose they had to be boiled to be fit to eat after coming out of that canal.I later learnt they were boiled alive.After that, maybe the best fate for them was to be put in jelly.You have to feel sorry for those poor eels.It makes me wonder what pain they felt.I don't eat fresh crab because of that. They boil them alive.That phrase about Jellied Eels slipping down a treat will never sound the same again.

As I see it, the eels are the cleaners of the canal;they are the Refuse Collectors; they keep the balance of the river life in check so their lives have meaning as part of nature's great plan. I'm no expert on the life cycle of the eel but maybe I just feel sympathy for them.Let's forget the jellied eels. The only thing I can say is that I ate them because Dave ate them and he was, in today's 'street cred' talk, to quote my Granddaughter, Zoë, 'cool'.I had to have lots of pepper and vinegar on mine.For me, they were really just something you bought - kind of take them or leave them. You could get them outside any pub in London, usually on a fish stall in a car park.Pie and Mash with Liquor on the other hand was special. This was God's gift to Londoners.The best pie and mash shops were the ones at "The Elephant" and in Leyton, East London.Swimming in the morning, pie and mash at lunchtime, and the cinema in the afternoon were sheer bliss to us.

After a few pints of shandy, Dave and some of his cronies who tacked on to him for a life, got their kicks out of upending BSA bikes with sidecars.

Throughout my early childhood, my family continued to live at my Grandmother's house in Greenford, which was located opposite an iron foundry;a massive place from which I used to see Indians and people from several other ethnic groups swarm when it was time to go home.

My attitude towards them was one of genuine fascination and admiration.

The women looked nice in their native dress. I saw every one of them as colourful, an array of lovely reds, yellows and so on, passing by.It was pure brightness and contrast all at once and plenty of jewellery, including gold - not that I understood gold then. Gold had real value. I didn't know that as a child.To me it was just beautiful to look at.

I recall how Dave would not accept that I liked people from other ethnic backgrounds.His habit of insulting their cultural differences, ranting about the way they formed tight packs in the street or on buses, concerned me.

"Look at them. They're like sardines," was a typical observation of his. To Dave, they weren't his equal. Having no sense of equal rights for white British people other than himself, let alone ethnic minorities, from his point of view they might as well have been another species. He would have been a staunch member of the Hitler youth had he lived in Germany in the 1930s. It came out very early on in our friendship that he wanted me to think like him.

Thoughts on the subject of discrimination led me to remember a young boy who joined our class. I can't remember any black people living in Harlow when I was really young. That's not to say there weren't any. I just can't remember meeting one. When this boy joined our class, I was intrigued by him. I envied him because he didn't have to pretend. He stood out, everyone looked at him and it didn't matter.

He arrived in my class not long before I left school. Of course, in that classroom he was different, yet he was able to be himself and people liked him for it. He didn't have to pass in a classroom full of white kids. He was comfortable with his difference and so it seemed was everyone else. If I had appeared in my class looking and behaving like the girl I was convinced I was, which would then have been in the crude form I called Tammie, I would have stood out. Known to my teachers and fellow class members as a male because that was the sex my body fitted, I would have looked different, would have been looked at and their reactions to it would have mattered to me. I would have loved to have been like that black boy - different but accepted straight away. No one was against him. No one saw him as weird. They all liked him.

My upbringing and exposure to Dave's discriminatory behaviour, that included his constant bad mouthing of anyone who stood out - spitting and sticking two fingers up at the world - just didn't add up. It led me to believe that had the situation in my class been such that it was full of kids like Dave, that black boy would not have been accepted. If I'd shown my true self both in that classroom and at home, I reckoned, from what Dave had told me of his parents' rejection of him because of his difference, I would have been thrown out of the house.

By this time Dave and I had become good friends. Flickering between naiveté and streetwise arrogance I was easily led. Dave excited me. I fancied him. I'd never met anyone like him and would bet with confidence that however long I live, I never will. However, I would not say knowing Dave helped me. He used to call me "darlin." Two young people besotted with what we could not have and constantly experimenting with new ways of trying to become what we could not be, we were almost inseparable. My relationship with Dave wasn't sexual. Everyone knew we were together. Where I was, he was and where he was, I was. It was about looking right to other people and he helped me do that.

My relationship with Dave was one of infatuation, kept topped-up with excitement. He did something for me; he was my drug and I was hooked. He was my sixties cocaine. I needed him. My attraction to Dave became compulsive and I had to have my regular 'fix', going to London nearly every weekend to get it. Potentially dangerous though this was, my ignorance of what Dave was, it protected me.

I had known Dave for a few months, his revelations about his sexuality, started to clash with and affect what we had. We were sitting on a wall together and we'd just been talking…or at least Dave had been talking. Having gone on about something in his usual manic way, he suddenly paused, and for once he actually stopped talking. Looking at me with what was for him a rare expression of concern, he said:"You know I'm gay?"

I was twelve and to me gay meant happy. He had to explain to me what he meant:"I go with blokes," he continued in a matter of fact tone. "At night I go to the city".

Talking to me as if I should have known, once again he was irritated by my naiveté. My first reaction was: Wow! I know someone who's gay I did not really know what he was talking about.

As I look back to my twelve year old self, l naturally and immediately feel emotions similar to those experienced in my youth. Little flutters of excitement tumble through me, joining that ticklishness in my stomach. For seconds that passed too quickly, I was mentally returned to those days which were some of the happiest of my life. I'd love to be twelve again, and be really back there, but with the awareness and understanding of my adult self.

I would not have wanted to have sex with Dave because that would have been wrong. I will try and explain - I was biologically male and even given that my thoughts and feelings told me I was female, I had been conditioned to believe that a person labelled male never went with - and remember that at that stage I didn't know what 'went with' meant - another person labelled male.I'd been told that men always went with women and it should never be any other way."For goodness sake, it can't be any other way, can it?"I remember thinking to myself... *can it..?* The idea of gay sex would not have crossed my mind at twelve years old, but then I can't remember being aware of sex in any form at that age.

Here, I was physically a boy, yet in my head I was a girl fantasising about being Dave's girlfriend without even understanding let alone thinking of the idea of us having sex together. The motto was very much: "I enjoy being with you but I don't want to go beyond what feels comfortable for me."The reality of the sex act didn't exist in the mind of my twelve year old self.

I had this thing in my head about Dave being my boyfriend. I would have loved him to have been my boyfriend. If only he could have seen me as the girl I felt I was.Iwanted him to be my boyfriend in an innocent, romantic 'girl meets boy' way, dreaming that eventually we would fall in love with each other.With hindsight, I realised that he wanted me to be his boyfriend; he saw me as everyone saw me - a boy:that was why his way worried me. I didn't want him his way, which was boy meets boy and falls in love - if love was the right word for it.I wanted him the right way for me.

Even today after all that's happened, I'm still in awe of Dave, or rather, my ideal fantasy of him, which has got nothing to do with the real world.

At about seven years old I began to look for things that made me feel good.When I discovered girls' P.E. knickers there was no turning back.Given the chance, I'd walk around in them all day long.Soft and green, they felt comfortable, so it was natural for me to want to keep wearing them. I wasn't being spiteful by stealing someone else's panties, were so much more comfortable. My fetish continued when I changed schools and went to an Infants' in Harlow.Cross-dressing before I even knew what cross-dressing was, because it felt right, was only a problem for other people.If I wanted a wee I would use the girls' toilet. There were those rare moments I got stopped in the girls' by a female teacher or dinner lady patrolling it, but that was when I was very young and I could still say I'd lost my way and ended up in the little girls' room by mistake.The girls' toilet was cleaner and smelt fresher. The teachers were probably just grateful you didn't wet yourself.

I never stood to go. I always sat on the toilet seat. Most times it was only possible for me to use the boys' toilet. Now, as an adult, I'm disgusted with what are called 'gents' toilets.I traced my dislike of male toilets back to my days of using the ones at school.For me, male toilets are still some of the filthiest places on the planet.

I went to schools called Waterhouse Moor and Purford Green both of which took infants and juniors. They kept shifting me and my brother Mick around. Being juggled between two schools, I never had time to get settled at either so my knicker wearing fetish was put on hold.We ended up at Purford Green Juniors where we stayed until the summer of 1962. We left there to start at a Secondary Modern that September

During my time at the new school, the usual mix of friends drifted my way. There was one who I really identified with. I felt closer to her than I did any of the others. She wasn't exactly like me but we shared something special. Her name was Tammie Martin. When I was with her it was like looking at my ideal self: she was everything I wanted to be at that time.

Tammie was the ideal role model for me in those days. The way she expressed herself was how I imagined I would have expressed myself had I been born with the right bits: she came across as strong, assertive, and definitely feminine. There were things I liked about my life then that Tammie didn't have: for instance, I was happy with my family background, so I would not have wanted to swap that for hers. I wanted to be the kind of girl she was, yet at the same time keep everything I liked about my existing way of being, which included my values, attitudes, memories, skills and so on which were essentially me.

There's no doubt I was obsessed with Tammie. I used to look at her all day long. I could see my real self in her. To my young mind it would have been perfection to step out of the male body I was stuck with and into her beautiful female one.

Those were the selfish thoughts I used to have. I certainly wasn't concerned about what would happen to her soul. She could have taken over the male body I had if she had liked, but given the choice I'm sure she would not have wanted to go near it.

That period of my life consisted largely of me giving off the wrong signals to others. There were times when I wanted to deceive people, and these acts of deception got more sophisticated. I used Tammie as my alter-ego and flitted between what I saw as my male persona and my emerging female personality.

I just wanted to be like her. The problem was I didn't

even know how to look like her. All my efforts to do so bombed. At best I looked like a second class transvestite. Getting my appearance right had to be done gradually otherwise it would continue to look phoney. I started at a low temperature, simmering away on the back burner for years. As I got older, I turned up the heat until one day I boiled over.

I was forced to keep up a gender identity which I had been stuck with since birth, so that 'male mask' I wore to continue to pass and function adequately in society was only removed on special occasions. I had to be careful only to let my Tammie self out of her box when it was safe. My lies got complicated. Lying became such a habit for me I even lied when I didn't have to. When I arrived home after a day out, if anyone asked me where I had been l would invent something, what I did on the day in question. Having lived my life the way I wanted in my own wilderness in the short space of a day without feeling lonely, part of me wanted to share that experience with my family and friends. Instead I ended up lying about it because they would not have accepted it. I would say I'd been to the fair and tell them about every single ride I had not been on. If I'd told Mum and Dad the truth it would have destroyed them. That is why I had to keep my meetings with Dave from them. He had to be kept as far away as possible from my home life.

I was so caught up in those lies, I started to believe them and act them out. Dave told me what his Mum and Dad did to him and, in my confusion, I began to think my Mum and Dad would do the same to me.

Dave could live without his Mum and Dad but I

knew I couldn't live without mine. If Dave was telling me the truth, his parents had thrown him out because he'd been caught by the police doing something he should not have. They had to go and collect him from the police station. When they found out what he had been doing they disowned him.

Now, at fifty, I could see how stupid my lying had been. In order to look like a boy to my family and friends, I told them I had been meeting a girl when actually I had been meeting a boy. What difference would it have made I was being totally paranoid? I was frustrated to think that that the only way people would accept me was in my male persona. This belief of mine turned out to be wrong. Recently, my Mum, and a number of friends in Essex I have known for years have told me they would have accepted me as Carol.

Secondary school wasn't good for me. I didn't learn much there and left as stupid as I was the day I started. It was my fault. There was no room in my head for things I should have learned. Swimming was the only subject I could cope with. I got quite good at that. The peace I experienced while I was in the water made me feel whole, like I was in touch with my real inner self. I would have stayed in all day if I had been allowed to. Every time I got out of the pool, I rejoined the world and carried on with the lie.

I soon discovered the real differences between boys and girls by hiding in the girls' cloakroom at school. There was always a big risk with doing this and how I ever got as far as I did without being caught till a few weeks before leaving is beyond me. All I wanted to do was to see how they looked and behaved in their natural form. When I look back on my Tammie Martin persona - and it was only a persona - I realise how guilty I was of stereotyping females. That was my male side trying to be female.I wanted to be genuinely female, not a stereotype, yet I was becoming that stereotype.

In my younger days, I had my female clothes made at a small place which was on the Old Kent Road. The Jewish tailor who used to make all Dave's clothes was a darling, bless him.Dave's taste for the good life was gradually rubbing off on me.I found myself wearing his choice of clothes.The only problem with this was he could afford them and I couldn't.He did help me with my massive shortfalls, always coming up with money from somewhere.My naive fourteen and a half year old self could not have cared less where that somewhere was.

I was well into mod culture in those days - all scooters and khaki parkas from the Army and Navy Stores.Rockers were the exhibitionists of leather and motor bikes.I wasn't into any of that.I was passionate about Ford Escorts - the fashion accessory for many of my generation - but I was too young to drive one legally.I loved mod clothes, basking in two tone mohair which I had in many different colours.Black brogue shoes and Ben Sherman shirts filled my wardrobe and my soul. The tailor used to come out with sayings that cracked me up like: "Don't worry - it's only a few pounds" which really meant: "many pounds" or "what do you want from me, charity? Rags you can have made up the road."

For my male role, my suits were also mohair and tailor-made by Willoughby. I wouldn't wear anything off the shelf. It had to be made to fit me. Willoughby tailors would alter something as many times as it needed. My body demanded that my clothes needed several adjustments to get them to fit right. According to my Mum, I was so skinny you could have played a tune on my ribs. Fourteen and a half and wearing a three hundred pound suit must have been rare. Thirty-five years later I can only describe that taste of being all right for money as pride over achieving adult sophistication in my early teens. It was being smart without putting on a dress. In other words, I really wanted to express myself in a feminine way but this was as far as I could go without being lynched.

From a very early age, I had to clean my shoes every day. I blame my Dad for that. He had this routine where we all had to stand in front of him to be checked for dirt and lice. It was like a military inspection. This ritual, which took place on bath nights, was Dad's way of seeing that we behaved the way he had to when he was a boy. Checking every nook and cranny of me and my brothers' bodies for hidden grime he could be merciless. If you failed the inspection, you were sent back to the bathroom to redo what you had not done properly, or if he'd had a bad day, everything. That meant having to have more than one bath - a kid's nightmare. Shoe cleaning had to be done with military precision. Acceptable wasn't good enough. Shoes had to shine. If they didn't it was back to the tin of polish.

During the dinner break one day, just two weeks before I left school, I sneaked into the girls' changing room. Unbeknown to me, I'd been seen going up some stairs by a teacher who was on patrol. He called the headmaster. Ten minutes was enough time for me to find what I was looking for in the girls' changing room - that beautifully laundered uniform hanging invitingly from a clothes hook. Safely outside on the school field wearing her P.E. gear, Tammie was taking part in a 'rounders' practice session.

Handling the uniform with the care of an antiques expert studying a valuable and delicate object, I put it on. The velvet caresses of its material warmed and soothed my skin, bringing it back to life. Unsure whether my quivering was due to my anxiety over the likelihood of being caught or my pleasure from living that moment - which could have been several moments - at least then I knew what being truly alive felt like. For a short time I could be truly *me* in a feminine role. I savoured this little sample of Tammie's life, stepping into part of her world which she'd stepped out of for a short while as if to give me the chance to experience it as my own with just a touch of the danger I thrived on.

I had just changed into her uniform when I heard voices coming from the swimming pool side of the changing rooms. Treading the fine line between staying hidden and being found, I tried to blend with the clothes hanging on those red plastic-coated thick wire coat hooks. Another teacher had also come in from the stair side, cutting me off. It was impossible for me to stay hidden when a further teacher also came in from the stair side, trapping me. The headmaster shouted: "Whoever is in there, come out!" I froze and could not move but I was still able to think. The headmaster shouted at me like a crazed sergeant major. A pair of hands slapped down on my shoulders, shunting me back into the present. I felt sick. That was the fear turning over inside me, making me unsteady on my feet. I was in trouble and I cared. The headmaster's disgust was shown in the strict tone of his voice. With the violence of a playground bully he pushed me in the direction of his office. Every one of his harsh words affected me worse than if he had punched me. I was filth to him and had to be dealt with before I damaged the school's reputation. He hustled me along the corridors. I was no longer in control having even lost my gift for backchat which I was usually full of whenever I had grief. He was following me closely, his breath touching the back of my neck, the words he said spoken with urgency.

The journey to his office was uncomfortably drawn out. I'll never forget every part of every corridor and doorway leading to it. The embarrassment of still wearing Tammie's uniform can only be compared to having a football stadium full of people watching me go to the toilet. Unable to get comfortable, the slightest move I made caused another wave of sickness to roll through me. I wanted to retch.

We arrived outside his office and the headmaster told me to wait where I was. With only ten minutes to the bell when almost the whole school would walk through there to get to afternoon registration, I was worried. Most kids had to pass down that corridor to get to the main building. I tried to will the minute hand of the clock on the wall near me to go backwards but the inevitability of time moving on and the punishment I was going to get increased my feeling of powerlessness. Knowing my freedom had gone when the headmaster said: "You pervert!" His scathing words cut into me and I began to wonder if he was right. I felt rejected. Amongst a school full of hostile kids, I was alone.

My school friends had great fun at my expense. I think everyone in my class and most of the pupils at the school must have walked past me. I can still see some of them gloating, their faces distorted with laughter.

After I'd been left standing outside his office for about an hour, it happened. Tammie and her dad walked towards me. Her Dad's face looked grotesque, pulled and twisted by a rage he couldn't wait to take out on me. As far as he was concerned I had soiled his daughter's uniform. He went to grab me, just in time the headmaster came out. The head greeted Mr Martin, his uncertain voice just holding on to its authority that was slipping away by the second. He was angry and painfully embarrassed but desperate to protect me and the school from further damage. Mr Martin was still shouting at me as he entered the head's office, describing in graphic detail what he was going to do to me when he came out. Through the door I could hear him ranting at the Head Master. Once the Head had used his interpersonal skills to turn Mr Martin's thermostat down, the atmosphere settled and the latter's shouting stopped, then became short occasional outbursts in a slightly raised voice; a gentler but chilling boom that still shook what self-confidence I had left as I stood outside. After about an hour they came out. Not a word was spoken. Old man Martin and Tammie pushed past me and I was told by the headmaster to "get inside!"

I flinched when he ordered me to stand in front of his desk.

Don't move, you little pervert he erupted. I felt like

I was dissolving right there in front of him. (Hopefully it would not happen today). He told me I'd caused a big problem for both myself and the school and that he was considering calling the police. He kept calling me a thief. "Look at you!" he yelled, tearing away every last layer of defence I had. What do you think you look like?" he went on, shaking with the force of his delivery. "I'm going to cane you, boy.

Well bloody well get on with it," I said to myself.

Then I'm going to expel you," he promised.

I didn't care about being expelled. I was leaving anyway. He warned me I was going to have to pay for the uniform and that it would cost me thirty shillings. That was daft because, like me, Tammie was leaving in a matter of weeks. It was her Dad who wanted the new uniform. He wanted me to pay for a new uniform for Tammie as a matter of principle. That was his way of getting me to compensate him, not Tammie, for what I'd done. I'd disturbed the balance of his world.

The headmaster wanted to tell my parents. I begged him not to. He struck a bargain with me. If I told them then came back to see him the next day with the money for the uniform, he would think about it. His offer was my only escape from social death. When I think what could have happened it seemed like I was being let off lightly. On my agreeing to his conditions he ordered me to report to his office the following morning at eight-thirty.

Nothing of this was mentioned to my Mum and Dad by the Headmaster or any school official and certainly not me. I had a fearful respect for my Dad. As agreed, I turned up with the thirty shillings for the new uniform that could be bought from the school shop.I had to take the money out of my secret fund I was building up at the time.The source of that fund was the pickings from what I'd believed to be my dab hand at shop-lifting. My Mum has since told me that she'd known what I'd been up to all along.Discovering late in life that I had not got away with everything was a shock to me. Her intelligence was helped by the fact she was a friend of the shopkeeper, who used to watch and log my crimes. Thanks to their friendship of several years, I remained at large.Enjoying a reasonable profit from my weekend car cleaning business which I ran from the local high profile car park behind the market, I no longer had to bring in cash by using less than honest means. The market car park accommodated most of the cars and vans owned by the stallholders. Driven by my desire for money, I was always going to get it somehow.

At about eight-thirty the next morning, I stood outside the Headmaster's office. Only having to wait about ten minutes this time before I was called in, the Headmaster was cooling off and had become more understanding about the mess I'd got myself into. His voice was calmer. Happily, it turned out that because I only had two weeks left at school and to save Tammie and me any more embarrassment, no more would be said of the incident.He obviously realised that damage limitation was the best option. He left it as an unfortunate affair to be put behind us rather than let it become an ongoing saga of pain and humiliation.I respect him for that.He told me I could leave school immediately.

Spending the next two weeks pretending I was going

to school hoping my parents didn't find out what had happened there was like having safely blasted off from a troubled planet then getting stuck in orbit around it.

Chapter Five

When I was in my teens, Dave and I had great fun out on the town most weekends. Our friendship had reached a stage where I'd accepted he lived for the hell of it and didn't worry about anyone but himself. If he slagged someone off, instead of telling him not to do it I just let him get on with it. We made a career out of breaking rules. The stronger I got, the less notice I took of anyone who got in the way of how I wanted to live. It did not bother me that Dave, at sixteen, was already claiming his stake in the world and living dangerously for himself. I followed him around as his willing partner in chaos.

He loved cars. The problem was they were always someone else's. He was really into Ford Consuls. The harder they were to 'borrow', the more he liked them. Sometimes he'd keep them for days. Many were left for the police to find. What fascinated him about these cars was the faster he drove them, the more erratic their windscreen wipers got.

Look at it. It's doing it again, he'd chatter. It didn't matter to me what the car was doing: I was just glad to be with him. In the driver's seat, he was like a kid with a lollipop. At each petrol station he visited, he would tell an attendant to fill up the tank of the car he was using at the time, and then ask him to go and get some oil. While the attendant was walking back to the station shop to get the oil, Dave drove off. Probably having 'borrowed' petrol from every garage on the A13 in the mid-1960s, Dave was a wanted man, though one way of looking at it was that the police would have been pleased when he left the area; car crime would have plummeted.

We'd travel down to Southend in one white Ford Consul and come back in another that was a different colour:green; black, convertible - you name it. He was always happy if it had petrol in it and a Motorola radio installed as he liked to push the great big buttons which were a main feature of this early car entertainment system.

More often than not we would go to Southend, but sometimes we'd venture to Brighton or Hayling Island, which for some reason is a destination for Londoners. Why we kept going to those places I do not know. I think it was just to be with the Mods. Certainly that was Dave's thing then. He was a Mod of a sort;perhaps a Mod in passing, as I was. Now, looking back, I find it boring, about as interesting as going to Canvey Island – with apologies to Canvey Island. That's only my view. To me it was just a place to go - full of petrol terminals. For someone else it could be a romantic haven, certainly if they were under the influence of an illegal substance. I nicknamed it 'the Isle of Oil'. Whoever thought of building houses around petrol terminals needed professional help. Here was a potential bomb waiting to go off if ever there was one. The island reeked of petrol fumes wafting through the smelly breeze, like Southend when the tide's out. Sometimes it was difficult to get off it as all the visitors seemed to want to leave at the same time. The estuary decided when you left the island.

Measuring sticks marked off the height of the water in feet for the high tides. Take the Isle of Dogs, similar to Canvey: there you didn't have the tide; just a single road near the Blackwall tunnel. As far as Canvey Island went, Dave liked it because the last word of its name was 'Island'. For him it meant 'seaside' and a day at the seaside at that. It got Dave's marine instincts frothing like the surf breaking at high tide. Those instincts really amounted to him getting overexcited by what was a novelty to an urban guerilla like him. Going to the seaside with me was also his idea of being grown-up and taking care of me, which was lovely of him, especially when he showered me with ninety-nines and candyflosses with the odd toffee apple thrown in.

As a child, I enjoyed many happy times holidaying at exotic places like Walton-on-the-naze, Frinton and Clacton-on-Sea, so you might say I have a lot of affection for these and other resorts. My Dad was the proud owner of a villa that was actually a caravan on a site at Dovercourt.

Nearer home, my social life was just as hectic. My friends and I never stood still for anything or anyone until one day we all went to Streatham ice rink and I had my first taste of violence. Standing in a group at the edge of the rink, I was in somebody's sight for a reason that was to prove bad for my health.

He was on the balcony sitting at a table watching us. Hearing a crack then immediately feeling this pain in my side as if I'd been hit by a cricket bat, I did the best pirouette of my skating career, never to be repeated, spinning me across to the other side of the rink at the speed of a camera flashgun going off. After I'd finished my party piece, the blades of the skates must've been red hot. I'd been shot with a 2.2 fairground rifle. In the seconds following the rifle crack, bewildered and hurting, I strained my sight in the direction which I thought the shot had come from. Focusing on the balcony, I saw a boy get up rapidly from his seat and run into the protection of shadows. I recognised him as a lad who had kissed me the previous week. Embarrassingly, I couldn't remember his name. I think it was something foreign. He would have been about nineteen. My guess is he wanted to get me because he felt I'd deceived him by pretending to be a girl in his company. From the way he grabbed me, he didn't seem to mind at the time; nor did I because I well snogged him back. I was flattered he wanted me enough to do that. I never set out to deceive anyone. He must've thought I was a girl to snog me like that. Somebody spoilt it by deciding it was in his best interests for them to tell him he had been snogging a boy without giving me the chance to tell him myself. What a shame his view of me had to change for the worse because someone couldn't mind their own business. The events leading up to my first insight into the way I affected other people began a week earlier at the picture house in Camberwell. My friends and I were all messing about in there. Afterwards, we hung around outside talking to blokes. That was how he knew we would be at the ice rink that Saturday morning the following weekend. Repeating our pattern of the previous week, after seeing the picture we all waited outside for male talent to come our way.

We'd watched this film - I think it was 'The day the earth caught fire' - but it was a long time ago and as far as that's concerned my memory is a blur. All I know is none of us were interested in it. The cinema was somewhere to go and the film was something to watch. Both were secondary to the fun of being irresponsible in our exciting little teenage girlie gang.

This bloke and I kissed each other. So what? That's what young people who fancy each other do. I bet that person who ruined my moment with him just told him I wasn't a girl. They would have put it like that. We're thirty-five years down the line and people are still doing that to me. I confided in my friends - or those I thought were my friends - that I was going to have gender realignment surgery, then they took it upon themselves to let everyone else know about it. I ended up being pointed at while shopping in the local supermarket. They told people who were their friends but definitely not mine. The young yobbo who becomes dangerous the moment he gets in a car lets everyone know that the one thing he can do is drive, the sound from his speakers audio-bombing the streets with the amplified basspounding his undersized brain. Passing me breaking the speed limit - the resulting rush of air almost pushing me over - he wound his window down, shouting: Where's your cock, Carol! How did he know? A friend I'd trusted and confided in told him, that's how. Another friend saw me in the supermarket, turned to the person she was with and called out, There's Carol. She's half and half you know!" and the whispering between them started. There was also the woman on the delicatessen counter at Somerfield calling me 'Sir', plus a guy on the frontline at the post office always ending whatever he'd got to say to me with 'Mate', all of which told me they just couldn't see me the way I wanted them to.I'm never totally free of that question running through my head:do I pass or don't I?

Sorry I got side tracked.Someone looked at the bit of me that had been hit.There was a hole with a lot of blood coming out.It hurt like a red hot poker being pushed through my skin.I borrowed a handkerchief from someone and pressed it down firmly on the wound.A taxi got me to the casualty department of the local hospital.The bullet had chipped my pelvis.The hospital doctor who examined and treated me told me it'd hit the best place for the least amount of damage. The best place for him maybe, but he hadn't got pain there.What he meant was that, for example, if the bullet had penetrated muscular tissue six inches further down I could have been left with a permanent limp.

Made from a small piece of lead, I stand by what I said that it wasn't a pellet as some of my friends today argue it must have been.Lodged underneath my skin, at first I didn't know it was a bullet. I was looking away as the doctor and nurse removed it.Even watching people taking bits out of others in a television medical drama - never mind the fact its fictional - or worse still a documentary, because that's real-life, upsets me.

I suppose you could say I'm a tough wimp. There's another contradiction for you.I can be hard when I want to be but deep down I'm a softie.Once accepting what happened I became calm.Being shot was all right if you take away the shock and the pain because I got all the glory for withstanding something that could have disabled or even killed me. The bit after it though, with the blood, the cleaning and dressing of the wound, more pain and the damage it did to my skin and pelvic bone where the bullet went in, was terrible:that was male ego versus girlie vanity.I think I told you I wasn't scared when I had some tattoos done.I regretted it later though.Both my arms have these ugly pictures that were scratched on them with sterilised needles.Now I cannot wear anything short-sleeved.People ask me:"what's wrong with tattoos?Lots of women have them." "Yes," I say, "but they don't have these bloody things that scream 'male!" at you the moment I roll my sleeves up. There's a picture of a girl, a dagger, an anchor and other depressing symbols of masculinity.

This bloke who went crazy because he'd snogged a bloke. It got to him very mad.It would most men.I was young and beginning to grow as a person, wanting to be like the girls.They were doing it.I wanted to do it.It was all done with their approval.They knew who I was.

I have to say I was driven by the excitement of it.That bloke didn't scare me.Remember I had a lot of clothes on.According to the doctor that dampened the impact of the bullet, but then he wasn't and I certainly wasn't a ballistics expert.I was in a cold place so I dressed for winter. To me the wound was more blood than injury. One of those big plasters was put on it to protect it.I was still in some pain, yet I was up and walking.It didn't occur to me to go home.The day wasn't over.Getting all that attention and excitement drew me back to the rink for more.Also the fact I'd been shot with a real bullet raised my status in the group.At the pull of a trigger I'd become honorary member.If I had not been there encouraging everyone to live for the moment, everything would have revolved around other people's stories. That would mean we would have been slagging off our Mums, Dads, teachers, friends who weren't normal - there's irony for you - and so on. Yet, there we were, a tiny community pulling together after one member had been attacked:me. There were all these others in orbit around us fascinated by what we were saying and doing - by what we were being, if you like - asking questions. For that moment in that place, we were at the centre of other people's universes. We were at the rink till about six o'clock that evening. The other girls found their blokes and went round the back for a snog. The bloke who'd shot me was crouched behind a big metal dustbin on wheels. I walked round the corner and he caught me with a machete across the top of my legs in the area of the hem of my skirt. Thinking he was going to cut off my manhood I jumped clear of my last position. He swung the machete towards me again and I was scared.

There was a problem I had at hospital. They wanted to call the police. One of my friends said we would get into serious trouble with our parents if we didn't stick together. Foreseeing big trouble if my Mum and Dad found out I'd been attacked - particularly my Dad - I agreed to cooperate with an arrangement suggested by some of our gang to keep what had happened from all our Mums and Dads.

We were all saying different things so after talking about it at length, we decided on a story we would all stick to. By telling the hospital staff we did it and that it was an accident, we got the strict Ward Sister's compulsory advice on how to behave, which we accepted. Her bossiness may have been an outlet for a hormonal imbalance, her worst fits of bad-temper leaving an emotional wake behind them that made you realise what a woman was capable of if you messed with her.

"You're old enough to know better" was wheeled out again which we all took great pleasure in ignoring. When she tried to smile, I knew there was hope for her, as if her humanity was trying to find its voice.

Our version of events was that we got hold of a fairground gun and mucked around with it. We were only experimenting. It was curiosity and stupidity typical of teenagers."

The point here is that it was covered up by me as a bit of fun that went wrong and the other girls confirmed that was what happened.

The injury I had sustained was not serious. Had it been a high-powered gun it would have smashed my hip or even killed me however many clothes I had on. In that situation, police involvement would have been unavoidable. What with the two wounds putting me through more physical agony to match and at times outdo the psychological, I spent the next few days at home trying to disguise the pain. Eventually, the wounds healed without further hospital treatment.

As for my attacker, I don't know what happened to him. There was what can only be described as a war between him and Dave. As far as I can tell, Dave went after him like a scud missile. When I later asked Dave if he found the bloke, he said with a Calmness rare for him: "Don't worry. It's been dealt with."

Violence seemed to follow me around. At about eight o'clock one summer's evening in 1971, when I was twenty-one an incident that did involve the police happened to me.

I'd just got back from a long day at work delivering furniture all around Wales for a friend who was on holiday. This was well before they built the M25. Dad came with me to share the driving because we had a long distance to cover and a lot to do in a short time. To use the haulage lingo, we were on a 'multi-drop run'. On our return to Harlow, I had to drop Dad off home first.

I stopped outside the local pub a short distance from Mum and Dad's house, feeling relaxed after successfully completing the Welsh job on time. After going to the pub's off-licence to buy a packet of cigarettes, I walked through the foyer thinking of getting myself a small, relaxing glass of shandy, which I never had.

From the direction of the bar this man came staggering into the foyer, a rat-arsed Irishman stinking of beer, about to lose his balance. Guinness might be good for you, but not in the amount he had drunk. We collided in the foyer. Trying to keep upright, he swayed back in my direction, he then quickly regained control of his movements to avoid falling over.

Out of the slurred sounds he made, all I could hear were expletives. The only sentence he could manage was: "gi's a fag you little s***". I can't explain the contrast of being calm one moment, to full of rage the next, but that drunken sod was responsible. My anger gave me the energy to push him away, without me seeing what he was up to. The sensation of a red hot poker burnt into the muscle of the upper part of my left arm telling me something was very wrong. The whole limb felt as if it was alight. Before I had time to take my jumper off to see what he'd done, he was launching himself at the nearest exit. I took my jumper off and could see some blood soaking through the material. When I rolled my shirt sleeve up I noticed bits hanging out of my arm that should have been in it. Muscle, veins and whatever else holds everything together there were spilling out of a three inch slit opened by the knife that Irishman must have had hidden on him. Seeing the damage he'd done, I passed out.

I remember waking up in an ambulance on its way to Harlow Hospital's A&E department, the person taking care of me in the back telling me I'd get fixed. I'd already been fixed in a way I could have done without. Accident and emergency staff put everything sticking out back where it should have been. It was like they were moving their fingers around in a bowl of spaghetti. Every time they pushed a bit in another popped out till they got it right. Once they'd patched me up with the required number of stitches they gave me a bottle of painkillers and told me to come back in about ten days' time. I was discharged and never went back. Several days later, I took the stitches out myself. That's probably why I've got a wider scar there than I should have.

On the night of the attack, I was picked up from the hospital by a gorgeous policeman who took me back to the pub where it happened.

You never know with drunks. He might not realise what he's done so he could have come back here, was this policeman's justification for returning me to the crime scene. Unable to recognise my attacker as anyone in the pub, I told my Chippendale police escort this, we parted company, and I drove the lorry back home. When I got there, the investigation continued.I had to explain my extended absence to my partner Debbie. Understandably, she'd been worried about me, so I got a good grilling. When she saw I'd been stabbed it took me a while to calm her down.

This and the attacks at Streatham ice rink - which are always linked in my memory - gave me some hard lessons in how violent human beings can be towards one another.

Chapter Six

In the mid-sixties, I started wearing flamboyant clothes to see how far I could go. That's how I believed most girls grew up, particularly the extrovert ones, who'd push their image boundaries as well as their Mum's and Dad's sanity to the limit. It was their time to test authority, which was just one way of finding out who they were, the more outrageous yet still 'girlie' they could be, the better.

Take female rockers in black leathers and boots riding motorcycles. They can be 'girlie' and 'macho', but once they've finished experimenting with male and female boundaries, they can tone down their macho side and settle into being their real selves. Like a butterfly emerging from a chrysalis, out of rough beginnings can come a stable sense of self.

My journey was one of trial and error - with a lot of error. I had to find myself. Part of that journey involved the girls deciding what clothes I should wear. I was being trained. I think they wanted me to blend with them. If I had looked weird it would have damaged their 'street cred'. They did not want to dump me so they tried to make me like them.

I made my own choices based on their advice and they told me if those choices were okay. I let them take the lead. On those occasions I was out with my 'sisters' I was 'one of the girls'.

I needed the right kind of support to help me on

my way. My female friends gave me that support. It's because of the start they gave me that I don't have to step in and out of the male and female role anymore to pass for different sets of people at different times. Now I can stay who I am, I don't need that support.

In those days, if I went off on my own I wasn't so at ease with myself because my female friends weren't there to get me out of any trouble

On rare occasions I was able to take on the guise of my alter-ego, Tammie Martin. When I remember this I cannot stop laughing to myself: I was a transvestite of the tabloid kind.

Dave Ingle gave me the opportunity to dress in women's clothes as often as I liked, and I did, but my cross-dressing was never a self-indulgent drag act. To me it was a necessary part of my becoming a woman. Each time I cross-dressed I hoped it would be an improvement on the last. Going into the girls' toilets at school at high risk of being found and punished wasn't out of some perverted desire: it was out of sheer need to be like the girls I admired.

Christine Moon used to say to me: "It's all right for you. You don't have to lug tits around the size of large melons, get the strops, put up with periods every month, and you've got that toughness that gets you places."

There were many statements like that; little half-jokes hiding serious concerns. The irony is I'm convinced that even then I would have accepted the down side of womanhood these girls were complaining about, just for the privilege of reaching it. At home I had no female role model to give me all the ins and outs of becoming a woman. Being female wasn't just about appearance. If I'd had a sister, I would have had a role model to compare myself with. My mum was no role model to me because she could only see me and accept me as a boy. I wanted her to see me as a girl and experience my process of becoming a woman with me. My Mum didn't know I was suffering. How could she? I never told her.

My headmaster told me to go out and be a boy. I turned into a young criminal because I didn't get the help I needed. That doesn't mean I don't accept responsibility for what I did. I rebelled against the lack of understanding. After the way I'd been treated, I didn't want anyone's help. From then on, I decided I was in control of my life. Whoever got in the way of that would regret it.

Dave gave me his own brand of support. I loved him, or thought I did. Going to see him was like stepping into a parallel universe where everything was exciting. There'd be that one magic day out of a whole week. That was the only time I was truly happy. I'd go home to my family as if nothing had happened during my weekend trips to London when really my time out of the house had been total fireworks.

I said to myself: They're never going to let me be a girl. I'll have to be what I'm not, and as I have to be what I'm not, I'll choose the way I do it", so I marked puberty by having these tattoos done. A week later, I realised how ugly they looked. I was young and already trying to destroy myself.

You may think I've skipped a bit here. In fact my childhood ended as abruptly as this suggests. I passed my driving test at seventeen and hit the road, getting through a succession of cars. Out of all the vehicles

I owned back in the late sixties, I had great affection for a yellow Ford Anglia van. It had all the noise of a sports car but the speed of a Reliant Robin. I remember paying sixty pounds for this little marvel with a gear stick that used to start vibrating at about forty miles an hour. It made your hand numb when you got hold of it to change gear at this speed or above. Its other irritating feature was the rear doors that rattled whilst the van was moving.

At nineteen, I was a mess. I drank heavily. During one of my calmer phases, my first partner came on the scene. I thought: Why not? Everyone assumed that because I wasn't married and didn't have a girlfriend, I was gay. This unfortunate girl was Debbie. Although I knew I was going to encourage a serious relationship with her, at the same time the sensible part of me said I shouldn't because I was doing it just to look right. In those days, if you were homosexual most people didn't call you gay. You were either a 'homo' or a 'poof' just as if you had learning difficulties you were a 'moron'. I hate those words as much as I hate transvestite and transsexual. Even Debbie's Mum had discussed my sexuality with her. That was because when Debbie and I were going out together I wasn't interested in sex. I wouldn't have sex with Debbie. I could not have sex with Debbie, finding it very difficult to rise to her demands. Her mum was angry that with all those virile young men out there who were basically sperm banks on legs gagging to deposit their donations on the spot, her daughter was lumbered with someone who stayed limp for England. Sex didn't work for me. Somewhere along the line I must've managed it because she got pregnant with my eldest child, Tracy.

Tracy was born on the 20th May 1971. Even though she's now thirty, she's still one of my babies. In an ideal world I would celebrate her life and how valuable she is to me. This isn't an ideal world so communicating with her about the deeper issues that involve both of us has posed problems because she's found it difficult to talk about her past, choosing to avoid raking up how unjust life has been for her without a Dad. She's told me she's not interested in the past. "The important thing is we're together now and we can build a new life," she says. I'm not sure really how this works?

This frustrates me because I want her to ask me questions. I want the chance to explain my life to her. She's been kept away from me all this time. I know less about her than I do my estranged children by my second partner, Jackie. Tracy came looking for her Dad and found Carol. That's how she put it. I appreciate how difficult that was for her. During our meetings I'm always asking: "Do you want to talk?" All she'll say to me is: "I accept you as you are and that's all that matters." I keep thinking there's a story here waiting to be told.

We both wanted to contact each other at the same time. I was anxious about how she'd take what she'd find. Her mother hadn't painted a good picture of me. Tracy told my Mum that she wanted to get in touch with her Dad and asked her if she knew where he was. My Mum answered: "Yes" and gave her details of my location, but at the same time tried to protect her from what I was. At first, Tracy wasn't told about my gender dysphoria as she was looking for her Dad. In my opinion that was wrong. We discussed it however and decided Mum and Dad were right;they knew Tracy better than I did. I didn't know how to deal with the prospect of meeting her, thinking it might be best if I stayed missing.It was then I realised I would want to know about my biological father had I been left in the situation I'd left her in.Having agonised over what it might do to her, I decided to arrange a trip to Essex to meet her. She'd been out of my life for most of her thirty years so she was entitled to an explanation.I asked my Mum to contact her and tell her what I had done.I thought this would help her decide whether she still wanted to meet me and if she did, soften the blow of what she found.Even after I'd been told she definitely wanted to meet me, I couldn't shake off my concern that on seeing me she might change her mind.How did I know she wouldn't be horrified at what I'd become?That concern was turning over in my mind constantly, along with the thought that she might reject me.

If ever I wanted to thank God in my life it was the day I was reunited with my daughter. I was very happy. In a way, I wasn't surprised over the similarities between us because when I last saw Tracy I was still with my second partner and remember thinking then how much alike my eldest daughter and I were. Looking back on our relationship eight years before this reunion, at a time when I tried to tell her about my gender dysphoria and what I had decided to do about it, I smiled over how far we had come since.Strangely, I had invited her round to my house twice during that period. Those meetings had to be cancelled because I was unwell. By inviting her to meet my second family, I risked upsetting the fragile emotional balance between Jackie and me. In the end, Tracy never came to see me while I was living with Jackie, Sophie, Ross and Alicia. It was just as well. Suffering from a mini-breakdown wasn't the best foundation on which to build a new relationship with my adult daughter.

In the car on my way down to Harlow, all I could think about was what I should wear or, more to the point, what she'd be wearing as I didn't want to out-dress her. The likely need for a quick change of clothes to look the best I could for my eldest daughter led me to take a suitcase full and I'd only gone down for the day. All eventualities hopefully taken care of by the unusually large amount of stuff I'd packed, I arrived in the morning with plenty of time still to worry about the outcome of our meeting that afternoon.

Tracy got to my Mum's at two-thirty. The knock on the door I dreaded came and I might as well have been going through the doorway to a job interview. Instead, it was through the doorway to a real moment of discomfort then happiness that has stayed with me ever since.

I was sweating so much I was beginning to fear I'd need a change of clothes without out-dressing Tracy, having one of my hot flushes that seemed like the ones described in stories of the female menopause. Unable to stay in control of my feelings, thoughts and behaviour, my speech came out all jumbled, giving the impression I was suffering from a nervous disorder, with interruptions for several seconds at a time when my mouth moved without any sound coming out of it. When the words did return they were still confused, as if I'd temporarily gone back to being a child. Most people who know me would tell you I never stop talking, but then this was my daughter. I was overwhelmed by her.

After that first awkward five minutes, I thought it best we went somewhere private so we disappeared upstairs to a room where we could talk comfortably. For about two hours, I poured my life out to Tracy. There were some emotional moments from both of us. At the end of our chat she said a lovely thing to me. She told me she approved of me. Having worried that she was going to be faced with a bloke in a frock, what she actually found was a relief to her. Since that day our relationship has moved forward. Tracy has been to stay with me, as I have with her. She accepts me as Carol and what with that and the bonus of knowing my granddaughter - Tracy's daughter, Zoë - a lovely, slim, fair-haired teenager who has also accepted me. I'm overjoyed that Zoë's first words to me were: "it's cool". That's a compliment in teenagers' language. Zoë has been to stay with me too giving me the chance to spoil her.

Tracy has a brother. I can't say much about him because I don't know him, despite the fact I'd like to, without there being any damage done to either of us. There's only the little Tracy has told me about him which is that he exists. He was very young when I left. I know nothing about his life today.

Missing the life I'd built for myself in the eight years before meeting Tracy's Mum, I had to get that back somehow. I'm not blaming Debbie because she didn't know about me. I was a bad person as far as she was concerned - or that's what I became in her eyes. She couldn't understand what was wrong with me, but then I couldn't either. My heavy drinking got heavier. I had to stay drunk to get through the day. It was close to my twenty-first birthday when I tried to get help. You would have thought that at that age I would have found the courage to put my life in order.

I managed to get myself to the doctor before end stage cirrhosis of the liver kicked-in but the effort I put into trying to explain to him how I felt was a total waste of time. That doctor didn't get one hint of what I was trying to tell him. "I fancy men and I like to dress as a woman. What the hell's wrong with me?" I demanded.

It was difficult to say those words. Before I'd finished telling him my story - which would not have been possible in the ten minutes he'd given me - he'd decided I was homosexual. In his expert medical opinion, my cross-dressing meant that I was still tied to my Mum's apron strings.

He basically told me to go and get a life. That was his answer to my pain. I thought I was going to get help. All I got was a feeling of hopelessness. With hindsight, I'm being hard on that doctor. I was disappointed and hurt he'd summed me up as gay. He hadn't listened to me. I remember exactly how I felt in that surgery. It was like nobody understood or ever would understand me.

Chapter Seven

Working away from home gave me some freedom. Getting back to the hotel after work I'd scrub myself clean. Psychologically, I was getting rid of all that horrible maleness.

Now I don't have to pretend anymore. There's no more hiding for me. During the hard times at home, I found going away to be female was easier than I'd imagined. Even so, I was concerned that someone would recognise me as the male I was known as at home and at work, so wherever I stayed I'd watch out for anyone I knew.

It was possible for me to stay in as many as four hotels across the country in the space of a week. One of my favourites was near Grantham on the Nottingham road off the A1 which was my main route up north. A husband and wife team ran it. They were a lovely couple. The husband always helped me set up my computer to do my invoicing while I was there. I've heard that many gender dysphoric persons go through this hassle just to grab moments being them self, often pre-dressed for their desired gender role. I did that to such an extreme that I got close to having a nervous breakdown. The company I worked for had a garage in nearly every town in the British Isles, which kept me busy.

One day, I was in the bar of the hotel in Grantham run by the nice couple. They joined me and together we put the world to rights. It was then I saw my chance to tell them about myself. They had a reservation for a male that was going to be paid for by a female.

The hassle involved with those trips away from home included having to empty virtually the whole contents of my car into my hotel room. I had to remove a false floor in the boot which covered the spare wheel compartment to gain access to my suitcase full of my girlie gear. There was my computer, briefcase, mobile phone, one suitcase for my dirty working clothes, one for my clean clothesplus my girlie suitcase. I turned the hotel room into an office and boudoir. One side was male, the other female. In that environment - where I was accepted for who I was - it didn't matter.

Once, I nearly got caught out by my workmates who had come to the hotel to have a meal at my expense. All the bosses of the company my firm worked for and the reps coming down for the merchandising of the garage shop that had just been completed, were at the dinner.

I decided to have a drink before my meal and I came downstairs to the bar. They were all sitting there laughing. I felt as if I'd had a mild kick from a low voltage electric fence. Feeling my face flush with embarrassment, I turned round and left them to it. I spent the rest of the night hiding in my room to save my reputation. Next day, they asked me where I was the previous evening. I was out, I lied. Getting the bill for their indulgence was a shock in itself.

When I first saw Jackie, I had to talk to her. Just looking at her seemed to switch something on in me. She had this charisma that brought everything around her to life, as if it was bathed in bright sunlight. I had to own her (what a terrible thing to admit). I stopped worrying about what I'd done in the past and began mapping out a future with someone I had only just met. Even in those first moments of making eye contact with her I could see she was special. I believed this beautiful girl had saved me.

Marriage was far from my mind. Savouring every second of her company, I went all out to be what Jackie expected from a boyfriend. She helped me rearrange my life, giving me some semblance of control over it. Through Jackie I had direction and consistency. Drunk most of the time during the period shortly before I met her, there was little chance I'd recover from my alcoholism. It got to the point where I was only working to drink. Immediately after leaving Debbie, I moved in with a well-known gypsy family. I knew John, the head of that family, he part-owned a pub in Harlow. That wasn't the only business he was involved in. I used to help him on his fish stall as well as drive a tipper lorry for his tarmac laying business. That is how I got my money before I met Jackie. I'd do anything that needed doing to get drink. I thrived on instability, stepping in and out of my male and female roles, tarmac laying macho man by day and, whenever possible, budding girlie by night. Enter Jackie who wanted a 'lovey-dovey' boyfriend-girlfriend relationship, which was all new to me. I'd never been in a 'lovey-dovey' relationship and while I was in this one I don't think I ever got the hang of it. The one point Jackie would agree with me over was that I was useless at relationships. Once we were a couple, she decided what our priorities were.

"You've got to do this, you've got to do that," I could hear her say without her saying it. "You need a proper job," she advised.

No longer a free spirit, there wasn't much chance of me doing what I liked when I liked. Every minute had to be accounted for. Marriage means commitment and I accept that.It wasn't long though before I had to ask myself where we drew the line between commitment and personal freedom.Just when were we allowed to follow our own interests without that taking anything away from the love and security of the marriage?Admittedly, if she'd given me the inch I would have taken the mile because that's the type of person I was.Perhaps she felt she couldn't trust me?My track record was crap:it was get up in the morning, earn some money, then go to the pub.Questions came like knives being thrown at me: "Where've you been?Who have you been talking to?Why are you late?" and "Have you been to the pub?"These were her most frequently asked questions. While I was following her regime, I smartened up and I accept I've Jackie to thank for that.Over the course of timeshe turned me around from being a drunken yob thinking nothing of laying tarmac on a road then going round hers to pick her up without having changed. The transformation worried those who knew me, including some members of my family, due to the fact that much of what they saw me doing was out of character. Gradually, Jackie helped me become a responsible adult. Buying the token family car, taking Mum and Dad-in-law out in it for little trips were all part of the package. Touring the Isle of Wight with them five times a year, carting their Labrador Ginger around, was one of the many events of family life I bought into.I wasn't a dog person then. Suddenly I had one.You could tell Ginger was around by his smell. This might've been due to his ill-health as he got older.

After him came a golden retriever called Rocky who had a smell all of his own. Being long-haired, it seemed worse than Ginger's. In smell, he took over where Ginger left off. Jackie always had a dog in her life. Following Rocky's demise, I bought Sophie for her.

Sophie was an Arabic breed called a saluki. They're racing dogs bred for speed, similar to greyhounds and whippets in this country.

I lived in a flat two floors up. Sophie worked out how to open the windows and with a kamikaze death wish, jump out. She was good friends with the law, used to walking round the inside of Harlow police station as if she was one of the staff. The police sort of semi-adopted her and Sophie like being there. If I couldn't find her when I got in I knew she was spending the day with the old Bill and drove to the police station to collect her. It was like going to pick her up from work. Curious to get to the bottom of her escape attempts, many of which were successful, her hypnotic whizzing round chasing her tail, plus her destructive habits with eating household furniture, I arranged with her breeder for her to be seen by an animal psychologist - a move that cost money. Even for those days she was an expensive dog. The diagnosis was that because she had been bred for the outdoors, confinement to a second floor flat in urban Essex had confused her. Perhaps she had a bi-polar disorder? If she had, according to the animal psychologist's report, the mania bit was set-off by us leaving the flat every day for work. Sophie was two bitches in one. When she was with us she was an affectionate, even-tempered animal and forgive me for going all soft here, from whose lively, soppy eyes shone love. I actually began to warm to the canine world through having her. Unfortunately, she had to go. She ate my flat. What do you do with a schizophrenic dog that was one thing with us and something else on her own? Common sense told us that in the end she was better off back with her breeder. One could say Sophie didn't know where she was or who she was without people around her. Jackie loved her so much she named our first child after her.

In our conversations with each other, Jackie had this way of suggesting what I should think. The sentences would be phrased something like: "Wouldn't it be a good idea if you took Mum...?" which is not a command as such - rather, a strong suggestion with a hidden condition attached to it. If she was annoyed about something I had or hadn't done I would want to compromise, though sometimes I felt a strong resistance to her opinion. Realising this feeling of resistance, which showed itself in my odd moments of irritability, was better kept to myself give me a quieter life.

Paying maintenance to Debbie and attention to Jackie was the only way I could deal with my domestic life, striking a delicate balance that if only slightly out would find me dashed on the rocks and finished. I objected to paying Debbie the exorbitant amount laid down by the court. The truth was that the amount I had to pay had built up due to my lack of responsibility to my children. Again Jackie helped me get that in order. It took a long time and had it been left to me, I would have gone to prison.

Chapter Eight

For the first two years of our relationship Jackie and I had a hard time. We survived on her money because mine was being used to pay-off massive debts I had brought on myself and we weren't even living together. Given my financial dependence on her we might as well have been. Johnny the gypsy's place was only ever a temporary roof over my head. Living in a shed and sitting round a campfire at night was difficult to justify to Jackie or anyone coming from my suburban Essex background. For a short while, I moved back in with my Mum and Dad whilst Jackie lived with hers. Her Mum and Dad used to feed me sometimes, mainly at weekends. I'd go to their house for Sunday lunch. I liked her mum's cooking but the house rules had to be followed. Jackie wouldn't smoke in front of her Mum who despised the habit.

It was two years before I could get a place due to having to clear my debts with the housing authority first. As soon as I moved into my own flat, I started cross-dressing again. Jackie went home every night. It was easier for her to leave from her Mum and Dad's house than from my flat as her place of work was only a short step up the road from where they lived.

I cross-dressed to feel comfortable. There was no sexual pleasure in it for me and I only did it at those times when I knew I wouldn't disturb anyone or be disturbed; it was a closet thing, private to me. I wasn't harming anyone so felt I could indulge myself. Those cross-dressing sessions were my refuge from the world when I needed it; my time for me when I would not open the door to anyone. I could still do that with Jackie in my life. Due to her orderly mind and excellent time-keeping, if she said she'd be round at five o' clock she'd be round at five o' clock. That was one of the few times I liked routine because I knew Jackie would not disturb me as she never took time off work unless she was on holiday, and never came round unexpectedly, so I was able to be Carol even if it was only in the safety of my own flat.

Eventually, Jackie moved in with me. I had the flat for about five years. We got married while living there. I still don't understand why I did it. I'd already been married once and didn't like it. Marriage restricted me. I kept Jackie waiting for years but she hung on. I know if I was her I would have dumped me within the first year of us meeting. I was no good to her. We could have carried on living together without being married but that wasn't Jackie. Her mum wanted her to get married. Most decisions, mainly the important ones were taken out of my hands, the arrangements being made by Jackie and her Mum. All I had to do was turn up. Both wanted the wedding with all the trimmings. They had it.

Our first child, Sophie, was born on the 27th July 1983. My Granddaughter, Zoë, has grown-up to look a lot like Sophie; tall, slim and blonde. Sophie was a 'together' person knowing exactly what she wanted and where she was going. A short time after she was born, we moved from the flat into a three-bedroom, semi-detached house which we ended up buying.

During the years Sophie was growing-up, she was a typical tomboy with her own edge to it no-one could imitate. While she was young, she didn't like anything girlie. She wanted to hang out with the boys, and she did, beating them at just about anything they happened to be involved in. From almost day one she was football mad which over the years cost us a fortune in Arsenal tops; she used to live in her Arsenal football club strip. Maturing quickly, she was a precocious child and developed into a strong character, doing well at school, later earning herself some fast track promotion at work. By seventeen she held a managerial post with a fast food company.

Ross, our second child, was the young man of the family, obliged to grow-up in an all female household, which was not easy for him. Sophie talked for him, directing him to do what she thought he should do. When our youngest, Alicia, came along, poor Ross was fated to have two very strong little ladies bossing him around. With two sisters to reckon with trying to mould him into their girlie world, it must have been difficult for Ross to balance that with his need to be a real boy in a real boy's world. His mother and sisters looked after him. I'm ashamed to admit I was not much good to him. I just could not relate to him the way I could the girls. Ross was a lovely, lively boy who tried hard to please everyone.

Later, he became angry. That was my fault. I didn't give him what he needed which was a male role model to look up to. He wanted a real Dad to identify with. I did not fill that role. I can't deny my responsibility for the consequences of not being there for my son as he was growing-up when he really needed a Dad in his life. I was still around for most of his childhood, leaving when he was eleven. If I'd been there during his teenage years I could have smoothed his path to manhood. Ross used to love it when I involved him in what I was doing. It did not happen very often but when it did you could see the benefit it had on him. Coming away with me, staying in hotel rooms, he could act grown-up and be with me and the men at the garages while we were working. He loved cars and could drive as well as any adult. When moving the vehicles round the garages, his ability to manoeuvre them in tight spaces was exceptional. Ross's spatial-mechanical skills were remarkable for a boy his age, backed up by the fact he never crashed any of the cars he drove, unlike some of the blokes working for me. Ross was as good if not better than some of them.

One weekend when I took him camping on a friend's farm near our home, I promised him he could drive my car on some of the surrounding land which was a very large area of cornfield that had been harvested shortly before we arrived. It was a big field of stubble. That made his weekend. He lived on that for months telling all his mates he'd spent it driving my car. Saying it like that does not seem much but that weekend he got through a whole tank of petrol. The vehicle must have seemed like a big lorry to him. It was actually a large Volvo manual gear change. Going up and down the stubble field like he'd always driven - sometimes at high speed for this was a car capable of well over a hundred miles an hour - Ross churned up enough dust to create his own desert storm. In my imagination, I saw this picture of people being able to see this huge dust cloud advancing in the distance, looking like the trail left behind from several wagon trains shifting rapidly across a nineteenth century American desert plain. Ross crammed as much excitement as he could into the time we had together. There were a few more visits to the farm that summer so he could act like a grown-up. Suddenly, those rare life packed days for Ross playing alpha male were snatched away from him. Due to my lack of input, he grew restless. His mother and sisters couldn't do anything with him, each passing day seeing his anger grow. At school, Ross would be moody and disruptive, whilst at home he'd be rude and aggressive. That didn't happen if I was around. When I was away he became a different person, hating everyone.

Knowing I've damaged him and that I am no longer in a position to put that right, I hope I'll be able to say sorry to him one day. That quality of love children draw from a healthy relationship with both their parents while they're growing-up can't be experienced the same way when they are adults. It is too late then.

Alicia was always several steps ahead of children her own age. She entered the world years ahead of herself on the 19th March 1987. She was my youngest and by the time she was six seemed more like a teenager. I have to use a cliché here - She was a typical 'little madam'. I used to ask her: "What are you?" and she would reply in her angelic little voice, every word well-pronounced, albeit in broad Essex: "A little madam."

Unlike Sophie, Alicia wasn't a tomboy. She loved being a girl, experimenting with clothes and make-up; a young lady who had the largest shoe collection I knew of for someone her age. If they had heels she had to have them. Her love of shoes was bordering on a fetish. Alicia had one of the cheekiest little faces going. She only had to look at you and she got what she wanted. That was a hint of how she might treat her boyfriends when she was older. Unless her personality did a U-turn, which I think unlikely, she'll be stepping into the adult world sooner than expected.

I really do miss them all. I'd give anything to have them back in my life. I have to hope that one day they'll contact me.

I had these shopping binges, usually after I'd been upset by someone. I would spend hundreds of pounds on clothes only to throw them out of my car window on the way home. I would leave the area at speed and be long gone before the dumped clothes had finished scattering across the nearest field. Imagine a farmer finding one of his bulls with a designer dress lying beside it.

I was horrible to Jackie and the children. Jackie could see right through my defences and for that reason almost anything she said made me angry. It is hard to explain what went wrong. My Partner used to do everything for me. Even if I got home at one in the morning my dinner would be waiting for me. Jackie put up with me working late nearly every day which showed real trust in me and an amazing tolerance of my bad time-keeping. There'd be no coded silences or angry confrontations over my lateness when I got in. Reflecting on the happier moments of my marriage, I realise how blessed I was having a Partner who loved me enough to understand me, putting up with the worst of me when the madness took over and I became a monster again.

I loved Jackie as if she was my sister. Jackie was in

love with me. Unfortunately, the 'me' she was in love with was an imaginary person.

"I love you," I would tell her, but to me these were simply kind words said by one sister to another. I could never return her love in the way she wanted.

Lately, having lost some of the arrogance which had stopped me from seeing a lot of the good that was around me, the idea of love has become more appealing.Still, it is easy to fall for the fluffy image, neatly packaged with an attractive, colourful wrapping, which is fantasy.

The neatly packaged fluffy image was my impression of how Jackie saw our marriage.I tried to keep that fluffy image going by playing the good husband and father, whilst in my imagination I was having an altogether different experience of intimacy with her.

I would not like someone to do to me what I did to her.Today, I realise what a privilege it is for me to have the freedom to look back on what I was doing then, compare that with what I've been through in recent years, and finally appreciate the value of love.

Chapter Nine

I was being slowly buried alive under a mass of papers with demands printed on them, figures that just didn't add up to me, like the senseless yet unavoidable conflict between my real inner self and my social self. The debts were my responsibility. I needed to escape. Perhaps that need left me open to Dave's influence? I could have resisted but I needed to see where he would take me, believing that he would get me closer to the truth about myself. Without the intervention of anyone else, I believe my struggle with the power of emotions would have killed me.

Finding Dave, or rather him finding me after all those years, could be seen as a weird coincidence. Convinced it was more than coincidence, I stand by my belief that it was our fate to meet again to settle unfinished business. I did *not* ask for what followed.

At the time, I was working in Bury St Edmunds doing an installation on a garage forecourt. Bollards had been left at the entrance and exit to the forecourt to stop people driving in to get fuel. Human nature being what it is, they still came. I'd spent a good part of the day telling the public we were shut. There weren't even any petrol pumps on the islands. The arrival of a public that was far from 'general' came with the suddenness and impact of a dam breaking, and my past flooded into my present. This powerful voice projecting a flamboyant cockney-Scottish accent called out: "Oy

Tammie!" causing me to look up from what I was doing. There stood this grinning, red-faced, slender, but muscular bloke. He looked strong. I didn't give a serious thought to him at first. Covered in diesel oil, dazed and embarrassed by hearing someone call me Tammie, I looked round frantically to see which if any of my men had heard it. I was about to say: "can't you see we're bloody shut?" when I recognised him. Dave Ingle was back in my life. I'd not seen him since I was twenty-one. We last met before I married Debbie.

My old friend had been to what sounded like a beer festival in Bury with his driver, known as Lovable. Like Extra Large in the café, seriously big Lovable took up the whole of the driver's side. You couldn't get a cigarette paper between him and Dave in the front passenger seat. When planning the ergonomics of the driver and front seat passenger area, the designers of the car hadn't allowed for the possibility of someone of Peewee's build using it, leading me to wonder if they'd based its dimensions on someone with the body frame of a whippet in sit up and beg mode.

This charismatic couple reminded me of Bonnie and Clyde, without the Tommy guns, on their way back to Scotland. We exchanged addresses, though I couldn't imagine Dave turning up on my doorstep. I knew if ever I was in Glasgow I could call on him if I needed.

For about six months my old friend didn't really enter my mind, when I got this job in Glasgow and thought I'd get in touch with him.

A company I worked for had garages all over Scotland, giving me many opportunities to go there. After all I was the boss. If anyone in my firm needed to go to Scotland I was the one who went.

Over the next five and a half years, I made several visits to Glasgow. Up there, with Dave, Dave's partner Frank, and Peewee, I found everything I needed to be sort of me. Unfortunately, it was a 'not quite me' but another virtual reality me, the taint of transvestism still there. Dave knew who I wanted to be from remembering our adventures in the 1960s. He knew I liked to cross-dress and this was often discussed during my stays with him and Ewan. I became Dave's idea of me, encouraged to carry on camping when I desperately wanted him to recognise that this was not his own personal drag act to be performed in front of him whenever he felt like being entertained. I was serious. He knew that but he wanted to put off facing the real issue concerning me. After all, we had a decade and a half to catch up with.

One evening, when we were sitting together having a drink, Dave asked me why I had changed. He couldn't understand why having lived the way I did when we were young within a few years of losing contact with him I had ruined it all by marrying a woman. Defending myself, I told him: "You went off and left me".

In my teens, he encouraged and kept my dream alive. I thought he loved me. My compulsion to cross-dress was driven by my excitement over being with him. Influenced by portrayals in old films, in my virtual reality world I was a gangster's moll, finding great comfort in this. At the same time, Dave was moulding me into his own fantasy figure. While that was happening, Dave and Ewen's relationship, whatever it had been, was breaking down. The atmosphere between them changed from the moment I was in Dave's life again. If I was there, Dave would ignore Frank unless he was telling him to do something. Frank would speak and Dave would carry on talking to me as if Frank wasn't there. That made me uncomfortable. I was coming between them. It was all me and no Frank. Frank was given his orders then told to p*** off. I didn't want it to be that way. I should have stopped it but I didn't. Frank was all right. I felt sorry for him. Dave gave me everything I wanted: clothes, money, absolutely anything.

During 1988, after several visits from me, Dave and Frank decided they would convert a room on the second floor of their house for my use. Given a choice of three I chose the middle one which used to be something perhaps best described as a large upstairs lounge. Four weeks later, I returned to open the door and see the room I had left transformed into luxury. The bare coldness of non-use with drab brown wallpaper and maroon walls had gone. The room, which was about thirty by twenty feet in overall size, now had an en suite bathroom built into the corner on the left as I walked in. A modern coal burner gas fire fitted the old style fireplace without taking anything away from its period charm. In my room, with that fireplace the old went hand in hand with the new. They fitted well together. It somehow seduced me, drawing me deeper into my world of change.

Recalling my room in its entirety, almost the whole length of one wall was made-up of built-in wardrobes. Half-way along that wall, there was provision for a bed, and then the wardrobes carried on. At the far end, although it looked like part of a wardrobe, I opened the door to find a walk-in office complete with its own telephone. Apart from the bit of history in my room the whole house was modern. Thick carpets, lowered ceilings, concealed lighting giving a soft glow from behind a picture on the wall, were all features of it I remember. There were also low-voltage halogens on the ceiling. It was a plush executive room that cost a lot of money. The bed was like being in the cockpit of an aircraft. You could operate all the lights and everything in my room from the bed. I know it sounds a bit seventies, a bit Jason King, or James Bond. It was Dave doing a modern Llewellyn-Bowen with his dangly bits, by that I mean L-B's dangly bits in the form of rocks all strung on string hanging from the ceiling giving concealed lighting. Dave, Frank and the contractors were being creative. With enthusiasm and energy they took on and played out this role, turning that space into my living quarters. I felt valued, comfortable, and totally safe there. It was to remain my room for a long time.

From 1987 till about 1991 my association with Dave was friendship and fun. He encouraged me to take part in his macho activities. Despite being gay, he had episodes when he appeared to be a 'girl loving macho male of the tarmac'. We shared a passion for motor racing. I hadn't lost my desire to be out there getting high on the slipstream action of the racing circuit. You could smell the high octane fuel. Sometimes I thought I could see Dave sniff hungrily at the air, drawing it through his nostrils to get high. The horrendous power of the superbikes Dave and I rode on the way to those speedway afternoons was a jet-fuelled heaven, recreating the buzz I got from pushing a formula one car to its limits round a race track.

Now in his forties, Dave's outlook hadn't mellowed, being, if anything, more extreme than that of the fourteen year-old boy he was when I first met him. To him, Glaswegians were all 'Jockstraps' who made good skivvies for a bit of beer money.Believing he was Scotland's answer to the Krays, Dave Ingle and Glaswegians were a lethal combination, like putting two highly combustible materials together.

Dave's anger and paranoia were disturbing.He had also developed his own version of a Glaswegian accent that was Rab C. Nesbitt before Rab C. Nesbitt appeared on our television screens.

Dave and some of his hangers-on, or mates, I don't know whether they were his real friends, had their own sub-culture.These 'mates' believed that under Dave's guidance, as long as they stayed loyal to him they were safe from other 'gangs'.This provided him with a health and safety insurance policy, partly for their benefit, but largely for his.

He always had money, which was what attracted them to him: he became their bank account and liked to control what they had.Buying friendship became second nature to him.If he liked someone, he would give, but he'd want a return on his investment.If he didn't like someone, he would let them know. There was no question of me or anyone being able to defend the unfortunate person he wanted to sort out.For a gay man, he was strong, his robust body, energy and charisma, challenging the gay male stereotype.He didn't do weight training and probably didn't even know what it was.His strength was greater than his physical appearance suggested, fuelled and driven by years of resentment concentrated inside that small, wiry, but powerful frame.

My Mum told me I had so much aggression in me but it wasn't mine. I was acting out stuff that was really Dave's, becoming one of the many channels for his anger. It was like getting a bug and suffering its symptoms, bits of Dave's negative energy broke off his aura, found mine, and clung to it. Sadistic and uncompromising or kind and generous, Dave's presence could be felt by those he had close business or personal relationships with. His hangers-on had to test the ground before approaching him. They could never be themselves with him in the room. In his eyes, they existed as mere extensions of himself. If someone upset him, Queensbury rules did not apply.

As time passed, I noticed changes in Dave that worried me. Like any physical expression of love, to me gay sex was the business of consenting adults who fancied each other. Perhaps I was naive, I don't know. Up till about 1991, I never thought Dave would step over the line. He was part of my history. I was troubled that this did not stop him trying to get off with me. It was hard for me to accept that someone I trusted who was gay wanted me to sleep with him when he knew I wasn't interested in him that way.

"No matter what you've done you'll still be a bloke," he insisted. I was under the impression that gays wouldn't want me that way if they knew and valued who I was, what I wanted, and what I didn't want. Why would a gay male want to have someone who was going to become a physical female? He wanted me to be the gay male transvestite I was in his fantasy.

Chapter Ten

Some four years had passed since my reunion with Dave at Bury St Edmunds and I still hadn't found the courage to tell Jackie who I was. Instead, I built this wall of hate between us to distract her from finding out the truth about me. One day I discovered it was easier for me to run away. Thinking that if I could make Jackie hate me so much my leaving would be less painful for her, I said some very hurtful things. I am afraid it looks like a pathetic plea for forgiveness but I didn't mean them.

In 1988 I was able to visit Russell Reid for a consultation at The London Institute, Warwick Road, near Earl's Court, to help sort my head out. It gave me such hope till I discovered it was all private. A GP had found Dr. Reid's name somewhere. He recommended that I went to see him. An appointment was made and I ended up in front of Russell all kitted out girlie style: bangles, dangly earrings, painted fingernails, all the things I now detest. Russell was a nice man. What struck me about him was that he was polite, sympathetic, and understanding. His professional manner was that of a gentleman. I looked upon him as a friend rather than a psychiatrist.

"Hello Carol. How are you? Come into my office. Now tell me what is happening," was his welcome. For once I knew I would not have to put up my usual defences to stop myself from being hurt. I didn't see him again till March 1997.

I moved out of the family home for about six months. During that time, I was there probably more than I had been in the previous four years put together, going back regularly to see if Jackie and the children were all right. Still working, paying the mortgage on the house, with hindsight both that, plus the fact I was missing my family, made my moving out a pointless exercise, except for giving me a tough lesson in how important they were to me.

Jackie thought I was staying with someone else. Actually, I'd taken a six month lease out on a flat in Leigh-on-Sea near Southend.

I had lived in Leigh-on-Sea for about a month when I had an eventful day. Early one morning, turning out of my street on to the main road, I came to a set of traffic lights where I had to stop. I noticed a police car pull up behind me. The traffic lights seemed to stay red for a long time. All I had been doing was driving my car which had only been serviced the day before so I knew they weren't stopping me for faulty lights. The lights turned to green and I pulled away. I had just got across the A13 when I saw blue lights flashing behind me. A siren urged me to pull over. Expecting trouble, I pushed the button for the window on my driver's side to go down. A policeman peered through the window. He politely asked me the predictable question: "Is this your car, Madam?" Without hesitation, I replied, "Yes, officer." Given I was dressed as a female with the voice of a scrum half no wonder he looked at me 'gobsmacked'. He must have stood there for about thirty seconds before he said anything else. When his brain switched on again he asked me if I had any documents with me. When producing my driving licence a lightning panic flashed through me. I suddenly felt very hot and flustered, and that wasn't down to the hormones: "Male driving licence with male holder dressed as female - "oops!" went off in my head like another siren, jolting me back into reality. I pulled myself together and thought: "No problem." I had my certificate from Russell's clinic that said I could dress in a way that fitted my desired gender role. Handing this document over with my driving licence, I felt sure there'd be no further questions. Instead, it put the interrogating officer into tilt mode. He kept looking at me, then my driving licence, closely followed by my document from the clinic. His face mimed the phrase: "This does not compute. This does not fit the norm." It was too much for him. He returned to his car to discuss the problem with his colleague. I knew that if they were going to stop me they would have done a vehicle check whilst they were sitting behind me at the lights. They would have known that the car was registered under a male name. I thought once common sense took over they would let me go. Wrong! I travelled thousands of miles every week and I'm arrested five hundred yards from my flat. It turned into a farce. These two Mr. Plods decided they could arrest me for impersonating a female. At first, I thought they had been seduced by my Volvo which was fairly new at the time. It was massive and looked like an aeroplane without wings. To me, as it accelerated it almost took off like one. Technically, it was a twenty-four valve fuel-injected job.

What might have started as two police officers' curiosity over my car ended up with me being arrested, If anyone knows Leigh-on-Sea you don't leave a thirty-five thousand pound car in one place for too long because somebody will decide to remove it for you or damage it trying. No matter how much I protested, these two audition cases for 'The Bill' decided I must go with them to Southend police station. The officer who came to my car first kept calling me by my male name which was on my driving licence; although the document from the clinic clearly stated that the name I used was Miss Carol Royce. Once we'd arrived outside the station I got out of the police car and the same officer said: "Mind your wig, dear." This upset me as my hair was mine not a bloody wig.

Having been taken to this dull room and told to wait, I wasn't happy. Gone for about half an hour, the two officers seemed to be making me hang about, then, when one returned to tell me I'd be there for a further half an hour and asked me if I wanted a drink, I felt relieved. "What's the problem?" I asked. "We're just checking something. It might take a little while," was his emotionless reply. It was about an hour before I saw the two officers again. Being made to wait to be charged with whatever they could lay on me made me angry. They had no reason to treat me like that for legally I had done nothing wrong. Although the male name on my driving licence didn't match my female appearance, the document from my psychiatrist which I showed both officers should have dealt with that. I suppose I ought to have been grateful I was put in an interview room and not a cell. There was no explanation why I'd been held. Unhappy over having spent six hours of my life sitting in a police station for the cause of British justice, I couldn't help thinking that the least those officers could have done was give me an explanation.

Chapter Eleven

In 1993, thanks to a friend of Dave's, I visited the Albany clinic in Prestwich, Greater Manchester, arriving there in an anxious state. The Albany is a fully-equipped private clinic that provides advice, support, and medical treatment for transsexuals.Everything needed for a successful transformation is under one roof.

At the end of the day its hatches have to be battened down to protect it from vandalism. The delinquent members of Manchester's population could not get its head around gender dysphoria

I remember arriving in my car on the very first morning, driving round looking for a small hospital, finding the address I'd been given, and being faced with a big metal grille that looked like something out of the Fall's Road in Belfast.Only the razor wire and searchlights were missing. If you arrive as early as I did on my first visit, don't be put off by this. The kindness and support you find inside make-up for the grimness outside.

I was put at ease as soon as I got through the door. The female staff treated me with kindness, respect, and understanding.That made it easy for me to talk to them.Apologising for coming through the door as a male helped me establish a good relationship with them from the start.

I realised how money made doors open.It gave me the choice to go there, and no doubt had an influence on the way I was treated, but I still felt the girls cared about me. What made the place work so well was that it was run exclusively by women. There was no need for me to prove to them I was female. They accepted this without question. Sometimes Jill used to listen to me 'run on' for hours. She had this way of making me feel better. Back then, I was a sad person, full of self-pity.

The other person who helped me was Marion. If Jill wasn't around I used to pour it all out to her. Both those girls saved my life. They were the first understanding women I'd spoken to about my gender dysphoria. I owe them a lot. I became attached to them, and I suppose, for a time, dependent on them. Their gender at birth was female: from their earliest memories they knew they were female, and never wanted to be anything else, yet they were able to empathise with me.

My operation had been booked for 1994. The door was slammed shut on this option when my money ran out. I couldn't afford to be treated at the Albany anymore. Grateful to the female staff there for what they had done for me up to that point, I accepted this without any bitterness. It was a business. I was running my own in Essex so I appreciated that, like me, they had to make money to survive.

I began to read everything I could about gender dysphoria. Jill and Marion encouraged me to do this, telling me where to look for books on the subject which I did not need a dictionary to understand. I've since learnt I could've received hormone therapy in my teens, delaying puberty to avoid the pain of becoming a man by staying a boy till I had my operation. One might say I could have been eased into womanhood rather than booted into manhood. Joining GEMS to get to know other gender dysphoric persons was a big step.

I can't help thinking that a lot of the social stigma attached to gender dysphoria comes from fearthrough continuing ignorance of the facts. Until that's reversed, those suffering from the condition will be seen as a potential threat to society, being both the perverted and the perverting.

Some of the things I read got my hackles up, such as the claim that people diagnosed with gender dysphoria are not really female because they have to have hormones and major surgery to be so. There are a lot of people out there who are totally negative to the plight of these sufferers.

Of course, the critics don't have the condition.It's even been said that when their youth starts to fade and the male role no longer works for them like it did, male gender dysphoric persons want to change sex to female. They can then use the female role to increase their opportunities for a better life as females from middle-age onwards?This attitude rubbishes many gender dysphoric people's genuine need to achieve their true identities, and the argument that gender realignment is not a simple matter of lifestyle choice. My world had not ended because I'd reached the menopause.Playing male would never be the best years of my life.It amazes me how some writers, with the amount of intelligence they should have, could come out with something so judgmental.

The career I chose for myself brought in good money.I could have minced around an office all day but I would not have earned much.My job was a career that even in the 1970s and 80s would have been hard for a biological female to do, let alone keep up, not so much physically as socially, so you could say the male role allowed me to enjoy a good standard of living for many years. As I keep stressing though, I've always been female, but with some useful masculine traits to my advantage.

Thankfully, the arguments put forward to justify blocking the alteration of post-operative gender dysphorics' birth certificates are being reviewed. The BBC television programme 'Newsnight' carried an item concerning this in the edition broadcast on Thursday 11th July, 2002. Justification for not being allowed to alter my birth certificate to reflect my newly realigned gender was: "if you suffer or in the past have suffered from gender dysphoria everyone has a right to know about it." Following gender realignment, former gender dysphoric persons like me are only trying to lead a relatively comfortable life that cannot be achieved if our previous history is still visible to certain others.

I did not like the way those suffering from gender dysphoria were portrayed on television and the media in general. My appearance on a television programme convinced me that its makers had invited people with gender identity problems to take part in it solely for the benefit of stirring up the public. The edition I appeared in was the equivalent of throwing petrol on a fire. They were warming up for a riot in that studio, the producers loving it. Sad people went on stage to be 'slagged' off by sad people in the studio audience. I wasn't one of the hecklers. I felt that those who were chosen to take part were both ridiculed and ridiculing themselves.

They were just men dressed as women who allowed the make-up department to go overboard.If you are a male, put a dress on, go to the pub, then act male, see what happens. You'd be laughed right out of the place. If you want to pass as a woman you have got to act like one.When a man enters a room and sees what looks like a woman in both physical appearance and dress, for a nanosecond he will almost certainly accept what he sees, because on the surface it fits the information he has stored in his brain as to what are the most basic features a person must have to look female.For the first few seconds of seeing a person who seems to be female, the male observer probably decides that person is female.After the first impression, received in a flash, watching how this person who looks female talks and behaves for a longer period adds to it, either weakening or strengthening it.It may take a while, but in most cases, sooner or later the observer will work it out.

Very little is known about Gender Dysphoria, or transsexualism as it is better known. Seeing portrayals of male 'transvestism' on television which always seemed like a cabaret act to most people. While I could see how the look and behaviour of some may attract critical comments, others may be suffering from guilt over enjoying cross-dressing.

As I have mentioned transvestites are usually men who feel the urge to act out their idea of being a woman by dressing-up in women's clothes, which may result in their getting sexually aroused and climaxing.

Most people have heard the word 'transsexual' and assumed that transsexuals and transvestites were one and the same. Worryingly, most people's understanding, or rather misunderstanding, of transsexualism was based on the idea that it was a sexual perversion. Transvestites are apparently fetishists but, as we will explain later, it is not that simple. Doctor Russell Reid expresses the opinion that: 'transvestites generally don't want to physically change sex.' While that is true, it seems that there are different degrees of transvestism. Sometimes the boundary between transvestism and transsexualism may be blurred.

It is just that some people know where they are and some people don't.

Visiting someone to clarify what they thought on the subject, I asked Barbara Ross, who is a trained gender counsellor, if transvestites can become gender dysphoric.

"Some transvestites don't want to change," Barbara told me.In some cases the wife or partner knows." She explained that there are transvestites who start their cross-dressing career wearing female clothes that are desperately over the top; wigs you can't miss and gearin colours that literally scream 'trannie!' at you. Once they have gone to these extremes to push the boundaries of what is socially acceptable as far back as they can, they may become more comfortable with their female personas. Their cross-dressing settles into a manner that is more in keeping with reality; they tone it down so their appearance is more subtle, which may be seen as naturally feminine. Transvestism is accepted by some employers, who will allow an employee to practise it as part of his working life: males who dress modestly as females in the workplace can be good at their jobs because they are able to successfully blend their cross-dressing with their professional role. These people are happy to stay physically male, but want to express the strong feminine side of their identities by regularly adopting a female persona because this way they feel at their greatest ease.

There are people who after having spent years being a transvestite discover that it is no longer enough for them. It is then that they seek gender realignment. Barbara suggested that they had probably always been gender dysphoric, but initially might have been too frightened to confront it, turning to transvestism instead as a halfway house until the emotional disturbances blocking their desire for gender resolution settled.

One psychiatrist told me I was a transvestite. When I objected to this he said I should know what I am. The fact I didn't follow the national health route right from the start made me a transvestite as far as he was concerned. If you don't want to be labelled 'transvestite' you must follow textbook procedure by shutting down your old life completely without going through the experimental stages developing your self-awareness naturally, a process that differs in character from person to person. The NHS way is only a fraction about this and mostly about following rules."

To me on the one hand, I knew who I was, on the other, medical professionals were telling me what I had to do to be who I was.

As the psychiatrist only saw me as male, which is what my birth certificate said I am, in his eyes I wavered between dressing as a female in places away from the family home and the workplace where I practised my male role, and playing male. To him, then, I was a transvestite; a man in drag.

What the television programme I was on did show was how gender dysphoric persons are judged with little or no attempt made to understand their condition.

Then in came the clever twat who'd been rehearsing the line over and over in his head found the moment he could claim his thirty seconds of fame by shouting: "Babies need operations before Transsexuals need their willies cut off!" Sorry, he meant to say male-to-female transsexuals. Females-to-males want one, don't they?"

The producers weren't interested in using the airtime to discuss how complex and tragic a condition gender dysphoria is. They could have encouraged a balanced debate on it. If people felt that much disgust in us, or found us that funny, I'm more than just worried about our society.

This narrow-mindedness can have serious consequences. At the time of writing, I believe that constructed - or those like myself I'd prefer to call 'realigned' - females are not protected by the current rape legislation. Imagine two females, one biological, one realigned, walking together in a park. Both are attacked and raped. Probably, the only charge the realigned female could bring against her attacker is assault. Surely rape is rape no matter who the victim of that crime is? The law states that a constructed [realigned] female is not a real female. Going by the twisted logic of today's society, it would probably be the realigned female who would get arrested for causing a public nuisance by being at the scene.

Around this time, with the medication from the Albany, my body took on a more female shape. I began to develop breasts. My face had a softer outline. I noticed my hair - once bombardment by the evil testosterone had slowed down - looked softer too. My body movements, which had to be learned and refined over time, became noticeably feminine.

This part of the transformation is probably the hardest for gender dysphorics. For people who aren't gender dysphoric, usually Mum teaches her daughters how to act female, Dad teaches his sons how to act male. I wanted to unlearn the male role I'd been socialised into. Experience showed me that unless I suffered total amnesia, there was no way I could unlearn how to act like a male.

Although I had many male traits, Jackie often picked me up on the way I did things because I didn't do them like a man.

"Why are you standing like that? Don't wear shorts," she'd demand, because I had girlie legs and she thought the weirdness of that would have a bad effect on her image. I don't know whether I copied it from other females without realising it or it just came naturally to me or it was a bit of both if that makes sense, but when I felt relaxed I stood like a woman. I didn't have to think about sitting or standing like a woman then. It just happened. That's what I meant when I was talking to you earlier about the left and the right hand. People saw me do everything right-handed. That right-handedness felt unnatural. I wanted to do everything with my left hand, which was the natural way for me. I had to hold that back for the sake of looking right. I'd always do that for Jackie because I thought that as she believed I was right-handed, if I didn't do it that way, which was the way she wanted it done, there would be a row. Sometimes I would forget and do it my way, she'd criticise me for it, I'd go on the defensive, and there would be a row. It was constantly in my mind to keep doing the right thing.

While honing the finer details of being female, I had this constant battle with the general public and the medics who were treating me. I felt they largely saw me as sick rather than just different, even though I was able to make rational decisions and run my own life as I always had. I had to be referred by my doctor to see a psychiatrist at Charing Cross Hospital, a second psychiatrist, and a gender counsellor in Norwich. If I could not convince these who I was, then I didn't stand a chance. Some doctors seem unable to become involved in more than just the medical side of the process. One of my doctors said that while he found the condition interesting, he knew little about it.

When I visited Charing Cross I only ever saw male psychiatrists. It's my belief that psychiatrists tend to be males whose idea of femininity is sometimes outrageously stereotypical, unless they've been winding me up as part of the real life test. One made a remark about me wearing trousers. "I see you're wearing trousers. That's not very feminine, is it?" he sneered. "Women wear trousers a lot these days. We're about to enter the twenty-first century remember," I retorted swiftly. "My wife doesn't. She wears nice skirts all the time. I think that's very feminine."

That got my hackles up. After a bit of verbal sparring with him, he told me I was argumentative and that real women did not argue with their men. I think the fact I was twenty minutes late for the appointment riled him. When he challenged me over my lateness, the thought flashed through my head that it was a woman's prerogative to change her mind or be late, so he could not say that wasn't feminine. He would've probably come back with the remark: "Come on, you've got a penis - you must be male." It's unlikely these psychiatrists will ever be able to empathise with those who are gender dysphoric.

Someone I knew in Romford had been waiting ten years for gender realignment surgery. She went backwards and forwards to Charing Cross. Unable to convince her psychiatrists she was genuine because she couldn't satisfy all the criteria laid down in some manual somewhere, being unemployed, living on income support, and generally isolated from other people, there was nowhere for her to go.

Chapter Twelve

Dave Ingle had connections with the pop music, fashion, and sporting worlds, pushing his way into the lives of those he thought would be of use to him. I called him the groupie with attitude. He got in with people he idolised, making sure he did well out of it.

Dave loved the smell of the petrol they used for the motorcycles on the speedway track, which I think was aviation fuel, a little bit of ignorance here. One whiff and he was high, looking forward to all his victories. He ran the master class on how to mix business with pleasure.

One day during the summer of 1994, it was decided that Dave and I and his back up team would fly down to Margate. Dave changed his back up team regularly. This lot were a real laugh. Manic conversation and laughter filled the plane for the hour and a half or so we were airborne. We became his crazy gang in his aircraft. Dave kept this plane, which we called the gang bus, at Prestwick airport. He always liked to make a point to everyone he knew that he owned a plane, even if it was only a bit of one. I think he owned a few of the rivets holding it together. It was his status symbol. His friends had fast cars, he had his aeroplane.

On the day, we got to the airport at about ten. It was a warm, sunny morning. When we reached the aircraft, the engines were purring as if they were in ecstasy over Dave's sexy pilot, Doug, doing the pre-flight check on them. This was the foreplay before the climax. You might say that from a distance I was doing my pre-flight check on Doug whilst he was talking to the control tower on the aircraft radio link.

Dave was ranting at Doug: "Why've you got the engines running? That's costing me." Doug would whisper to himself, smooth as Irish coffee: "Get a life and let me get on with being a pilot."

Doug was the cream of the Irish race, a thoroughbred, his black hair combed back as smooth and as glossy as the coat of a cat that'd been well looked after, showing up nicely when the sunlight of that glorious morning shone on it. His vagabond face, his deep blue eyes, his charm, made him the perfect young Irishman. He had little mannerisms that made his Irishness sexy. His personality - and he certainly had one - was very present and real compared to the others who were there, including Dave. Doug was like a sentence on the page of a book that stood out and hit you. He had a special charisma. I admired Doug, Jackie, and Dave because they all had charisma. Doug's was really special though. He had that little bit extra. My memory of him still fills me with this fantastic warmth; in fact, right now, as I'm speaking, it's giving me 'goosebumps'.

I don't want to leave this memory so forgive me if I draw it out a bit, savouring every second like when I'm watching the dishy barman of an Irish pub in Essex slowly pull me half a pint of Guinness on a scorching hot day. It must be the Irish in me. There I was the mongrel Murphy besotted with this Adonis of Irish masculinity.

Doug stood about six feet tall, was well proportioned, and mega muscular like a body builder. Talk about bend me, shape me any way he wanted me. I meant that as an invitation from me to him. I'd say he was probably in his early thirties at the time. Before coming to England he lived in Belfast.

We all got on board the plane. Once we were ready, the aircraft taxied to the main runway, took off, and we were airborne. Dave was on the turn, sitting in the co-pilot's seat pretending he knew everything that was going on, ranting: "Shift this f****** Airfix kit, Paddy. I want to get there today."

I think the plane was owned by one of these syndicates that about twenty people had shares in. It was a nice plane, not that I know much about aircraft. Accommodating up to ten or twelve people, it was a two propeller job, very posh inside, with leather seats. It even had a well-stocked bar which I thought was dodgy. Booze and aircraft could be a lethal combination. If the plane was going to crash Dave and the drunkards he used to hang out with would probably say: "Grab the malt" before parachuting out with the only parachute on board. I don't know whether there were any parachutes on that plane. Maybe they were locked away, in which case it would have been disastrous if they had been needed urgently.

Doug said it was one of those aircraft that would glide if necessary, unless it was blown-up or vital bits of it fell off during the flight. It had two engines but could be flown and brought down safely on one.

Don't worry, Carol. I counted all the bits before we took off and they were all there and looked as if they were stuck on properly," was an example of Doug's wit. According to him that plane was safer than a helicopter.

Until Doug told me this I was under the impression that if the engines were cut it just fell out of the sky.

Oh well, Carol I thought to myself:If you're going to die at least you'll have someone sexy with you when it happens.

We'd only been in the air a short time when I asked Dave if I could sit at the controls with Doug. This was like telling a small child I wanted to play with his favourite toy. He went into one before giving up his seat saying: "Go on then. A quick go."

"He'll suck his thumb in a minute," Doug commented. We both laughed together, excluding the others from our thoughts as if we were sharing a joke that only we understood. That made Dave jealous and he let us know it. He was hilarious. "Speak English, you f****** Irish git!" he yelled.

Doug had this lovely broad Belfast accent. His words seemed to blend beautifully, flowing in an almost musical way. He was always making me laugh with the things he came out with; his 'little ditties' as he called them. He'd always start with: "Back home we'd say..." suggesting he was about to tell some gem of Irish folklore, or say a few words of Irish wisdom to a fascinated audience.

About an hour into the flight, Doug switched to autopilot. He jumped up from his pilot's seat telling me he was going to the toilet which was in a room the size of a broom cupboard. You had to really want to go to risk using it.

"I won't be a minute," he muttered quickly, the speed of his voice revealing how desperate he was. "Be a good girl. Don't touch anything. She's on auto pilot.

She'll fly herself," all this said in one breath. For me it was like sitting in the front passenger seat of a car doing over a hundred with no driver. A funny feeling somewhere between excitement and anxiety caught me off guard when I looked at the mass of gauges stretching across the width of the cockpit, glowing with an eerie, luminous green, expecting them to start flickering like mad then fall to zero. I still don't think leaving people's lives in the control of gadgets is a good idea. My car had cruise control but I still had to steer it. That thing didn't need anybody. How, I don't know, but at some point I must've touched or kicked a serious bit that flew the plane because suddenly the radio erupted with swearing. The edited version was: "Who the bloody hell's flying that plane?"

Doug came charging back into the pilot's cabin, adjusting his trousers frantically almost catching his pride and joy in the zip. Removing all the "f" words from his outburst, if my translation of what I remember him saying is correct, I think he meant: "What have you touched?"

He wasn't a happy man so I avoided any jokes about what was happening in the cockpit and his untidy appearance through being interrupted mid-stream. Jumping back into his seat, he started doing a hundred things at once to put right the grief I'd apparently caused. He made excuses over the radio, then once the aircraft was under control gave me a lecture filled with expletives on how I could've killed us all. Delivered partly in Irish, it was more funny than upsetting, helped by the fact he didn't stay angry for long. I knew he was mellowing when he explained to me that the plane had been going up and down a bit and he was worried I'd lose him his licence. To this day, I honestly don't know what I did to take the aircraft off auto-pilot, except that my lack of aviation knowledge, and my temptation to fiddle with controls believing that whatever I touched the plane would remain steady, might've helped it on its way. All that, and I was only looking for Radio 1.

About two hours after take-off, Doug asked me to sit down as we'd be landing shortly. To avoid bringing him back to the boil, I got up and returned to where I'd sat at the beginning of the flight. We landed at an aerodrome near Ramsgate which I believe was called RAF Marston. Following touchdown, during taxiing to our allotted parking space, Doug told us in his lilting Irish tones that our return flight would be leaving at eight p.m.

We were like a group of small children moving in single file as we transferred to a people carrier. Dave had gone to so much trouble it makes me laugh now when I look back. I mean, why? I've often wondered if it'd all been a theatrical performance, written, produced and directed by Dave, in which he played the lead of course, to prove to himself he was number one. The vehicle, a posh Japanese mini-bus, was another prop he needed to guarantee the show's success. There'd only be one performance of this show and the many others that would follow, all part of Dave's agenda. His long-term objective was: "My life sorted first." He was first on and first off the minibus; he had to be first at everything.

Leaving Doug behind at the aerodrome to secure and watch over the plane, Dave showed off in front of the minibus driver by giving us orders before we left for Margate. Either at Margate, or on the outskirts of Hythe, some three quarters of an hour to an hour later, we pulled-up outside a pub. The amount of time without food was beginning to tell on me and the boys by the sound of our guts groaning and gurgling the basic notes of what could have become the world's first gastric symphony. To say we hoped they did food other than a bar snack cobbled together from yesterday's leftovers is an understatement.Dave was meeting somebody there. All of us full of nervous energy - 'on the hoof' through being 'hyper' after the flight - we found it difficult to keep still.I was starving and could not have cared less what Dave was doing. A couple of the lads and I made for the restaurant to order some of the most expensive items on its menu.

As Dave was paying we racked up quite a bill. We made the most of the opportunity by ordering steak with all the trimmings plus drinks all day long, encouraging everybody else to do the same. You could say we went out of our way to enjoy ourselves. After the meal, we were blobbed. Dave and Peewee didn't eat with us. They were too busy dealing with the people they'd gone to meet who turned out to be three extra large men who, with make-up, could have passed as Japanese Sumo wrestlers. The minibus driver who'd picked us up at the aerodrome was also with them. They spent the whole time huddled together in a corner of the saloon bar. We spent all our time in one bar in this pub in Hythe waiting for them to finish their business in the other. All of us well and truly 'rat-arsed', we turned out of the pub like a load of revellers having been slung out of a twenty-first birthday bash. It was close to seven before we all climbed back into the people carrier to return to the aerodrome at Marston. With no immediate remedy on hand for Dave's verbal diarrhoea, we had to harden ourselves to his ranting on and on about how much this trip had cost him. Ranking material wealth as more important than life, he was so annoyed about the minor losses he'd suffered that day he was in desperate need of an injection to slow him down before his heart burst out of his chest 'Alien' style. The word 'rant' might have been designed for Dave had he not been born long after it was first thought of. He kept shouting at the boys that he didn't see why they had to eat all the cows in Kent in one day and drink the pub dry at his expense.

"Ain't none of you got any money?! What do you think I am: your f****** bank?"

Dave didn't give me any grief over it but I was responsible for committing him to pay an obscene amount of money to settle our bill. What made it harder for him was that he didn't even get one pork scratching out of that restaurant. Without considering the financial implications of following his advice to "Go and sort yourself out something to eat and drink and I'll deal with it later" I invited his other mates to do the same when actually he only meant me.

Just add it to Mr. Ingle's bill. We're here for the day, I told the landlord with total confidence. I thought I dealt with it quite well. At fifteen quid a steak, not to mention the bottles of whisky at bar prices the 'joyriders' who were with me happily consumed, Dave was hundreds down as it was all added to his slate. He was ranting all the way back to the aerodrome. We arrived at the plane with about ten minutes to spare. I don't remember either taking off or the return flight itself, having given way to the alcohol. Awoken by the plane juddering on touchdown at Prestwick airport, my need to sleep hadn't been satisfied. By this time Dave was still furious, though with longer pauses between each session of ranting at the joyriding four - now the thoroughly p***** off four. Deciding to shut this noise out, sleeping for most of the car journey back to Hamilton Road was my response to this boring, long-winded speech from Dave. We got there about midnight.

I left Glasgow early the next morning as I had to earn some money. The long sleep the previous day had been necessary and, as if my body had anticipated that need, I was fresh to drive to Aberdeen which was some distance from Glasgow.

That day trip to Kent was just one of many absurd things I did during my confused phase. There I was with a family in Essex, acting like some irresponsible teenager.

Dave's little day trips were how he made his living. He had a lot to do with the haulage business. He was always meeting people who arranged the transportation and dispatch of various merchandise. Everything was merchandise to Dave. He would have sold air if he could. He had this deal going with somebody in London relieving companies of their consignments on a road somewhere. Dave would get a phone call one evening and the next day his big lorry unit would be mobilised. Sending a couple of his boys out to do the heavy stuff, he'd usually see them return with something that had to be got rid of quickly.

Gold was his favourite. It could be turned rapidly into cash: chains; earrings; rings; watches. If you wanted something gold Dave could get it for you. The logistics of his operations were complicated, an intelligence behind them all co-ordinated from his head. Unlike the rest of us, Dave had no need for a filing system. He had his minions make up sets of items in medium size leather attaché cases for people to sell all over Scotland. They'd buy the case from Dave then go off and make whatever profit they could out of each sale, which happened mainly in pubs and clubs. Drink, clothes, leather jackets - nothing was out of the question if it could be turned into money - mostly without Dave being involved. For the whole of the time I used to travel to Scotland regularly to see him he never involved me in any of this.

I can't even leave my car on a double yellow line for two minutes without getting a parking ticket or travel a couple of miles per hour over the speed limit without being stopped by the police, yet here was a man who crossed the finest of fine lines between legal and illegal practices on a regular basis, and always got away with it. His way of doing business was that of a virtual Robin Hood rather than a malicious, selfish criminal: he'd think he was doing everybody a favour by selling expensive goods at knockdown prices to people with low incomes, but it cost him next to nothing to make those goods.

Over the five year period between 1991 and 1996, I was involved with many other mad projects masterminded by Dave. As I was living in Essex, Doug used to fly down to a small airfield in Stebbing located on the A120 between Dunmow and Braintree. The airfield was about half an hour from my home. That was how

I was able to lie to Jackie about where I was without arousing her suspicion. I'd park my car and within three hours be sitting in a room in Glasgow having a cup of tea. I could get to Scotland and back in the time it took me to drive there. Due to the inconsistent availability of the plane, I drove to Scotland many more times than I flew, although with the speed I used to drive, always watching out for police cars on my tail - when I arrived I felt as if I'd flown. Sometimes Dave would travel down with Doug. Doug would meet me, and with his cheeky Irish grin and a wit to match tell me he'd had to bring 'the old cocker' with him. That caused me to crack up because it made Dave sound like he was Doug's pet spaniel when in fact Doug's term of endearment was a reference to his boss having cockney roots.

    I got stranded once. I'd been picked up as usual. We flew to Prestwick, landed, and I did my stuff in Glasgow. The following day, we returned to Prestwick where we were told the plane was in the hangar undergoing repairs. The car had already gone. I was just dropped there. That caused me all sorts of grief. I was supposed to be home that night as I had a big meeting with an oil company the next morning that couldn't be cancelled. A further complication was I'd not finished all the reports I needed for the meeting. When I finally got hold of Dave, which was about two hours later, he had to send one of his boys over to pick me up from the airport then drive me to Essex. Joining my car at Stebbing aerodrome in the early hours got me home with about four hours to spare before the meeting was due to start.

Chapter Thirteen

The slightest effort and I was exhausted.I would often spend the night downstairs sprawled across the couch.In the couple of weeks running up to this it seemed as if I'd had about a day's sleep altogether. On waking from recurring dreams of throwing my family into poverty, the fear of making the break to do what I had to was overwhelming.

Jackie would never accept who I really was.I certainly couldn't expect the children to. I wished I could be me and we could all stay together as a family.Her company and the children's energy and laughter making the house feel alive would all be lost to me.

I had a choice. I could either remain in the family home, became a glorified lodger and stayed financially comfortable but unhappy, or leave so that Jackie would be free to find someone who would love her the way she needed to be loved.At least if I went, the children stood a better chance of growing up in a stable home.

In the past, I have pushed the theory that my suffering - indeed the suffering of everyone diagnosed with gender dysphoria - is caused by a genetic defect. Admitting I had wrongly accepted this as being the only cause of gender dysphoria - perhaps because it didn't make me feel so responsible for the trail of destruction I had left behind me - has been a real lesson in humility. Making such an adamant sweeping statement about how I was a poor, confused person who nature had punished shows how desperate I was. Gender dysphoria may have many causes, none of which are proven: there's no black and white answer as to what creates the condition; possibly several factors come together to make it happen. More research needs to be done to test the genetic defect theory, amongst others.

Dressing as a female with a penis between my legs was depressing. A penis and a leotard just don't go together. That thing dangling down there stopped me from having the life I wanted. Before I had gender realignment, I was convinced that once my penis was removed I'd feel close enough to being a woman for my gender dysphoria to disappear, then I'd be in a state of bliss. I knew I would still have problems, but the major struggle would be over. With female bits, my transition would be almost complete. I could then have a go at tackling everything else as a woman. The excess baggage had to be removed. It didn't function. By that time it wasn't even a real penis. The medication shrunk it - I mean seriously shrunk it.

Seven years ago, I could not have laughed at that. Now I can sit back and openly discuss this, because I'm more grown-up about it. I'm so laid back, I'm dangerous. All those years ago, with my depression the way it was, I would've hacked the lot off and bled to death.

Realising that the penis I had was needed for my realignment to help construct the sensitive parts of my vagina, particularly my clitoris I had to accept that even old mister dangler wasting away down there had his uses. My male frame, along with everything else that told the world I was male, had to go and very soon would, so the male member was only a temporary inconvenience.

Dave had started bringing me clothes that tacky transvestite strippers and kiss-a-grams would have refused to wear in public. He wanted me to look stupid enough to entertain his friends - a sort of "Here he comes: the dumb blonde transvestite, game for a laugh, and the odd STD if he's unlucky."

He told me everything I owned belonged to him. I'd never heard him talk like that before. The clothes I wore were my clothes. I'd bought them with my money, yet to his mind they belonged to him. He told me he had loaned them to me.

Sometime in 1994, while on one of my working holidays north of the border - as up until then visiting Dave had always been a holiday - I dropped in to see him. Lovable treated me to one of his bear hugs which was like I had been clamped in a giant vice with cushioned jaws. I'd enjoy it in my girlie way, even if I was risking cracked ribs. I had not intended to stay there that night. One thing led to more than another. There were seven of us in the house. We all ended up having a drink ... several drinks ... together. In the end, the drinks had me. Out of those seven, which included me, I knew Dave, Frank, and Lovable. I'd never seen the other three men before and I would not want to again without the cover of a police marksman. There was something evil about them. They looked like they were about to kill somebody, and that was when they were in a good mood. They drank furiously from bottles clenched in their rough male hands. I imagined the stuff they were swigging trickling down their gullets, blending with the slime and gastric juices in their stomachs. The hate inside them was the nearest they had to a soul that like a wasp sting only a thousand times worse would be injected into some unfortunate victim.

All appeared civilised, and the evening went by quickly, or so it seemed. I had been driving all day and I felt very tired. That, plus the drink - which I knew I should not have had - set the agenda for trouble. Once again, I became the actor, this time, ironically, playing Dave's favourite gay male transvestite, more false than my much hated ordinary male role, catapulted bleary-eyed into a seedy world. This was nothing to do with being girlie. I take full responsibility for my stupidity in allowing myself to become so vulnerable. Talked into changing into what I'd wear for Dave on a normal visit, I walked on to a stage that included three strange men who would have looked at home in a boxing ring. When I'd changed I remember Dave saying: "That feels better, doesn't it?" Here I became a sad parody of femininity in a tacky burlesque where I was mocked with each turn. I felt cheap. Now, having been one of the entertained, I was the entertainment for the rest of the evening.

However much I drank that night, I'm certain it wasn't enough to put me in the semi-comatose state I ended up in. I am sure somebody spiked my drinks. I was spiked in another way too, or that's what it felt like afterwards. I passed out. The next eight hours were dreadful.

On waking, I thought I was in bed with my partner. I turned over to find one of Dave's unknown guests asleep beside me. My underwear had been removed. All I had on was the dress I'd been wearing the night before. The soreness in my rectum caused me to reach down and put my hand there. It was slightly wet to touch. Palpitations in my chest through my heartbeat quickening with the anxiety over what damage might have been done were so strong, I had to put greater effort into controlling my breathing to slow them down. I stared at my fingers. There was blood on them. I'd slept with a gay man. A person I didn't even know had got into bed with me, and the unthinkable happened. A sharp, thrusting pain jumbled up with bits of memories stained with my blood still attached themselves to me like mental leeches when I did realise where I was and worse what could have happened in that filthy bed, the bloke who had been in there with me had already got up and left. The worst thing that could've happened to me, short of murder, had. Once the bleeding stopped and the soreness eased it should have been all right. Later, after going to the toilet, there was more bleeding. A fullness in my stomach with a colicky pain gradually replaced the soreness and bleeding. It lasted on and off for several days. I started to think it was delayed shock, possibly a psychosomatic reaction to the assault.

Shouting at someone, at anyone, to tell me it hadn't happened, the effort of it beyond what I thought I was capable of, anxious, confused, like a helpless child abandoned by friends, that place took in the shape of hell. Dave and Frank knew I wasn't gay or wanted any part of that world. I'd always made that clear. For a while, I could think of nothing else. As far as my feelings for Dave were concerned, I hadn't any. If there was ever a time that put me off sex for life that was it. That did something to me. If I'm totally honest it smashed me to bits. Whether it is straight or gay, most of the time sex is more trouble than it's worth.

Lovable was an ex-marine. His training had been tailored to Dave's instructions on how to deal with people who upset him. The brute fact was, if you didn't return what was Dave's on time, you'd wish you'd never borrowed it. He was judge and jury. I think he identified strongly with the Krays, and may've even fantasised he was one of them. From the time we lost contact in the early 1970s, he'd developed a social network that would have protected him. For nearly twenty-five years, he'd lived off this, surfing on his popularity with other people who thought the same way.

By that time, Jackie and I were on different paths with ambitions totally opposed to one another. I had to tell her what happened in Glasgow. It took me ages to do this. I kept going upstairs and sitting on the edge of the bed fretting over how I'd break it to her. She kept probing me on and on and on. Pushed too far one day, I came right out with it: "I've been raped!" I yelled, silver stars in my eyes I had shouted so loud. The first thing she asked me after I had told her was: "Did you go to the police about it?" I told her it had happened about twelve to eighteen months earlier.

"I hope you haven't given me bloody AIDS!" she shrieked.

"You know I would not have risked your life like that," I assured her. "I had tests done at Harley Street."

"Harley Street! How much did that bloody cost?!" she went on.

Waiting for the results of those tests was agony. The worry of that alone left me psychologically and physically useless. For a while, I'd little more than the confidence of a small, frightened child. The results arrived and I was given the all clear for any sexually transmitted disease.

Telling Jackie about the rape had terrible consequences. We were still sleeping in the same bed, but we weren't having sex anymore. We went from sleeping in the middle to her sleeping right on the far edge of her side, and me right on the far edge of mine; in other words, as far away from each other as possible. Even if Jackie had still wanted me that way, it would never have been the same after the rape. In her eyes, our sexual relationship, which had always been initiated and driven by her, had been contaminated by me. There was no hope of any further sexual intimacy between us. It even destroyed our ability to be just physically close to each other. There was no more touching and kissing. The mutual trust we had was lost for good.

Chapter Fourteen

The beginning of March 1995 saw Dave becoming increasingly restless. Suddenly, the house in Hamilton Road wasn't big enough for him. He'd seen one for sale he liked that was even nearer the city centre. With a large price tag on it somewhere in the region of two hundred grand, the property had all the comforts he craved. He used to go on and on about that place as if it was already his.

One night, we were all sitting down having a drink when Dave suggested to me and Frank: "shall we all put some money into the new house, then? Havn't either of you f*****g heard me? When we get the f*****g place we can share it. Come on. It'd be a good investment for all of us."

His plan was that he'd sell the present home which was half Frank's, then whatever I could come up with together with the rest would make the asking price. I'd been putting money away for my 'being me' fund for some time. Explaining to Dave that whatever money I had I was saving for my future, stressing that I couldn't use any of that to contribute towards his house purchase, was my way of being up front with him. I already had a home in Essex. Those trips to Scotland were an added bonus, or had been before the rape. I wouldn't need them after my gender realignment. My words died on me. He treated them with contempt because they expressed a view that got in the way of his plans.

"A short term loan then" he suggested, this option "less complicated", as he put it, for him and Frank. Bells should have rung for me then. Dave didn't need any money from me or Frank. According to his endless rants over the years, bragging to all of us how much he'd got, he already had enough to buy the property himself. When I mentioned this, he came back with the excuse that all his money was tied up in an important project. Advising him that he could take out a mortgage given that the place he had must have been worth a fortune, I put it to him that surely this would go half way towards what he needed.

We don't want a f****** mortgage, do we, Frank? Too much bother. Why pay more than you need to?" he snarled. Tax-wise, I would have thought a mortgage would have been the best option.

Idle chatter wasn't Dave's style. He was only interested in buying that house, warning us we'd regret it if we didn't go through with the purchase. At the beginning of August, he changed tack, giving us an ultimatum: "make your minds up fast if you want to come in with us, or you're out."

Facing Dave head on, more forcefully than I'd ever been with him, I said: "Look, you know how important the money I have is to me. I don't want to tie that up in a house up here."

He waited a moment before answering: "How about a short term loan then, with interest? Lend me what you've got. Go on. All I need is a bit of cash now. I can wrap it up in a couple of days. Knock the price down. You know, do a bit of haggling. Save us some dosh for a few extras here and there. It already costs a f****** fortune more than it's worth. They won't find anyone up here with money like that. Come on, you old queen. I'll make it right with you."

I might've been listening with caution, but the alarm bells still weren't ringing.

"I've already got someone for this place," he went on, "so some of the money's already here."

Before, Dave had said he'd do a banker's draft for me. It was then I weakened thinking that if it was all right with Frank there couldn't be a problem. Once I'd said 'yes' I wouldn't listen to my intuition suddenly telling me not to be so stupid. There I was, off to the bank with Dave.

Unable to sleep for the next couple of days because the thought of that money kept nagging me, I had to check with Dave that everything was all right. That 'little bit of cash' as he called it was my fortune. It would've provided the safety net I needed to carry on having a reasonable standard of living as well as pay for my operation. Looking back, I can now see how I got my priorities wrong, putting myself above the needs of my loved ones.

The fact I was unwell doesn't let me off my responsibility for failing to take care of my partner, my children, and the rest of my family, including my Mum and Dad.

Rushing around, trying to get back a little self-control, lost in my anxiousness which aggravated my nervous energy, I tried to get Dave on his mobile, my finger stabbing desperately at the number pad of my own.

The Tuesday after the bank holiday, I'd phoned

Frank to see if everything was all right. All I got from him was an urgent request to meet him at the house in Hamilton Road that day because we had a problem.

Imagining all sorts of tragedies as possible reasons for Frank's desperation to see me, I couldn't understand why he wouldn't tell me on the phone what was wrong. All the way up to Glasgow I kept ringing Dave. His phone was turned off. Breaking all records driving up to Glasgow, there were several moments when I should've been intercepted by the police, the speeds I was doing up the M6. My poor car never stopped all the way to Hamilton Road which I reached some six hours later. Pulling up a couple of feet from the front door of the house, I was greeted by Frank who was pale with worry. My temper had been building-up during my drive north. Seeing Frank in a dither like that caused me to shout the crucial question I asked him on the phone. He was so white I thought he was going to need a blood transfusion on the spot.

What's the matter, Frank? Are you ill?I asked him.

"You had better come in," he mumbled. "You're about to become as sick as me."

"Had someone killed Dave, or had he had an accident?" I asked myself.

"What is it, Frank? Is it Dave? Has something bad happened to him?"

Starting to shake, a wave of disgust rolling through me, I went hot then cold. My sickness at Dave's betrayal of our trust went deep inside me; it felt as though I'd been struck instantly by a virus that left me temporarily helpless.

"He's done something with our bloody money, hasn't he?!" I roared at Frank.

Frank fielded my anger by dropping his hesitant behaviour to give me the truth straight up.

"It's worse than that," he revealed. "He's gone." What do you mean gone, I heard myself yell to the entertainment of the neighbours who found it impossible to mind their own business.

"There's been no house purchase made either by Dave or on his behalf, but there's been a sale all right: this bloody house. He's sold it behind our backs."

Over a stiff drink, Frank explained how Dave hadn't come back from a trip to the city the day after I last saw him. He hadn't been too worried at first because Dave was always playing games that kept him away for a couple of days.

"I looked for his passport which has always been kept with mine and it's gone. I've asked all the boys and no one has seen him and Peewee since Saturday. Dave told them all to stay away till today. I wasn't worried till I took a phone call for Dave this morning. The person phoning asked if our house had been cleared and could he drop the keys in on Thursday as they had someone coming up from Brighton on Friday? When I asked the caller what he was going on about he dropped the proverbial bombshell: the estate agents he worked for had sold our house!"

Have you phoned the police yet? was one of my first pieces of useless advice in reaction to the worst news of the century.

How the f*** could he sell the house without you being involved? That's stupid. You needed to sign everything as well.

"I'm not on the deeds," was Frank's pathetic answer.

Why the hell didn't you tell me you were nothing more than a lodger?My voice going into its unwelcome deeper male sound as I expelled my anger bit by bit. I had the bank on the telephone and while shouting at Frank on and off, I had to put up with being told by some stupid woman that I had to visit the bank personally for my account details. Ranting at Frank, my voice still raised, I reasoned that Dave wouldn't do this to us because apart from Peewee, who was really only his favourite fancy henchman, we were all he had. Slamming the telephone receiver down I got my energy back, strode out of the house, took the car, and drove to the bank like a formula one champion let loose round Monaco in a high performance car. The stereotypical male bank manager told me my banker's draft had been cleared.

cleared where? I demanded.

His manner was direct and clinical. Even though he'd told me his name he was just another man in a suit to me.

Had it gone into the account of a Mister Dave Ingle? I pressed. He said he couldn't give me any information other than that the money had been transferred from my account according to my instructions. Well and truly tensed up, the bank manager saw me leave his room in a fury that seemed to turn him girlie for a few seconds before he got his authority back as male chauvinist banker. Even I felt its intensity when I charged out of the building, hitting the gas all the way back to Hamilton Road to have another go at Frank. Frank, waiting outside when I brought the car to rest on the drive, gave me the rest of the story, unedited.His words so final, so damning, shut me down on the spot.

"He's got mine too," he stammered. "He's drawn out the bloody lot."

To this day, I've heard nothing more from Dave Ingle. He killed our relationship, including happy memories of the good times we'd shared. Frank and I hired a private detective to find him. He was traced to Canada, but we couldn't take the investigation further because we didn't have the money.

This loss had a serious effect on the cash flow situation of my company. Things started to get hard after that. The company I used to do most of my work for went into receivership. Even though I was broke, the dreadful events of the previous couple of weeks motivated me to get my life back into some sort of order. Dave Ingle had been manipulating me on and off for eight years. Now I was going to run my own show without the interference I'd put up with from some.

Chapter Steen

With three children you get to see the doctor a lot. Over the years, we'd built a good relationship with ours. He treated us as equals. He would ask me: "How's mum?" Meaning Jackie's Mum, then he'd ask me how Jackie and the children were. I felt I could approach him on any problem we had no matter how terrible it was except my gender dysphoria. My dilemma over whether to come out or keep my real identity hidden sent me into a tailspin. I thought: "What's the matter with me? Why don't I just come out with it? Why don't I just tell him?" I knew that all doctors are bound by a strict code of ethics that includes patient confidentiality, but I found it as hard to tell him then as I did my Mum years later.

He gave me prescriptions for all these tablets I didn't want: analgesics for headaches; sleeping pills for insomnia; anti-depressants for depression. It took me several visits to tell him what I had to have.

I need hormones, I insisted.

He said he couldn't give me that sort of medication. Hormones could only be prescribed to someone on the approval of a psychiatrist. I had to see one before I could get near any. Yet more delays. Unless I wanted to take the unhappy step of getting them off the black market, which without medical supervision would have left me vulnerable to being ripped-off or even killed, my only choice was to go through the proper channels.

On my doctor's advice, I contacted the Albany and told health care professionals there my problem. It was agreed that I visited the Albany one day the following week to go over all the treatment options open to me. No longer a patient of the clinic because I'd nearly run out of money, by paying only for what was essential, which was a blood test and a report for my doctor, it was still possible for me to be treated there until I received my first appointment at Charing Cross. As ever, the staff at the Albany Clinic were very supportive. They really looked after me.

I had an appointment every eight weeks which I used to pay seventy to eighty pounds for. Charing Cross wouldn't recognise anything the Albany did for me. When I started having consultations at Charing Cross, the experts there took control of my life. They decided that the advice and treatment I'd had at the Albany didn't count. A psychiatrist told me bluntly that my doctor had no right to refer me to the Albany. I corrected him with equal bluntness saying that my doctor hadn't referred me to this wonderful private clinic. It'd been my choice to go there. From my point of view, I was doing something active for my doctor in that through my attending the Albany he could get what I understood to be a bona fide medical report on my state of health, and progress if any, which wasn't at the expense of the NHS. The psychiatrist was totally unsympathetic and told me in a strong voice like that of my old headmaster: "When you come here you'll do what I say."

When he warned me he was going to take me off the hormones for a year, I just blew.

"That's not a very feminine way to behave," he scoffed. That phrase still rings loudly in my mind from time to time, often when I feel at my lowest, and it irritates and angers me. I remember how squashed that kind of interview made me feel; my memory of being patronised there, in spite of my assertive personality, still gnaws away at me. Pride got the better of me. Being treated like a second class citizen made me over defensive. What was thrown at me was a stereotypical male view of what is and what is not, the right way for a woman to behave. Given that we were living in late twentieth century Britain, I was shocked by the sexist slant of it: whatever the reasons were for this aggressive interview style, a large number of women taken off any street anywhere in the country would have objected to being spoken to like that.

Trying to get my head round why I did what I did to Jackie was like struggling to solve a crossword puzzle with cryptic clues. Perhaps it was the wanting to be like her so much that made it possible for me to love her and deceive her at the same time? She had a presence that set off extreme thoughts and feelings in me. Had I been born a biological female, I believe Jackie and I would still have been drawn to each other and become close without any sexual involvement between us to ruin our friendship. In my dreams, we would have been two straight girls who would chat together non-stop, sharing the intimate details of our lives, being there for each other through the good times and the bad times.

Like with Tammie Martin in my school days, my view of Jackie wasn't a realistic one: my idea of her as the kind of woman I wanted to be on the outside, whilst staying 'me' on the inside, differed from how she saw herself. When I met her I'd more or less convinced myself I'd never be allowed to become a woman on the outside so that I could be whole. That's why I had to keep playing male.

I make that sound like I just mentally switched on the male role, but was not really like that? When I first saw Jackie in that pub I didn't see her from a male point of view?

Here and there the conflicts inside me might have caused me to respond to her as a straight male would a straight female. Chatting her up was, as far as I remember, a natural, spontaneous move for me; I didn't fake it. The few times it did surface, 'attracted male seeks attractive female' didn't last; it was a mood I'd be in for an hour or so, then I'd go into a depression. I would describe it as going upstairs with my male head on, then, to shake off that depression, having to come down as myself.

My identification with Jackie was really my identification with my fantasy of her. My life was driven by the desire to be with her and like her. I married her because I loved her as the person I believed she was, not as the person she really was.

I don't want this to read as if I didn't think Jackie was sexually attractive. Of course she was. Remember that I wanted to be like her physically, but I didn't need her sexually. I felt I had this bond with her without sex getting in the way.

What we had at the start was enough for me to feel close to her and stay so. Another perhaps contradictory bit of me is that I have never been what I call a tactile person. If Jackie wanted me to cuddle her I'd do it but she would have to ask me. Sometimes when we were sitting on the couch together, during one of her passionate clinches I'd feel this incredible warmth pass right through me. Like the cuddles, if Jackie wanted sex I'd do it with her if I could, but I would never volunteer. I believe I grabbed the situation knowing that as long as I couldn't be a woman - and, more to the point, a woman like her, at least I could have her near me, and that was 'love' for me.

I had been giving my future some thought, analysing my relationship with Jackie. I was sceptical that I would ever be able to be my real self and meet somebody with whom I could have a *full* relationship. It seemed to me that whoever I got involved with would have to accept my condition and be practical about it. I'm not waiting on anyone. That doesn't mean I wouldn't do things for my partner. What it does mean is that it would have to be an equal relationship; my partner would have to have the self-awareness and maturity to cope with the baggage that came with me. Perhaps my earlier statement was arrogant of me, but I know without the slightest hint of doubt I'd never put up with being downtrodden. If that means my expectations are too high then I probably won't end up with anyone because I won't change. In my male existence, I learnt how to do most things for myself. My ability to fend for myself would rule out any man who thought I'd be there to attend his every need twenty-four/seven. He'd be waiting forever. Whoever had a close relationship with me expecting that I would sort all the problems wouldn't last five minutes.

In my male existence, sex was either bottom of my

agenda or right off it. My hope was that it would be top after everything that needed doing had been done. That hasn't happened yet. I've always preferred to think of myself as having a loving relationship without sex. When I admitted this to my partner she got angry because sex was important to her. She couldn't see how I could talk about relationships without mentioning sex. She felt I'd deprived her of a sex life. Male-to-female transsexuals in a male-female relationship tend to have a very low sex drive. I had the libido of a corpse that had been warmed up. One of my goals was to keep Jackie in my life. Sex had to be part of my life because it had to be part of hers. I found it difficult to get aroused though. When I did get an erection I had a problem keeping it up. My head was telling me: "No. This is a possessive love, which isn't love at all. I want to lose myself in her, yet I have to be really pushed to get just a little way towards meeting her very physical needs. It's not right."

I wanted to be like her. She was the image of my ideal self. I screened out any details that threatened to spoil this.

Really, I imagined myself into the sex act with her. In my distorted world, I was always being made love to. When Jackie and I were in bed together and if sex was suggested by her I'd often just let it happen. I encouraged her to be on top. Jackie was the most desirable woman any man could have wanted. I told her I accepted that I'd been selfish in holding back from her, and that I still loved her. I also told her that the moment she felt she couldn't wait anymore and had to find another partner, I would leave. I'd leave not because I wanted to but because I wanted her to have what she needed which I couldn't give her. There was another selfish reason though. I couldn't bear the thought of her getting ready to go out and meet someone else while I was still living there. As stupid as it sounds, I had this idea in my head that someone else would soil her. The thought of another person touching her, however innocent it was, made me jealous.

If I'd had sex with Dave before my operation, from a physical point of view it would have been homosexual. The very thought of that is disgusting. If I'd had sex with him after my operation, then because I'd finally got the right bits, it would've been psychologically and physically heterosexual. Dave was gay though, and no matter what I had done to adjust my body to make it right he would always see me as a gay male transvestite. Whatever I did at the height of my confusion was wrong, but in terms of social labels I was neither heterosexual nor homosexual, and I hated being called transsexual even though I've used the term sometimes in this book for the sake of clarity, so perhaps you can appreciate how confused I was. I can well imagine a psychiatrist puzzling him or herself to death over this.

Thinking myself into the sex act with Jackie meant: "I've got to have sex with her". When she said: "let's go to bed" imagining myself into the sex act was more a, dare I say it, looking forward to being close to her, almost feeling those cuddles and the warmth and laughter that went with them before they happened. I loved the cuddles. They made it bearable.

Was this another contradiction? What I meant was I'm not usually tactile in that I don't rush up to just anyone and touch them. Jackie would always have to initiate a cuddle between us. Once my barrier came down and we did get together, that warmth, like electricity conducting through me making me fragile as if I was in the early stages of drunkenness, ended in me feeling protective towards her and comforted by her. Although it never lasted, it happened and it was real.

My idolisation of Jackie was a delusion. I was living out my fantasy of wanting her as she existed in my head. When we had sex it was an opportunity for us to get really close. What was actually happening for her, I don't know, but you can be sure it was a long way from what was happening for me.

I loved her beautiful femininity as it flowers and grows towards maturity, guiding the outward development of my own inner femaleness, but also I could have loved her in the sisterly way I wanted to, free of any sexual obligation to her.

I'll never stop loving Jackie my way. She wanted me to love her like any husband would in a happy, loving relationship. My way and her way just didn't go together. Our marriage was doomed.

Chapter Sixteen

Roughly a year before I left home, Jackie discovered my secret. It was common practice in our household that if my car was available Jackie would use it. Scratching around for clues as to what I was up to she discovered my appointment card for the Albany. Looking back, I realise that subconsciously I wanted her to find out. I'd left the card in the car for her to find. Having already told her I was attending a clinic that dealt with alcoholism, at first I used this to explain the appointment card, but she was already many steps ahead of me. The card had a picture of a fairy in its top right hand corner. It was like one for a boutique or somewhere really girlie. Jackie had to investigate. She rang the number printed on the card and got through to the Albany.

"Is this a clinic for people with an alcohol problem?" she asked the girl on the other end of the phone who replied: "No. This is a gender clinic." Quoting the male name I was known as, Jackie asked if I was a patient there. The girl told her she couldn't give her that information and neither could any other member of staff there due to their strict rule of protecting client confidentiality. She did, however, go into great detail about what they did there.

When I got home, I felt as if I'd walked into a tornado. Jackie and I had a dreadful row which lasted for three hours. After she'd unloaded the full strength of her feelings on me, Jackie just walked out. She had to tell someone, so she left me indoors to go about a hundred yards up the road to confide in her best friend.

That row saw every destructive emotion going exchanged between us. I still think about it today. On the one hand, I was glad it was all out in the open, on the other there was this sense of everything we had emotionally, being destroyed. She kept shouting at me to tell her it wasn't true, then asked me why I was doing this to her and the children. I wanted to hold her, she wanted answers: she was laying out every detail of everything I'd done over the years that hadn't added up on her emotional balance sheet. The shouting became screaming. As far as she was concerned, there was no money because I was spending it all on my perversion. I tried to give her honest answers to her questions. The more I told her, the more upset she got. Her short breaks of calmness brought her no peace. There'd be a few moments of quiet then another explosion. For the first time in my life, I was telling the truth and it hurt the person closest to me more than if I'd carried on lying to her. As we sat down and discussed the crisis, I noticed her eyes. They stared into mine coldly, like they were just seeing me, tolerating me because I still had information she needed.

This lasted for several months, then Jackie seemed to mellow. For a very short time family life ran smoothly except for brief eruptions between me us. On the whole, it appeared that Jackie was trying to understand what was happening to me. During our calmer moments, I told her how I felt, and explained why I acted the way I did for all those years we'd been together. The way it looked to me was that the bond formed between us in the days when we first went out together had rekindled, touching me at a deep level. With hindsight, I now know this wasn't real.

I saw a person whose youth I'd taken away but who was prepared to listen to me despite what I'd done to her. It really did seem that Jackie had accepted the worst from me and still valued what I said. Apparently, she'd forgiven me.

Several visits to my doctor and two or three to the NHS clinic and I was still kept off my medication. Trying to stay calm about myself was an effort that failed, marked by the return of old tensions. My life had started to go back to how it was before I went to the Albany. I'd been off my medication for three months and had virtually returned to being the thing I hated. There would be the odd 'stiffy' in the morning - very odd - as if it was saying to me: "You can't get rid of me that quick." You might say it reared its ugly head.

Shaving was probably the activity I hated most about that phase. The more I shaved, the more I had to, frequently ridding myself of what weren't soft, girlie wisps, but rough, prickly male bristles popping out of my face and chin as well as from under my nose like they were made from strands of coconut hair.

I thought I could go to my doctor, tell him the mess I was in, he'd say: "No problem", and carry on prescribing what I needed. That, of course, was another of my fantasies. Whatever I might've thought of the medical profession back then, I must admit that my GP, Doctor Smalley of Harlow, was marvellous. He put himself out to help me even though I'd caused him mega grief. The poor man was having to swat up on gender dysphoria and the effects of hormone therapy because he had never come across a patient suffering from this condition in his entire medical career. Dr. Smalley managed to refer me to Dr. Dein who'd dealt with people with my condition at Charing Cross.

When I went to see Dr. Dein, who was a top consultant at St. Margaret's Hospital in Harlow, he asked me: "Do the children know what's happening to you?" and I had to say "No". He said: "They should be told." Dr. Dein recommended that Jackie came to see him accompanied by me to try to help her understand gender dysphoria.

In my head, I was jealous of her femininity. Now I was able to tell her how nice I thought she dressed, and let her know I liked the things she bought. In all our time together, I don't think I'd ever done this. To be able to talk about underwear; make-up; shoes - the works - but as two women who were just friends - at last brought out the better side of me again. I had found I could still be sensitive and loving. During our chats, I'd learnt that Jackie didn't have any trendy skirts or a smart suit to wear. There was me happily going on about what clothes I had, when she broke down in an upsetting show of tears. Over the years, I'd been so into my own world I hadn't even thought to ask her if she needed any nice clothes for her wardrobe. The two of us shopping together was another change with me showing genuine interest in what she bought pleased her for the wrong reasons. My latest problem was the struggle I had to contain myself in that situation. In the old days, if my partner asked me to go shopping with her, nine times out of ten I would say "No". On the odd occasions we did, we'd spend more time walking round clothes stores than supermarkets or any other type of shop. She always insisted I bought some things for myself. Of course, those things had to be male clothes. My male wardrobe was the most pathetic collection of 'uncool' crap you could imagine. Even by most men's standards it was sad. You could have kept it in a few plastic bags from the local supermarket, yet you would have needed an articulated lorry to move my collection of female clothes down from Scotland.

Jackie and I agreed that the children were far too young to cope with the shock of me 'coming out' so we didn't tell them about it. If it could ever be possible for the children to know, that would have to wait until they were much older. By keeping my secret from them, I could save them a lot of grief. If I'd told them then, I think the emotional trauma they would have suffered would have been even greater than what actually happened in the end. They would have been bullied at school and probably in the neighbourhood as well. I couldn't let that happen.

Our financial problems had to be solved. I've already mentioned the enormous debts I had. Jackie and I agreed I would stay for as long as it took me to pay these off.

Jackie gained strength from within to cope with the challenges and changes that lay ahead of her. I learned from her. As I got worse, I watched her change into a strong, confident woman. From then on, her priority was to focus on what was right for her.

Towards the end, I just sat around. I couldn't be bothered with anything. The mortgage still had to be paid. I was still working, though nowhere near as much as I had been. That was because I didn't need the high income necessary to live a double life anymore. I was doing it properly now: I was doing it the way my partner wanted. All I had to do was settle my debts.

One day Jackie got hold of the subject of Dave and squeezed it dry of anything good it had ever meant to me. She sussed I was meeting other people on a more intimate level than business. Given that she now knew my secret, there was no longer any point in me keeping quiet about Dave.

"Any normal person being showered with the gifts you've been given would have suspected, if not known, there was something behind it," was the gist of her argument.

"Nobody gives anybody anything for nothing," she lectured. To give Jackie some time on her own I took off to Scotland for a few days. After that row, I had dramatic mood swings. One minute I'd be all right, the next I'd lose it. The situation at home had become so sensitive that even when I was calm I couldn't move without upsetting Jackie. From the moment she found out everything about my life in Scotland Jackie continually cross-examined me. That put me on edge all the time, shortening my temper so much it would go off over a little innocent remark taken the wrong way.

I had to give her a complete timetable of everything I'd done and was going to do. She wouldn't tell me anything about herself though.

It became my priority to try to cushion my family from the inevitable break-up that was coming. What increased the chances of a confrontation between Jackie and I leading to another row was the fact had been off my medication for a while. All I could think of was that those bloody male hormones were taking me over again.

I still wanted Jackie in my life. In the early days of our marriage, she'd put a huge effort into our sexual relationship. She had enough libido for both of us. Always beautiful, tactile, passionate, her sensual nature moved her to respond keenly to the mildest sexual hint or touch from me.

It saddens me to think I've been capable of deceiving someone I loved. We tried to talk about what I was and she kept telling me I was throwing everything away. That made me shout at her: "I'm not choosing this. I'm already this. You're looking at the real me."

Everything I loved about my life up till then was about to be taken away. Jackie said my decision was so final and the result would be the ultimate selfish act towards her and our children. She asked me why if I had managed to control 'it' as she called my condition, for all the years I'd known her, during which time we'd had three children together, I couldn't stay as I was?

She didn't know what she'd tell the children once I'd gone - or if she'd ever tell them who I really was - feeling it would be too traumatic for them.

There was a time I believed she'd always help me if I needed her. Towards the end, I wasn't sure. Her friends were eroding whatever tolerance she had towards me.

For years she had helped me with the accounts side of the business. She never once asked for a penny for all the work she did for me.

No amount of self-awareness on my part could

override the destructive forces in me that I took out on Jackie. Additional stress for her came with her Dad's tragic death. Quite apart from her grief over his sudden dramatic passing, she was trying to look after her Mum, deal with me, be a Mum to our children, not to mention keep her career going.

I was just about existing, going to work and nothing else, feeling tired all the time because I wasn't sleeping properly. Jackie was having the same problem. The fact that we knew we were both constantly tired didn't do anything to improve our relationship. We became less tolerant of each other. When we were in the same room together, sometimes the vibes would be so bad one of us would have to leave. A difficult path to tread, the psychological and practical effects of her Dad's death caused the rift between us to widen, so the end of our marriage was inevitable.

During a rare moment when we were actually in the same room together, discussing my condition, Jackie asked: "If there was this good looking man and a pretty woman standing side by side who would your choose?" My reply was: Neither - they'd just be two people to me.

There wasn't a sexual thought in my head then, all the energy that would have been my libido having been used to satisfy the only ambition I had, which was to sort myself out. I told her I'd sooner stay with her than have to make choices like that. She came back with, surely if I wanted to be who I said I was, I'd pick the man? That was when I had to tell her again, however ridiculous it sounded to her, that sex wasn't important to me. I didn't know this hypothetical man or woman. Why should I pick either?All I wanted in my life was her.Finding that I couldn't handle anymore complications, particularly as I needed all my reserves of energy - easily drained at that time - to deal with the essential details of my life, I began to shutdown on her.I'd like to have said that I would have preferred the man, but I would have been misunderstood:Jackie would have taken it to mean I was gay.

Jackie referred to my way of being as it or what I really was, rather than who *really* was.

Chapter Seventeen

Jackie told me I'd treated her and the children badly. It was true I'd become self-centred, using the bottle to escape my inadequacy. Whether in the long-term gender realignment would help me become a better human being was worth waiting for. You know how much I want to believe that my gender dysphoria was caused by a genetic defect. Even if that's true it doesn't alter the fact I still had the freewill to make the choices I did. I chose to lie to Jackie. At least, despite what I believe to be a number of different factors influencing my destiny - including perhaps a misbehaving or even missing gene - I eventually tried to make the situation better.

Forty-five years old, unable to see any way forward other than achieving gender realignment, I went back to my doctor to push hard for this. Agreeing to prescribe the hormone therapy I needed to carry on, he insisted I went back to a gender clinic like the Albany or Charing Cross before he would sign the prescription form. I wasn't going to the Albany then because I'd promised my partner I wouldn't continue my treatment until I'd paid off my debts. My worry here was that the clinic would say: "If you're not a regular patient then you're on your own." That would have meant having to wait ages to be seen at Charing Cross. As each day passed, the male hormones were taking over again.

There are now legal changes that can be made to documents such as driving licences which were not possible at the time of writingi.e., those concerned with all personal insurance and tax; and passports, that show the identity of the holder.As I explained earlier, just a boring bit of paper like a driving licence can cause emotional distress to a person who has gender dysphoria. On my driving licence, my gender was described as male.My biological gender *was* male, which is the sex somebody decided I was at the time of my birth because I had the normal body of a male child, but that is *not* my true gender. The Gender Recognition Panel (GRP) for me, was set up in 2004 to alleviate these problems.

After my gender realignment, you could not marry in your new roll, or if you were in a new relationship adopt any children who were related to you or your new partner.You had no rights.We seem to be perceived by those who don't understand gender dysphoria as sick individuals who have our precious bodies tampered with, which lead's them to believe we can't function adequately.For me, it was more irresponsible to go through life as I was, not caring about anyone other than myself.I walked around the house full of anger.

How can you expect someone who can no longer function as a male to carry on going through life looking and behaving like one?Many countries accept gender dysphoria.The United Kingdom appears to be stuck in the slow lane of dealing with this condition.

We learn a lot about people through what they wear. Sometimes, their choice of clothes may cross generally accepted boundaries for how to look and behave in either the male or female role.Like anything else in life, dress code doesn't have to be set to a rigid standard.

A psychiatrist said to me, "How can you want to be

a woman if you don't live in frilly dresses with bouffant hairstyles, and wear bright red nail varnish?"If some of them genuinely believe women don't normally wear trousers they can't be living on this planet.

I fully accept that the decision to allow a person to have gender realignment surgery has to be made carefully. By watching how people seeking gender realignment dress and behave over years rather than months, a psychiatrist can judge how serious they are about living in the role of the gender they want to be recognised as.People who know their body's look and feel wrong genuinely want to put this right by having their shape, size, and detail adjusted to fit their beliefs about who they are.

We all have to follow basic social values and norms that help us tell males from females.I wasn't going to follow a stereotypical female dress code for the sake of looking 'girlie '.Trousers were right for me as long as they were female trousers - which the ones I wore when I saw the psychiatrists definitely were - so what was the problem?Certainly for a reasonable time, I had been watching my partner, making a note of what she chose to wear each day.Naturally feminine, and proud of it, as a modern woman, Jackie knew how to dress.In a total of twenty-one days, she only wore a skirt twice, with tights and a nice top.The rest of the time her dress was casual: ski-pants; leggings; and jeans with a jumper and boots.Wait a minute.Something must have been wrong with her: she didn't want to wear a dress very often, paint her nails red, or wear high-heeled shoes!With the wildest imagination, you could never accuse Jackie of not looking feminine.Smart, and caring about the way she looked to herself and others, she expressed her femininity in a suitable way for each occasion, both naturally and uniquely.

Today, re-examining what I wrote at that late stage of our dying marriage, I can see how I would not let anyone trick me into believing I wasn't Carol Royce. I can't pretend anymore just to satisfy what others want of me. They tell me: "You're male - get on with it!"

I love my partner and my children. Jackie should never have been dragged into my life. I should have seen all this coming; that there was a real danger that even if I innocently fantasised about being a woman, the themes and issues of my youth would return.

It really hurt me when we were all in the same room together and my children went straight to my partner and clung to her when they could have come and sat with me. All positive communication between us had been destroyed, yet there were still things left to say to each other. Not being told the kind of details that couples in happy relationships tell each other, no matter how trivial they are, was another side of family life I missed.

My partner kept digging at me to answer her questions about gender dysphoria. I wanted to talk to her about clothes, make-up, and how we both felt. She said I was perverted. I had to talk in her language to get through to her: I have to say I was guilty.

It was awkward at home and at work. I could not carry on with the job I had been doing. Right from the moment I knew I was eligible for gender realignment surgery, sooner rather than later, I eased off on the amount of manual work I did for the business whilst stepping up my contribution to the office side of it. If I wasn't out there doing it myself though, it was never done right. I'd even tried taking on partners. That didn't work. To go back to how I was - constantly switching between the male persona and Carol – would have upset the psychiatrists. Given that I'd have to travel the country like I did before, I saw myself spending the rest of my life worrying about having to explain why I was impersonating a female if I was caught out in male role. The company employed me because of my expertise and knowledge built-up over the years, so if they knew I was staying in the office rather than going out to do the hands-on work, the business would have suffered.

Although I tried to deal with my condition on my own, I would not recommend this to anyone. Some people would need as much support as they could get. They would need to mix with other people, and not just those diagnosed with gender dysphoria.

A culture where it is easier for gender dysphoric people to blend with the wider society as valued individuals would be a dream come true. I am *not* saying that being in a group of people all suffering from the same problem is not a positive step to becoming whole. It is nice to have someone who is going through exactly the same as you offering words of comfort - even the odd bit of constructive criticism by telling you you're not doing something quite right - without destroying your self-esteem.

After the fallout, Jackie and I did not stop analysing our marriage. It felt like every sentence spoken in the whole of our married life was being slowly and viciously dissected.

One dream I hung on to till the very end was that when I walked out of the door for the last time Jackie would still be my friend. As I had created most of her problems, I wanted to support her in her future attempts to solve them.

In March 1995, I returned to Scotland. My room had been emptied. All I could find of my stuff was a pair of earrings and a bracelet which I ended up giving to Jackie. I only had these because Frank had them. Even giving something to Jackie wasn't easy. I had to reassure her they were presents I had bought for her. The earrings and bracelet looked better on her than they ever did on me. I hoped she would keep them. Knowing she liked them would have meant a lot to me. A few pounds worth of gold wasn't going to help her come to terms with who I was, but if she did decide to wear them I wanted it to be special for her. If only in little flashes now and then, I wanted her to get back in touch with the happy memories of our good times together.

Towards the end, Jackie would check up on me and find I was in Manchester when I should have been in Liverpool. At first, it was easier to go back to lying, then, one day, I realised it wasn't even worth doing that anymore. The irony was, when I told the truth she wouldn't believe a single word of it. "You're just a liar", she'd say to me. I think she was gathering as much evidence for her case as she could.

Chapter Seventeen

The seventeenth of July 1996 Jackie, the children and I spent our last day together. I was sick with anxiety over what might happen to us all, and found it difficult to raise the energy to pack. It was hard to stop myself from saying goodbye to my children but Jackie and I stayed with the decision that it was best I did not.

I'm not blaming Jackie for anything. Everything was my fault. I am responsible for everything that's gone wrong. Jackie had nothing to do with it.

She was determined our children would never know who I really was. She became quiet and distant towards me. If she ever told them, how would she do it? What would she tell them? How would Sophie, Ross, and Alicia feel when they knew?

That morning, with unbearable sadness, for the very last time, I watched my children leave the house to go to school. My throat tightened. I kept swallowing hard to relieve the aching fullness there. That pain, working its way out of me, was all the anger and sadness that had built-up over the years, the last bit let go in a final, pitiful scene marking the break-up of my family. I felt as if I'd gone back to being a child, I cried, the final groan that came out of my mouth ending that release of tension, allowing my throat to relax and feel comfortable again. The tears mildly stinging my eyes, all that was left of my hope for a reconciliation with Jackie that I'd been clinging to, dripped on to my bags like a few sorry raindrops that would soon disappear. We'd been together for twenty years. This was going to be so hard. Once Jackie had departed with the children, I loaded my cases into the car, then left. I haven't seen them since.

Closing my eyes then sticking a pin in a map was how I chose where I would go. The pin went through Cromer in Norfolk, so this was to be the lucky place where I'd start my new life.

From 1993 till about the beginning of June or July 1996, I was on and off hormone therapy. Summer lightened my arrival in Cromer. I remember there were two summers running that were quite good. When I got there I was shocked at the pace of life. For me, it was dead stop.

Everything was in slow motion. I wasn't used to having to wait an hour for a bus. The shops in the town were small. Where I'd come from they were huge: they had about twenty-seven aisles. Then I went to Safeway in Cromer where I had to queue for about half an hour to buy food. I'd get so angry, I would leave the trolley I had been using behind, and walk out.

Everyone seemed to be on a mission to delay me. I'd be walking along the pavement and somebody would be just ahead of me blocking it, talking to somebody else. They would have died first if I had not have asked them to get out of my way. Some people don't look, do they? They don't see you; they don't see anything. Summer was the wrong time of the year for me to go there. If I'd arrived in the winter when there were less people around I could have got my shopping done in less time by practising walking along the pavements dodging the natives who were in a trance, then by the summer I would have been trained to deal with them and the dozy holidaymakers. Why don't people look where they're going? Are they on something? Many a time I've asked myself: "How do I cope in a place like this where time is slowed down so much it's almost freeze-frame?" It was like life itself was on permanent hold. I've got over that now.

Being without money and a roof over my head were my biggest worries. I'd been used to having everything, so poverty came as a big shock, which is an understatement. Up until then, I'd never had to worry about whether I had enough money for a packet of cigarettes, a tank full of petrol, or my car tax, insurance, and so on, then all that and more was taken away from me. It's like somebody asking you to give up smoking. You get anxious. Not knowing what to do with yourself and the realisation that even if you did you wouldn't have the money to do it with was about the size of it. Having to pay an amount of rent for your room that ate up most of what you got for your fortnightly social security benefit meant you spent all day there getting bored.

I was trapped. Sleeping in my room in the afternoon helped to fill the long days. I felt as if I was in prison. I wanted to escape, but when the black thoughts and the confusion were bad, I couldn't move.

The eighteenth of July 1996 saw a new beginning for me. So much concern was shown towards me over that weekend - a level of friendship I was grateful for. I'd got on very well with another person who'd been diagnosed with gender dysphoria who I met at a party in Norwich run by two friends, Steph and Maxine. We seemed to click straight away. Her name was Nicky.

Nicky was from Cromer. I felt good about her and the party's hosts, convinced that at last I had found friends who didn't want something from me. They just gave to me. I was so happy. Nicky, my first true friend during my struggle, showed me what I thought was genuine friendship. Moving in with her to start my new life was a timely relief from physical, emotional, and social shutdown. Here I was, able to retreat from the advancing ranks of insanity.

A force to contend with, I imagined Nicky and I taking on the whole world. We sat for hours talking about everything we could think of from cooking to what we wanted out of life. As I saw her in those first days of living with her, Nicky's finest quality was that she was a person who cared about others. When I looked back over the previous few months to consider what I'd achieved, which was nothing, and then at what I'd achieved in the week I met Nicky, I realised I had changed from being the defensive, depressed prima donna with barely more substance than my shadow when I walked into Steph and Maxine's house, to the self-assured person who believed that she had a way out of her problems. At last, there was the feeling of having the choice to live again, and it was exciting. I belonged here. I looked forward to building my life the way it should have been. Having waited forty-five years for fate to be on my side, I wasn't going to let it slip away.

A couple of weeks after moving in with Nicky, we had a girlie night out. I'd looked forward to it all day. An arrangement was made to pick up Steph and Maxine on the way to Barbara Ross's. The highlight of the evening was Nicky driving there and me driving back. While this may seem insensitive to those who enjoyed the evening, the people who went to that dinner weren't really what we, or should I say I was about. The transvestites took over, which irritated me, yet I felt I had to try and mix with them so I didn't spoil the evening for the others there who were genuine. I felt compassion for the Transsexuals who had turned up, and I wanted to help them, but that do wasn't for me. Resented by the 'TV' majority invading the event, who treated it like a fancy dress party for perverts, I knew I wouldn't make it to the end of the evening. I couldn't help but see it that way. Keeping to their end of the room, the 'TVs' glared at me as if I hadn't the right to breath the same air. I made it clear I didn't like them through my body language, which was tense, upsetting their enjoyment of this play-acting they did for cheap thrills. Where was the subtlety in their choice of clothes or the dignity in their behaviour? Why didn't they dress as I thought females liked to dress for an evening out instead of going to extremes? Overhearing one of them telling another that the clothes he was wearing belonged to his late wife really got my hackles up.

My time with Nicky was short-lived for unbeknown to me she was suffering from clinical depression. She became very ill. On the fifteenth of August 1996 I moved out of her house. Finding a note asking me to leave wasn't easy to take. With hindsight, there were many problems with our friendship. There were several years between us - not that an age gap should stop people being friends - though a young mind versus an older one is often a cause of friction.My laid back approach to everything was impossible for her to accept.Everything in her life was urgent which I couldn't stand.We clashed several times.Having problems getting my benefit payment, the reason for which only the benefit office could explain, meant I couldn't pay rent to her for the first six weeks. That certainly didn't help our relationship.Maybe the council thought that if they delayed my benefit I'd go back to Essex?

Six weeks after arriving in Cromer I found myself homeless.On the plus side I still had my car so at least I didn't have to sleep on the beach.After about an hour of sitting in my car parked by the sea front I got myself up to the District Council housing office on the Holt road. Waiting again, this time for an hour to see somebody to help me find somewhere to live, got me nowhere. Promptly told to go back to Essex by the member of staff I saw, as the North Norfolk District Council was under no legal obligation to house me, I realised how desperate I was.Pleading with them that they must know somewhere I could get a room, they came up with an organisation for homeless people called Saint Matthews. An appointment was made for me to have an interview there at ten the next morning.

That night, it sleeted heavily, high winds sounding like I was in a blizzard in the middle of the Antarctic keeping me awake for most of it.Unsettling me with their doleful moans, those winds tipped my emotional balance: this was my winter in the height of summer. What tiny slivers of confidence I had would be lost for several seconds, then come back.I'd rather it hadn't, but the next morning came and I faced a dilemma.Did I go as Carol or as Ray? I decided to go as Ray as legally that was who I was. I'd not yet officially changed my name.

Saint Matthews was made-up of three houses. Arriving at the one where I was to have the interview ten minutes before my appointment was a sign of my need to grab any scrap of certainty in my life that came my way. Knowing I'd at least get a roof over my head that night was a start. Had I been my old self I would have arrived at any interview with barely a minute to spare, loving the 'back against the wall' feel of that. As it was, my uncertainty about what I was doing and where I was going, and the need to be careful over what I said and did, ruined my natural spontaneity. Spending the night trying to sleep in my car wearing what for me were androgynous clothes, in a layby displaying a 'no overnight parking' sign (I still took some risks) because I didn't have much petrol and had no money, was uncomfortable. Aware of the slightest unusual noise in the eerie spaces between the cries of the wind, I was worried the police would find me and ask me to move on. The clothes: pink shirt; pink jeans; and flip flops, which were all I had, I wore at the interview as Ray. If I'd gone as Carol Royce, I would have had no chance of getting accommodation because I didn't have any valid documents to hand to support the fact that Carol existed. My hair was probably as long as it is now, that and my hazardously long fingernails made me appear gay. After a short while, this lady appeared and announced that her name was Moira. Straight away, she reminded me of a nun. She was short, I suppose no taller than five feet. Her soothing smile was a relief to me. Moira was the house manager of one part of this set-up. She interviewed me. Moira was one of those helpful people who inspired confidence in you, however physically and emotionally battered you were. The way I felt, a halo above her head would not have gone amiss.

She showed me into her office, at all other times the kitchen, encouraging me to talk about myself, which isn't always a good idea. It was more of a chat than an interview. During our hour together Moira told me I'd also have to be interviewed by a lady called Sheena who wouldn't be able to see me until that afternoon. Asked to come back at two, which I did, I repeated my story to Sheena. It was agreed that I could move into one of the hostels immediately. For the time being, my room was at the top of the house. If anyone moved out I could move down. The house was big, with a lot of living space crammed in. My room was on the fourth floor the size of a small garden shed. No bigger than eight feet by six with just enough room for a single bed and a wardrobe, it was home. Luckily, I was only in that room for a week as a girl on the next floor down moved to the ground floor.

In those days of nowhere to run from myself - which was in bits with no manual to help me put it back together - despair was often turned into creativity. Almost every day I wrote things down about my life - critical incidents that described the horror and the funny side of being human.

On day one I was introduced to everybody and taken to the sitting room. Two brothers who I hadn't met on my first tour were swearing at each other. The moment I came in, they stopped, looking at me as if their brains were telling them: "This does not compute". Both giants, they were well over six feet tall, the one called Richard the shorter of the two, the one called David at least three inches taller. They were covered in tattoos, the bits of their bodies still untouched by the needle likely to be filled with more words and pictures of death and decay, advice from Satan and other voices from the dark side unless they kept taking their medication. Any references to God would be added for the wrong reasons. Those two lads had to take medication that would knock an elephant out for days. They smiled at me in a way that meant friendly to them, showing their teeth which in the state I was in lacked a certain human quality. Starting a conversation with them wasn't as difficult as I'd expected. David offered me a cigarette, which I took out of fear, forgetting that I hadn't had a cigarette for well over a year. I was shaking whilst they were both trying to light the end. The heat coming from two lighters full on, plus my nervousness, made it the most dangerous light up I'd ever had. The first inhale brought on the giddy feeling I'd been getting without smoking. That night, I smoked about twenty cigarettes with my new friends who were chain smokers. I joined their club and became a chain smoker again.

You didn't need to be a doctor to know Richard and David were unwell. Revolving their wrists or moving their feet up and down as if they were pumping up tyres very fast with a foot pump, ash falling on the floor from the glowing ends of their cigarettes held precariously between their quivering brown fingers, it was clear these two needed help. Schizophrenia and manic depression stopped their lives from even reaching the point where they could be ordinary young men. I was in that room for hours with those two pouring their lives out to me.

Where an individuals way of being - such as that of someone like Richard or David diagnosed with schizophrenia or a severe personality disorder which is usually kept balanced by drugs - threatens our safety, the position changes. It is then unavoidable that awareness of the illness with which that individual has been diagnosed takes on the weight of a moral judgement, and we act in ways that protect us from the danger we are in.

Even if there is no obvious threat to our safety, can we always suspend our judgement of a person - a judgement based on incomplete knowledge of their condition in our first meeting?

Anyone who stands out because they appear strange and fail to function adequately can be valued and appreciated simply for their humanness.

Later, I found Richard and David both blamed their Dad for their grief. Hating their parents one minute, more their Dad than their Mum, the next high over the news their Dad was coming to see them, which was a rare event (in the two years I was there I think he visited them twice), it was difficult to keep track of their continually changing mental states. After several months though, they seemed to be calmer in my company. Once I'd listened to their whinging about what was troubling them, there would be these moments of comfortable silence with them when I could temporarily forget they were unwell and touch on their humanness.

Sleep was something I had built up a resistance to, the over-stimulation of fellow residents coming back and forth to see me, filling my room and me with their largely negative emotions, turning me into a night owl with attitude.

Painfully early the following morning, concerned over having to tell somebody about my condition, I took this to Sheena who was in the kitchen getting breakfast.It seemed the only way to end my agony of keeping up this pretence in order to be accepted by my fellow residents.Although I wasn't able to tell her what I had held back at the interview with her and Moira the previous day, I made Sheena aware there was more to me than I'd let on.Sheena set aside time the next day for us to have a chat about what was really happening for me.

Traipsing to the Job Centre to sort out my housing benefit was more urgent than 'coming out' to Sheena with the awkward truth that was my life.Otherwise, I would not have been able to stay there, the rent ninety pounds a week, was punishing to an unemployed person.Once my housing benefit was sorted I would be housed and fed, food being included in the rent.

I came back from the Jobcentre armed with my B1 which Sheena helped me fill in for my interview the next day.From there, disappearing to my room to write my letter to Sheena, I was all day and most of the night trying to put into words what the awkward struggle to be the real 'me' felt like, not to mention how I'd break it to her that the person she thought I was didn't exist, following that with the bombshell that I was gender dysphoric.I was pleased that I had managed to get most of my life on to two sheets of A4 though on the second read through it still looked as if I was apologising.I was always apologising for who I was.

Why did I have to change back into something I hated just to be accepted?Sheena was marvellous.

She said to me that when she first interviewed me she thought I was gay or an artist of some sort. That was all right. When I wasn't 'me' I gave off confusing signals. I might as well have been 'me' as the openness of everybody there made it pointless being otherwise.

The three Saint Matthews houses were home to a diverse bunch of characters all with their own true stories. I had this idea of their life streams trickling into mine, and I realised how we can all connect as human beings whatever our individual differences are.

At the first of the houses there were eight residents, the eldest being this lovable man called Walter. He had the nickname 'the eating machine'. Seventy years old when I arrived, I gather he is still going strong today.

Jessie, twenty-two at the time, suffered an eating disorder. She weighed at least twenty stone. Between them both, Jessie and Walter could empty a well-stocked fridge in a day. Kelly had a distressing problem with one of her legs which was swollen with fluid. She also had cerebral palsy.

Gavin, arguably the least troubled of all the people living at Saint Matthews then, was the only one in the house who worked. He used to do long hours at the Cromer crab factory. The hardest person to talk to till he got to know me better, Gavin did have a refreshing realist streak about him.

"If you want to be Carol, I like Carol, no problem," he reassured me after a tedious session explaining to him all the inroads and cul-de-sacs of what it was like to be me. Sadly, Gavin left the house a few months later.

Moving from the first to the second house was funny. During the week before I left house number one, the residents of my new address had all discussed whether I should be allowed to move in with them. My reputation for being strong-willed and argumentative followed me wherever I went. Arriving with a bang, I tried to be fair to everyone from day one right through to the end. By confronting most of the other residents hiding in the kitchen before I even put my belongings down, I stopped the place from turning into a social wasteland. I could hear voices - not in my head yet, though I was getting close to it - coming from behind the kitchen door, some slightly raised, some giggling like infants. Those of them who could string a sentence together were talking about me as if I was being tried without jury. The silence I got when I opened the kitchen door was like the whole world had shutdown for two minutes.

"I'm here, you know all about me and I am staying. If you don't like it *you* can leave! Have you any questions?" Then, an expanding grin relieving myface of the tension gripping it before I broke their cycle of whinging and piss-taking with myopenness, I picked up my stuff and asked to be shown to my room.

The second Saint Matthews house I lived in was next door to another belonging to the same organisation. Spread across the two homes were twelve residents including the House manager. This set-up was different from house number one. It had two self-contained flats on two floors. Many small rooms were furnished. There was a large communal kitchen in each house which residents shared, taking it in turns to cook for one another. Each side had a large sitting room that was nicely furnished. These two houses were seen as the residents' final step towards returning to live in the real world.

A lot of friendships I formed in those houses continued after I'd left, one of which was with Damon Albarn - not to be mistaken for the lead singer of the '90s pop group 'Blur', although this has happened more than once with hilarious consequences - whose birth name was Gary, which was what he was still being called when he first set foot on Saint Matthews' property. Damon was a young man of twenty-one when Sheena brought him to live at the house where I was. His life up to then had been an emotional minefield. Confusion and misery filled his days. I worried about him as if I was his Mum. Six years later, he still worries me. Damon looked at the floor a lot when he tried to talk because he was so shy. For the same reason, he couldn't look at people while they were talking to him. Very insecure, the energy he had stemmed from his nervousness and might have explained the fact that Ihad seen more fat on a rasher of bacon than I'd seen on him. His skinny frame, which at a glance looked the width of a deck chair side on, seemed to reflect the damage his traumatic early childhood experiences had had on him. He later found out he had a thyroid problem. I'm glad he's improved since our first meeting, gradually coming out of his shell. Nowadays, he has his own flat in North Walsham.

Leon, who was a guy we all found difficult to accept, moved into house number two with me. I became his Mum too. This young man wasn't only dangerous to himself, but anyone who came across him. He took a lot of understanding: if we were Venus, he was definitely

Mars. This poor lad had been hit on the head with a baseball bat, so he had to have a metal plate put in it. I loved him as my temporary adopted son. Being impatient, never standing still, always rushing round with nowhere definite to go, he had to go somewhere. For me, his manic way was a challenge to keep up with, for others something to steer clear of. The plate was somehow fitted over his skull, giving it support to stop it caving-in. Most of the other residents called him 'metalhead'. As cruel as this was, he took it well.

The day Leon arrived he stank. Living on the beach for as long as he had, he certainly didn't smell of Chanel number five. He reeked of rotting fish, seaweed, B.O. and tents. The bath he needed was something along the lines of a sheep dip, followed by a tub of hot water, carbolic soap, vigorous scrubbing, then, a cold shower just to be on the safe side. Unfortunately, he didn't agree. His smell got everywhere. When I was first near him I gave a controlled retch to ease the rolling ache in my throat which spread to my stomach. I wasn't there to do his washing for him and tell him when to have a bath. At least he was happy. I admired his ability to keep his past separate from his present. There was no reason for anyone there to know his past. No-one ever found out about Leon's family. He wouldn't talk about his Mum and Dad. All we ever knew was he was from Norwich.

Gerald seemed to me to appear and behave like an indoor tramp living on bacon sandwiches and toast, famous for shuffling around holding his mobile phone against his ear. He was another person who found it hard to have a bath. Gerald's signature was his long greasy hair and dirty, untidy appearance. His clothes looked as if they needed prising off of him. Either they'd eventually rot away or they'd have to be surgically removed he'd worn them for so long. He wore his jacket in the hottest weather, walking round Cromer with his toes poking out of his shoes. There was no need for him to be like this as he had money put away, but he didn't like spending it. What happened to Gerald was sad too. He worked in the kitchens of a Norfolk school for most of his life. He never got over being sacked from that job for not obeying its rules on health and safety. Because he was uneducated, he had little or no chance of getting another job.

The lovable JT was yet another of my surrogate sons. A young man in his thirties unfortunate enough to have learning difficulties, John Thomas was vulnerable to exploitation from other boys in the house. That's why I took care of him. Committed to stopping this slow, pleasant, always eager to please young man from being used, I befriended him. I showed him kindness which I don't think he'd had much of up to the time I met him. He became emotionally attached to me, so much so he got confused, thinking we were man and wife.

Coming to in the very early hours of one memorable morning was fortunate because it gave me time to react. An orange glow radiating from an outside light filtered through the darkness. It gently touched the walls and the chaotic ruffle of my bedclothes, the groggy, half-aware sub-light of my consciousness pushing itself towards full alertness. Like the morning after in a film or television programme, my vision slowly phased into focus to see this large male appendage, both in length and girth, dangling in front of my face apparently talking to me. Surely I heard it talking to me, its words spoken in a deep, stretched-out voice, delayed, slowed down to near stationary, begging: "Carol, will you sleep with me? I'll wear me pants in bed." It was JT, bless him. While most people I knew spoke at forty-five revolutions per minute, JT was a forty-five rpm record playing at thirty-three and a third.

Pulling myself up, swinging round with a force and speed that surpassed my usual reflexes, my discovery that this appendage was attached to JT didn't make the situation any less disturbing. Throwing him his dressing gown, relieved that he was already putting his pants back on which he must have had either in his hand or nearby, saw me telling him straight up that we couldn't be together like this. Once I'd settled him down, he sat on the edge of my bed and seemed to agree that a passionate affair between us would be impractical, not to mention disastrous.

His Mum visited the house and came to see me to thank me for looking after him. JT had told her about my condition using words like: "Carol used to be a man" and this woman treated me as if I was sad and to be pitied. Though I was glad I'd eased JT's own struggle at the house by befriending and protecting him, to me it felt like his Mum was only sympathetic towards me because I'd done this. I didn't need her sympathy. Acceptance was what I needed and I seriously wondered whether she would have been able to have given me either if I had not looked after JT.

People saw him as a child in an adult body. Everybody at the house liked JT. He was blissfully unaware of what was happening in the real world. He had an exceptional gift: he could remember almost any pop record released between the mid-1950s and mid-1990s and tell you the name of the artist who recorded it, the song title, and the highest position it reached in the charts.

Although the residents here were, in the main, mentally children, they were physically adults with sex drives to match. If I encouraged JT to help me in the kitchen he would think it was a 'come-on'. Corruption hadn't got to him and I don't think it ever will. Strip away that politically correct label 'intellectually-challenged' that had been slapped on him and you had a human being who was simply nice whenever he was in my company

Someone else who lived at the house was Martin. He suffered bouts of deep depression. If he didn't like you he'd soon let you know. He had worked at the same school kitchen as Gerald 'kinky shoes' Bean, but he left due to ill-health. We discovered that Gerald and Martin were brought up together in the same institution. Martin was a clean person, always in the bath. He seemed to fall in love with me, his idea of affection towards me expressed in his buying me something every day. The trouble was that something was always from second hand shops which meant it was usually junk. I had so much clutter dumped on me made up of unwanted gifts from him I was running out of space, nearly having to take on another room to use for storage. He loved my cooking but then they do say "The way to a man's heart is through his stomach", except I didn't want to get to his heart by any route, least of all his stomach. In sympathy with Martin too, I wanted to show him a bit of kindness to help him on his way. When I left he broke down. I did go back to see him a few times. There was a little improvement on what he'd been like when I lived there.

Nineteen year old Josh moved in a week or so after me. Here was someone else looking for maternal love. Like Leon, Josh wanted me to be his Mum. He'd never talk about his parents. I must've asked him many times to talk about them but he always refused. A very smart young man wearing designer clothes that he got out of all the people he knew, who were mainly from London, he looked seriously out of place in that hostel. Always a complicated person, it struck me that Josh was troubled about his sexuality. He tried to prove he was a man, not an easy ambition to achieve for someone so young and mixed-up. Also running against him was the block he had with young girls that caused him to treat them like dirt. I asked him if he was gay. He said no. Although he often surrounded himself with girls, he appeared to be happier in male company. His need to control both sexes echoed throughout our family, as I liked to call it. Definitely gay, Josh ended up in Florida with a male partner who owned a bar and night club.

Taylor, who like Josh was smart and about nineteen when we met, already lived in the house before I moved in. I met him the day after I arrived. He was sitting in the kitchen. Before we opened our mouths we hit it off - what you might call instant rapport. We fascinated each other. One of these people I felt I'd known all my life, I was so comfortable with Taylor my first words to him were "You're definitely gay." He was so frank, which helped me. That made it all right for me to talk openly about my life which up until then I'd not discussed with any of the residents in those two houses, only Moira and Sheena. Sometimes, Taylor and I would go back to our childhoods, perhaps part of the effect of ending up poor and having to live in a hostel for the homeless.

Damon had this weird idea of hanging my childhood teddy bear, Ted. When Ted got to fifty I stuck a badge on him that said "I am fifty and loaded." He was a symbol of my childhood. Still having the original bit of ribbon round his neck, evidently I'd looked after him. I'd never part with him. Damon and Taylor decided that Ted was suicidal after spending too many years with me. For them, it was kinder to put him out of his misery. An ultimatum was given to me in the form of a ransom note warning me that if I didn't stop nagging Damon and Taylor I'd never see my Ted alive again. What went through my mind was that I'd had that Teddy all those years then two young men still wet behind the ears come along all set to destroy him. They did have the decency to bury him in a plastic bag afterwards so they had some respect. As Damon explained: "We did treat him with a bit of dignity. We gave him a cross and a funeral service that Carol failed to attend."

They buried an important part of my childhood. I didn't even know about the funeral. Taylor is still a close friend, often phoning me for a good whinge as well as to make sure I'm all right, in that order.

Patrick shouted at people. He was one of two residents who worked in the house and it had gone round Cromer he was a pervert. He really paid a price for that label; he might as well have worn a badge with the word 'pervert' on it, or the same printed onto a bright red tee-shirt in large black lettering.Much as I don't tolerate child molesters, it wasn't certain he was guilty of this allegation.The trouble he found himself in started before I arrived so I found it easier not to judge him.Still, Patrick reminds me of how difficult it is to see people simply as ways of being without wanting to give them a label of some sort.He pushed me to the limit so I had to confront him.He shouted at me in his girlie voice, which you could barely tell apart from that of the average female and I flew at him.I shot off my bed, found where he was, pushed him into the kitchen with me and slammed the door behind us in one great dam burst of energy.We had a good crowd watching.I could've charged them for it and made some money. People wanted to get in there to see if I was going to hit him.I stuck one of my fingers between his eyes and told him at a volume louder than his: "Don't shout at me or I'll rip your head off!"The look on his face was pure shock. He was a child in a strong male way with a girlie voice that didn't fit."

Some people would say that is being judgmental but you don't know how much that bloke asked for it by the way he wound me and the other residents up and interfered in our lives.My story illustrates how difficult it is for me not to judge people when they won't accept me as I really am.As long as it doesn't interfere with other people's lives or put them in danger, do I not have the right to be who I really am? Doesn't anybody who follows this general principle have that right?

Once I'd shaken Patrick up I'd done my bit, leaving the room telling everybody gawking outside:Right, I'm girlie again. Our Pat went from maniac to mouse.

Everybody had been frightened of him. He never raised his voice to me again over the whole of the second year I was there. Since I left the house Pat's been round to see me at my flat in North Walsham because he knows I'm one of the few people who won't judge him on the basis of what he's alleged to have done but if he still treated me the same way he did at Cromer before our run-in we'd be sworn enemies. His voice is still irritatingly high, which I know he can't help and I've learnt to tolerate, but by the time he's gone I've usually got a headache from it, and that does interfere with my life.

A second Martin, who I saw little of, had one of the self-contained flats. He seemed like a recluse to me - the Howard Hughes of Saint Matthews. When he did manage to leave his room, he'd come downstairs to talk to me about horse racing, a subject I knew nothing about. I once saw inside his flat. It was decorated in designer nicotine. The walls were yellow-brown caused by his full-strength capstan cigarettes. You'd be a passive smoker simply by sitting in his flat on a hot day without him there, the tar on his walls and that absorbed by furniture and carpets coming to life.

The next person I liked was Colin who was the house manager after Moira. Although Colin and I started off on the wrong foot because I'd applied for the manager's job when Moira was leaving and he never told me he was also up for it, we too became good friends.

I liked Colin very much. When he realised it was me who'd competed with him for the job, he came over to console me, staying with me for about three hours.

I felt sorry for Jessie. We watched her make a sandwich once. It was a whole loaf and a block of cheese stacked on a plate. "It's only a cheese sandwich," she protested.

"That's not a sandwich," Sheena roared. "That's a four course meal." Sheena decided Jess should go to number twenty-six where she could fend for herself. We all had our own fridges with locks on them. The privileged had master keys so your food wasn't as safe as you thought. One time, Jess charged me £7 for a dinner she cooked me. It was spaghetti Bolognese. Only a few of us sat down to it. I was the only one who was charged for the privilege. "I'll give her due though," Damon remarked in her defence. "She did nice cakes."

The roast dinners were Tudor-style banquets. This girl ate a five pound chicken which she tore to bits like Henry VIII. Twelve Aunt Bessie's Yorkshire puddings, two pans of roast potatoes, plus a whole cauliflower with the chicken ended in grief when during her struggle to digest all that her stomach would go into trauma. Despite the setbacks she suffered caused by her large form, Jess was a lovely person. I remember her coming into my room as I was sorting out my clothes to ask me if she could have one of my skirts. Given that I was a size twelve and she was a twenty-eight, I nearly rolled off the bed swallowing the cigarette I was smoking at the time. It was my black lycra skirt she fancied.

"I'd like to think I could wear that one day," were her words, which really made me sad. Wanting to give her hope, I gave her the skirt aware that if she tried to get into it it'd be like putting a bandage on one of her legs. Still, it felt nice giving her something that made her feel good. All the girls took my clothes. It was a wonder I came out of there with anything.

Theresa, walking round the house in bare feet, didn't have any shoes so I gave her a pair of mine I'd bought but never used. They were brand new worth about £80 and she went out and wrecked them. She walked them straight through the mud down by the boating lake.

One day Steph and I gave her a makeover. It took us hours to turn her into an attractive young woman. Her boyfriend walked in, saw how nice she looked, and ripped it all off of her. He wanted her to be scruffy because he could only feel comfortable with her if she was like that. Before coming to the house, Theresa lived in Sheringham. There were so many bin bags in the flat where those two lived, some full of maggots; they were evicted for being a public health hazard. With them, money came before safety. Theresa's boyfriend had taken all the lead off the roof of the building which housed their flat. He then stripped the tiles from it and sold them. Open to the elements, the loft space filled with water and the ceiling collapsed. They were instantly homeless. It was this that brought them to the exotic location of Cromer.

When she was younger, Theresa had been in a serious road accident. A car dragged her for hundreds of yards causing brain damage. She was a child in an adult body constantly struggling with her surroundings. Damon used to see her walking round Sheringham. "She looked as if she'd come out of a coal mine," he recalled.

She was on medication, her boyfriend was a ciderholic. Their highly individual ways of being were to a large degree caused by the substances they took.

Steph and I were inseparable for a few months till Damon came into the equation. She used to say to me:

"Do you like Damon? I really fancy him?" I used to say to her: "If you fancy him, tell him," because I fancied Barry, Steph's on/off boyfriend, sometimes called 'roll-on/roll-off' for reasons I'm not going into. Most times when Steph was out of the way, distracted by the ever confusing world of Damon, Barry used to come and sit on my bed. Like a great big teddy bear he was ultra cuddly, confiding in me about Steph because he was gutted when she left him for the demon Damon.

"I was probably the male slut of the house," reflected Damon.

I had a job keeping Taylor and Damon away from my clothes and make-up. When you see somebody who's six feet four in a twelve inch lycra skirt it's something you don't forget. If Damon was to stand in water you'd have a job distinguishing his legs from those of a stork. He had the skinniest pins I'd ever seen with tights on. They weren't for walking with, in my imagination more useful as oars. Visions of his legs slotting into the rowlocks on the side of a rowing boat haunted me.

Chapter Eighteen

Over seven hundred days passed while I was with Saint Matthews, each one having its own unique character. There was always someone coming to live at the hostel or moving out. Sometimes, the chaos was wonderful. My friends taught me how to live on nothing. They gave me more than I gave them: the teacher became the pupil.

During my time at one address there was a huge turnover of residents. Somehow many of these people's lives became part of my own. My dive looked something like an old railway station waiting room. Often the smoke alarms would go off because there were so many smokers dragging away in there - sorry, wrong choice of word - puffing away in there. Sometimes it was so bad I couldn't see my hand in front of my face. Then I had to put a cover on my bed to tone down the stink of fags on my bedclothes. Some evenings I had my own tropical cloud haze in my room, with the smoke line hanging around for hours causing me to have to open the patio doors to let the draught suck it out.

My stay in Cromer had its moments. From where I am now, it's clear to me that I needed to go there to learn to do without things I had taken for granted before. Living on next to nothing was a steep learning curve for me. All the boys in the house made sure I didn't want for much as far as cigarettes and wine were concerned. I soon knocked the house into shape. One of the changes

I made was to arrange a kitty for the food. That meant we all ate well. The other girls and boys who made up my team were unemployed. They were probably eating better than some people in full-time work. Money I used to collect from eight residents amounted to £15.00 a week each, allowing us to get quite a kitty going to pay for the wholesome food I believed everyone needed. Beans on toast was strictly off the menu when I was in charge. Satisfaction at seeing their lethargic, directionless lives transformed into healthier ones improved the quality of my own there. A structure to their day and the value I put on each of them, which they could see by the way I cared they ate properly and had some order to their existences, helped them.

To me they all seemed like tramps with no purpose in life, prepared to stay in bed all day then get up to go to the off licence and squander their benefit there, or on drugs, sooner than pay their rent. I'm not claiming I changed their lives for the better as if I'm a nun with no faults of my own whose sole aim in life was to put them right. Neither am I trying to get credit for helping them. What I will say is that before I sorted them I was washing and ironing mostly boys' clothes. That was because their hygiene was so poor compared to the girls. Not only was the boys' stuff offensive to my nostrils because it stank, they just dumped it in the washing machine without any washing powder expecting it to come out clean. They were a potential health hazard. Once trained to a basic standard of social responsibility, they were doing their own washing and ironing. Tactical was my middle name. I used to say to them: "go and have a bath and while you're doing that I'll wash your clothes and iron them later."From small beginnings, I got a community going there.My team, who I saw as my new children, achieved a better way of living through learning by example, as had my own children back home.Within the limits of their resources, they became social rather than anti-social, largely through my showing them life skills that slowly sank in.They found they could help each other, sharing their experiences good and bad.Above all, they could solve their own problems because they thought in a more focused, adult way.In each case, I didn't want to take away their individuality. It was more a matter of smoothing their rough edges to give them, and all of us for that matter, healthier, richer lives.Telling a twenty-seven year old to leave the toilet in a hygienic state after he'd been isn't something most people would imagine having to do anyway, but that's another example of what it was like.Of course, I was grateful that person actually used the toilet in the first place and not the garden.The next step was to encourage him to care enough to wipe the seat if he'd peed on it, press the flush lever, then wash his hands in the washbasin.Remember that most of these young people were ill-treated from an early age, kicked out to fend for themselves when they couldn't, so they saw any demands made on them as unreasonable, retaliating either in an introverted way by withdrawing, or in an extroverted way by answering back or being aggressive.

I work on the belief that there's good in everyone. Ask people in a civilised way to do something instead of demanding it to be done and it will probably get done.When I was looking after the boys and girls at the second home I lived in, I used to make sure they completed all the cleaning we were expected to do on our side of the house on a weekly basis. The kitchen was my job because I was the one who used to do all the cooking with a little help from Damon. Spelling out to my team that household chores were necessary because if they weren't done the house would soon become a health hazard with so many people living in it, gave them a reason for doing them. A community needs leadership and organisation with a good balance between authority and love. Over time, a bond of trust leading to friendship was established with most of the residents there, evidenced by how today they take the trouble to travel from Cromer to North Walsham to see me when they don't need to.

Staff at Unwins' off-licence knew us well, stocking-up for our sit-round-the-table-all-night drinking parties, full of bad behaviour including the x-rated humour, releasing our tension through the most spontaneous and enjoyable of all therapies: laughter. The language may have been a tad blue during those crazy sessions of human contact and the exciting energy that flowed from them, but it was living in the moment for the moment.

The first time Frank saw me I was dressed as a male. The second time Frank saw me I was dressed as a female. No wonder the poor man was confused. His friend Jim asked me in a less than subtle way: "Did you used to be a bloke?" to which I replied angrily: "I still am, but it's not my choice. I didn't ask to be like this." He responded with a phrase that was as aggravating to me as if I had been poked with something sharp then having it corkscrewed into my skin.

"Are you a transvestite then?"

No.

"What other sort is there?"

This dumb conversation between us came up like indigestion at regular intervals over the next two years. On days when Frank and others wanted to know things about me they were straight to the point with their questions, but however clear I tried to be with my answers they just couldn't understand, and again however much I tried to accept them for who they were the label 'intellectually-challenged' was difficult to put aside when dealing with them.

I want to see everyone for their humanness. It's a fact of life that some of the bits that make-up a person's way of being can be dangerous to others. Similarly, people will find traits of mine that irritate or hurt them, or both, which block their acceptance of me, causing them to place a judgement on me that's usually attached to a label that's socially discrediting.

Frank used to come to see me up until a short while ago. Although he told me he liked the way I always gave him straightforward answers, those answers always turned into big debates that exhausted me with their repetition. It was the same old thing every time. Frank had been in the army. He had probably been a cook there, but he often talked about being in the SAS. The problem with Frank was that his whole life revolved around his medication. He'd say: "I've been to the doctors. I'm on more pills," before he even greeted me. That was the gist of his mindset. He liked everyone to know he was ill. You can see why I felt like a Mum to him. Frank would go home then think about something he'd forgotten to ask me and have to come all the way back to ask me it. He couldn't let anything go. Whatever played on his mind kept him awake until he had put it right. It takes some imagining to guess what he would have been like without his chronic anxiety, which was eased by a high dose of medication given to him regularly by his community psychiatric nurse. Sitting in my flat for days, coming on a Friday, leaving on a Sunday afternoon, I used to let him pour out his frustration. Frank would stand on my doorstep greeting me with those ominous words that told me he would be staying the weekend: "Can I have a bath, Carol? I listened to him to show him acceptance and valuation. However, on another level 'Frank's not a well man' was never far from my thoughts. His repetitive behaviour was, if nothing else, wasting his and everybody else's time and energy and when I was with him, as much as I tried not to, I could only see him as obsessive and compulsive to the point where it did my head in. Sadly, Frank is no longer with us.

Towards the end of my year at number twenty-six, sadness was a part of my life again. In the two weeks prior to his death I'd become close to a young man called Joe. Turning to drink with his friends, who were the drunks of Cromer, Joe found his way back to the downward spiral he had never really escaped. One of the drunks who Joe called a friend had used syringes in Joe's bedroom to inject himself. Unfortunately, there was a random search of Joe's room that discovered the syringes there. Given they were found in his room, it was assumed they were Joe's and Joe had used them.

Without any discussion, sentence was passed on him. He was told to leave. Within a few days, he was dead.

Keith, who was in his mid-fifties, was a problem at first. "I'm not calling you Carol. That's a girl's name," were the less than supportive words I got from him. I soon pulled this relationship into line. By the time I left, Keith had come round. I actually got a kiss from him as he happily called me Carol.

Bleaching the work surface in the kitchen lacked the glamour I wanted in my life, but for hygiene's sake it had to be done to keep the salmonella, e-coli, or anything else nasty that was bound to hit us if I didn't do this regularly, at bay. Sexy, with the loveliest black hair, dead straight, that went right down his back, perfect tanned skin as if he'd just got off his horse in the Arizona desert, Richard was unique.

Claiming one of his relations was a Sioux Indian, he exploited the assets nature had given him. Richard was a disappointingly English name for someone with alleged American-Indian blood. When I looked at the gorgeous Richard, who was a hunk and a half, I could see the Sioux in him. He only wanted a horse and some war paint.

Asking him not to sit on the work surface or stick his feet on it after I'd bleached it was an invitation for him to reveal his maverick streak by climbing on it just to wind me up. Grabbing his feet then pulling him off the side of the work surface, I watched the shock capture his face as he landed on his bottom and bounced off the wooden floor. That marked the beginning of our understanding of each other. Once Richard knew I was capable of carrying out a threat, from then on he was straight with me.

I remember an exciting time we had during the Cromer Carnival celebrations of 1997. The day started like any other. First thing in the morning we all sat round the table smoking, and drinking coffee, having a chat about what we were going to do over the next twenty-four hours. Earlier in the week, the subject of the coming annual highlight of Cromer's social life was raised by one of the residents. I can see and hear it now. "Why can't we have a float?" someone protested. What about the organisation involved with it? I remember saying. There was a short silence. "Let's do it," enthused Sheena. "It'll be fun."

How can you join the carnival without transport? You need a float. This takes time to arrange. Next morning, battle plans were drawn up as to who was going to do what. It was decided that we'd see if we could get hold of some material and try to find someone who would lend us a lorry for the day. The lorry was harder to sort out than you would imagine, although when you think about it, who in their right mind is going to lend a lorry to a group of delinquents they don't know? Out came the yellow pages. We must have phoned every haulage firm in Norfolk. It seemed hopeless, then, as I was coming to the end of the list I dialled this number. A man with a polite voice answered. I went through my rehearsed patter expecting him to say what everyone else had. He told me to hang on while he found out if he had a spare truck that weekend. He was gone for about five minutes. During this interlude, cheap sounding high street store music played distractingly in my ear. I remember having everything crossed, his voice came back on the line saying: "You're in luck." I asked him what he'd charge, explaining we were a charity that couldn't afford a lot. "You can use it if you have an HGV driver and can get him to come and see us in the morning with his licence," was his welcome reply. As luck would have it, Robert could drive a lorry so he agreed to go.

On the day, I spotted our float in the procession, shaking my head. There they all were, pale, lifeless ghosts on the back of this lorry with Robert driving, looking as if he'd made the public relations mistake of his life. Big Wayne, dressed as the grim reaper, was doing his version of robotic dancing to heavy rock. The lorry passed so slowly through the mass of happy people it was agony to watch. I wanted to hurry it along to get it out of the way. Each member of my little community had a mask on that was enough to terrify the children running around. They wore hooded capes made from old rummage sale clothes. The cardboard sickles they wielded were unconvincing. The irony of it struck me. *I wanted to live and they all wanted to die.*

December 1997 saw me experiencing symptoms that over the next eighteen weeks made me think of giving up smoking. A circulation problem in my left arm due to a collapsed artery coming from my heart was the cause. On the wedding ring finger of my left hand an appearance began to cause me concern. Beginning as red dots under the nails of that finger and the ones either side of it, the doctor diagnosed Reynaud's disease. He prescribed drugs for this then asked me to go back every week for about a month so that he could keep an eye on it. Growing worse, the pain made sure my nights were almost sleepless, spent largely pacing the floor holding my hand under my arm pit. My finger looked as though it had been hit with a hammer. During the day I tried not to bang it doing what had to be done. All the doctor did was give me different tablets. Tablets weren't going to stop the drawing, knife-sharp spasms. Swallowing alcohol to deaden their slow, stabbing rhythm, contained in black, swollen tissue that was my finger dying on the end of my hand gave no lasting relief. Common sense told me I needed an x-ray.

Snow fell and the rare experience of confronting a blizzard in Cromer doubled my pain bringing me to the limit of my tolerance of spending my days and nights pacing up and down my room to stay above the agony.

Unable to take my glove off during an emergency visit to my doctor, he removed it for me, saw the black, seething flesh where a finger would normally be, picked up the telephone and called an ambulance. The drama had an imaginary romantic tone to it, for the ambulance whisked me off to the Norfolk and Norwich Hospital where I met a lovely physician who treated me, called Doctor Clarke.

Every medical doctor their except lovely Doctor Clarke seemed to be saying that my bad finger had to come off. Keen to preserve my painfully embarrassing digit closely resembling a feature of the male anatomy I didn't want to be associated with, he vowed he'd try to save it for me. About two o'clock in the morning on or about the second day I was there I fancied a cup of tea. Venturing into the nurses' station one of them asked me: "Can we help you?" The only thing I could think of was to display my infected finger in front of her bewildered face and say: My hand has grown a penis. I think I need a cup of tea. As I said this she spat her coffee across the room, nearly showering everyone with it. I don't know what made me say that. Most of my life had been spent wanting to get rid of a penis and now I had one growing on my hand as well. Even down to having a hole in the top of it that was in the middle where dead tissue had fallen away, its helmet right down to the first joint of my finger.

The room was in uproar. That frivolous outburst on my part, pun intended, helped the week go by better than it would have done. Getting to know all those lovely nurses who used to come into my room to see how I was doing, guaranteed a good injection of my humour to brighten a stressful working day.

Doctor Clarke had a stock phrase when he arrived at my bedside on his morning ward round: "It might hurt but it's still there, isn't it?" Over the next week regular tests were done to analyse the state of my blood. Worried about the gangrene in my finger, Doctor Clarke kept his promise by saving it. It's still safely attached to my hand in as near to its original form as possible. Though more slender, it blends with the rest of my left hand.

If my understanding is correct, the tiny blood vessels at the end of my finger were blocked. Blood was unable to circulate there causing the existing tissue to slowly die. I couldn't even have a collapsed artery properly. The hospital had to send abroad for a tube to go inside the blocked artery that was the cause of the restricted blood flow in my finger. On the fifth day, I went down to the operating theatre. The surgeons had to make a hole in the artery of my right leg to allow a tube to be inserted into the hole to go right up the main artery to the heart. My artery didn't collapse on a straight bit; it had to collapse on a bend. Anaesthetic was injected into my leg at the site where the tube was to be put in. This only deadened that small area, so I was still able to feel much of what was being done to me. Like a worm wriggling up inside me, the sensation of the tube going in with a fibre optic camera was the start of about two and a half hours in the operating theatre. The length of time in theatre was necessary because they couldn't stop the bleeding at the site where the tube entered my body.

Warforin is glorified rat poison. I'd taken a lot of it over that week to thin my blood down, which was like water. The moment the tube was in position there was instant relief in my finger which was by then getting a supply of blood flowing into its dying tissues. Within hours my finger had changed from black to pink, except the damaged area still painful to touch, a good dollop of pus there promising that the worst would soon be out of my system.

One of the reasons I moved from Cromer to North Walsham was to protect my anonymity. Too many people saw me and believed they knew me as a body labelled 'transsexual'.

One Friday, while signing-on at Cromer Jobcentre with a friend who knew about my life because she'd lived in the house with me a short time, everything turned bad. This friend happened to take it upon herself to explain my life to her boyfriend who didn't need to know about it.

She signed on ahead of me, left the signing point, and told me she would wait outside. Whilst I was standing in the queue, she was telling my precious secret that was, literally, my life, to this thug, whose hatred of me was based on his ignorance and fear. She had no idea of the damage she had done until it was too late. Her bloke had his army of mates with him and he was going to impress. When I came out of the jobcentre they thought they'd have a bit of fun winding me up, then give me a good kicking.

Tired of Cromer, tired of the crap life I was living, I'd had enough of everything: the house; the people who lived there; the whole f****** mess. Stripped of the power I had - if you could call it that - I was going nowhere, like a robot, cooking; cleaning; thinking twenty-four/seven about those youngsters. I'd spent the whole year in that place worrying about them and putting *me* on hold. When I walked out of the Jobcentre I didn't hear what that bloke said to me. Whether I could hear him or not I knew that kid was 'slagging me off'. I hit him hard on the side of his head. He just went down. It was one of those moments when I reacted badly to what was thrown at me, then the situation became desperate, with his mates standing round me, staring. Down on the floor, 'Thug' had lost his power. He looked vulnerable, as if in seconds I'd reduced him to the fragile state of a small child. By hitting his ear I'd forced air into it. Blood was coming out of both of his ears, his nose, and his mouth. Seeing the state he was in, I panicked and ran from the scene.

I pushed past the gathering crowd and walked briskly back to the house. I went straight to my room where I sat on my bed shaking. Feeling supported by everyone there, who wanted to know what was wrong - Colin, Sheena, and Moira in particular - I realised how genuine my little community was. Paranoid that the police were going to bang on the door and come in and arrest me for killing someone, I stayed in my room. Regretting what I'd done, fearing its consequences, I thought my life had stopped.

After about an hour and a half the doorbell went and it was Jane, the girl whose boyfriend I'd hit, She had come to tell me he was all right, yet even after hearing that reassuring news from her I continued to feel uneasy, unable to understand why I'd done it.

Sheena and the social worker told me I had to get out.Emotionally, the other residents were keeping me there.They were growing and I wasn't: arriving as these poor, homeless, unwell people, I directed them towards improving their social skills by teaching them to live and work together, but in the end it was taking so much out of me I had nothing left for myself.

I went into those houses confused but still strong, a strength that was gradually whittled away by my fellow residents over a period of nearly two years.It took four weeks from when it was decided I should leave, to get my flat in North Walsham.The help I got from Sheena, Julian Housing(where Sheena had started to work full-time), and the social workers, was marvellous.

One of the hardest things I ever had to do was tell my mum about my new life. I'd not seen her since I left Harlow in 1996.Before leaving Cromer I saw a clinical psychologist and in my usual way tried to explain my whole life to him in an hour, which was the time allowed for my appointment.He listened patiently to me then at the end of the session advised me to do something I had been avoiding.

"I can see what the problem is. You need to contact your parents, especially your Mum," he said.

Throughout the interview I kept mentioning my Mum and the psychologist picked up on this.

"Why are you talking to me when you can talk to your Mum?" he queried, with a logic that left me gob smacked.

He also made the point that where I was living in Cromer lacked the stimulation I needed to progress. Here was someone who wanted to move you on. The desire to move on was always there in me. The psychologist helped me realise that I had stopped my life to help others. I wasn't growing. I was hiding in that house instead of taking responsibility for improving my own life. The only time I went out was when I had to. I'm grateful to that psychologist. Without him I'd probably still be in Cromer, or even dead.

It was fate that I went to Cromer. Life dealt me some tough lessons there. Before that experience my arrogance left no room for understanding people less fortunate than me. When I moved into the hostel some of my fellow residents were so down on their luck I was made to think. I found myself in a world I knew existed but would never have believed how bad it was until I was part of it. Unemployment wasn't new to me although up to that time I had never been out of work for long. Young boys and girls with mental illnesses that made them unpredictable was a new concept to me. I'd never had such problems with other people before. Some of these youngsters barely functioned. Out in the real world they were hopelessly lost which was why they ended up being looked after by 'Saint Matthews'.

Writing a letter to my mum brought back harsh memories of the upheaval of leaving home in July 1996. Here is that letter.

"Dear Mum,

I'm sorry it's taken me so long to write and it doesn't seem as if I care about anyone but I do.It's taken so long because of the way I live my life now.I'm no longer the person I was.

This letter is probably the hardest thing I've had to do since I moved away.I need to know how you and Dad are.I hope you're both well but I'll understand if you have disowned me.What I did up to the time I left must make me seem insane.It wasn't just my sanity that was in danger of going under.I would have ended it all if I'd not done what I had.I don't know if Jackie told you anything about me and our life together but it wasn't easy for her towards the end.She put up with hell from me.So did the children.I took my hatred of myself out on them.They now think I've disowned them.I haven't but it is best they think that way at the moment. They are too young to take what I've done.I hope they'll forgive me when they are older.

It's not easy to explain but here goes.I suffer from a condition called gender dysphoria, better known as transsexualism.This is something you are born with. You don't become transsexual.I've known for most of my life that I've hated my male form but not knowing what was wrong didn't make life easy.You can't talk to anyone - even those closest to you.I found out in 1987 what my condition was called and I did try to tell you many times.What with dad and the boys and my marriage and the children it was easier to turn to drink or that's what I thought at the time.I even nearly managed to kill myself with it but I even got that wrong.The two women in my life and my children should not have been in my life. What I mean by that is I should not have married my two partners, set-up home with them, and had children by them, but it was the only way to look normal. I love Jackie, Sophie, Alicia and Ross to bits. They are all of me, but I can't put into words the way I've treated them all over the years. My lies and deceit to them and everyone I knew is unbelievable. My selfishness took over. I've robbed my family of many thousands of pounds leading my double life. We should have been rich with my income.

I've changed my name and live totally as a female. I have a flat in Norfolk with many friends who accept me as I am. I know this letter is a shock confession but there's no easy way to tell you how I feel for everyone - you, Dad, my brothers, Jackie, the children. I just feel so alone. I need to talk to Mick as well as you. I've so much to explain. I don't know where to start, Mum. If you can come to terms with all this which I know won't be easy - even I've found it hard over the years - would you come and stay for a while? I need to talk to you. I cannot put it all down on a few pages in a letter. What I've done to my partner and my children I've done to you, Dad, and my brothers as well. I just can't come to terms with how I treated you all but at the time it was easier to keep my life secret. I didn't want to appear a pervert, which I'm not. I wish it was something easy like I was gay or something but life isn't that simple for me. All the anger I've carried around for so long has gone now. I now help people instead of use them and the friends I've made are my true friends. I know Dad will find this hard to accept, as will my brothers. I know the truth must come out now.This isn't a guilt trip.It's just that I need to explain my life - the reasons why I just couldn't handle my life as it was.Not being able to tell you how I felt, the being dragged along in life and making a mess of everything I did soon took its toll and one mess became another, lie upon lie, deceit, and the anger pushing away any friends I had, making life hell.Towards the end I didn't trust anyone.I was on my own.I couldn't handle rejection by you, Dad, Jackie, or any of my so-called friends.If it makes sense I wanted things to stay how they were but I've had to change my life and lose everything I had.I suppose that makes me insane?

If you can handle this and meet me as I am, because I won't change back, it's too late for that I am now who I really am - I would plead with you to come and stay.I live in a small town called North Walsham.It's not far from the coast and I think you'd like it.It's more like a small village.You'd like the shops here.There's plenty of everything.If you're unsure what people would say or think, don't be.They only know me as Carol Royce.I've spent nearly three years building my new life and my neighbours know nothing of my male life.They all think my voice is deep but lucky for me I have a female friend with the same problem.I'm not making light of the problem but I need you to know that no-one knows.Do you remember Alan's party when you said how much I looked like you?Well now you know why.I was already changing then.I was already taking hormones.Please write to me Mum.Yours with love, Carol."

Being on my own in a small flat in rural Norfolk

was at odds with my outgoing personality. I needed people around me. This became a hunger that had to be satisfied. Lately, I'd been more able to take on what was around me - when there was sufficient stimulation around me to take on. Becoming interested in the comings and goings of the neighbourhood, I noticed things I'd never have taken the slightest interest in before, believing this change was due to my inner self finding its way to the surface at last.

Chapter Nineteen

When I arrived in North Walsham, I decided it was time to do something useful with my life that would occupy me. I chose voluntary work because I wanted to help people, and promptly contacted Jenny who worked at social services. Jenny was the coordinator for the North Walsham district of Norfolk Voluntary Services based at the town's cottage hospital. I spoke to her at length, telling her that if I was going to do this type of work in an honest way, which was what I wanted, anyone I befriended must know the truth about me. Jenny had a lady in mind she thought I'd like to meet. I decided to go ahead and meet her. That lady was Diane.

Diane was to be my first befriender and befriendee. We'd both joined the scheme for the same reason. I made up my mind that if Diane could not deal with my condition we'd not see each other again. Jenny had discussed this with Diane before I met her.

All went well. I hit it off with Diane straight away. She turned out to be a very open-minded and talented person. It was decided that at first my visits would be limited to one hour on a Wednesday morning. That one hour soon became three, then four, then every other day. That was in the autumn of 1998. Today we are good friends who see each other regularly.

Her husband Peter is also talented and her son David kindly agreed to help me write this book on his computer.I've every admiration for Peter.He's a brilliant cook and that's the understatement of the decade.He spoils me.He is one of those rare people who can make time for everyone.Since knowing him, I've never gone without food, keeping my larder stocked to the hilt.For my money, Pete makes the best meat pies in Norfolk. His survival kits - small bags of food that he gives me on most of my visits - are typical of his generosity.He's so kind.Working very hard for the Women's Institute Market that nowadays allows men to take part and help with that side of the organisation, his products have become well known to many of the older, and some of the younger, residents of the town.He is also a brilliant painter, a talent he hasn't exercised for years, that and his practical skills come together to make him one of the most versatile people I've met.

In her younger days, Diane was a successful performer with the Chelmsford and Witham amateur dramatic societies. She was involved mainly with Chelmsford Operatic and Dramatic Society but at different times was also a member of Chelmsford Festival Players.In 1948 she was the youngest person ever in Chelmsford to be given the lead role in a production.The production was "No, no, Nanette" and the performances took place at the Regent Theatre in the town.She was just fifteen.Her reviews were excellent.I was impressed.Diane's other talents include drawing and poetry.I've read and would recommend a couple of slim volumes she has written that demonstrate her talent for producing traditional poetry and prose.

David Berthelot is a kind, gentle person who tries to understand everyone he meets.It's an impossible task.

In the short time I've known him I have become more tolerant.

My friend Gail who I've known for six years has been an inspiration to me. I don't know where I'd be without her. She's also one of the most selfless people I've met, helping me through some difficult phases since I moved into my flat, often giving up a lot of her time to support me. Through her, my eyes have been opened as to how I really feel about myself. My perception that I was the most hard done by person on the estate was changed greatly when I met and befriended Gail. My problems were put into perspective when I saw what this poor woman had to put up with. What she does for her friends and family is remarkable. With so much zest for life, and drive, she can stand up to any obstacle that stops her from getting on. I don't think she gets back the good she gives out, but Gail doesn't give to receive; Gail is a giver. She is in pain most of the time, yet it seems to me that some of the people around her don't understand what is happening to her. It's her will to struggle on, always hoping and striving for a better life, that keeps her strong. Gail is the sister I had been searching almost all of my life and found in 1998.

We're both the same age, bar a few months. We have a marvellous rapport. Our lives have been similar in the choices we've made: you know, been there done that. We either can't find the tee-shirts or their colours are faded and they don't wear too well. Marriage, children, money, have all given us grief. Now we're both without partners, our children flitting in and out of our lives, and, much to their inconvenience, we haven't any money.

Looking at us both together there's one feature that

sets us apart: I'm extrovert, while Gail probably leans more towards the introverted side. We complement each other, which makes our relationship work well. People think we're sisters because we spend so much time together. My Mum and Dad have even adopted Gail into our family as though she's always been there as their other daughter.

Most people treat me like a person. The process of gender realignment largely doesn't allow you to be a person. That's certainly how I found it.

For consultants to agree to someone having gender realignment surgery, strict criteria for eligibility have to be met. This clinical approach may increase the likelihood of gender dysphoria sufferers withdrawing from the world, or be too concerned with what looks right to other people rather than with being honest and truthful about how they really feel. A further effect may be that they withhold information about their experiences that may help improve other people's understanding of their condition, causing them to be more alienated than if they had been open about what's happening to them.

I also argue that the confrontational interview style I had to put up with may do more harm than good to other genuine sufferers of gender dysphoria. They feel hurt and dismay at the often total lack of understanding from other people. We can't make this journey alone. Once diagnosed with a gender identity disorder, I became a non-person; a label: I was classed as 'mentally ill'. Trying to keep everything within the psychiatrists' prescribed timescale, from initial diagnosis to surgery, has led to some who suffer from gender dysphoria becoming a tragic mess. They've tried to struggle whilst following doctors' orders, which they need to do just to get to first base.

One female doctor said to me: "What do you want to do this for? You're being selfish. You've got children you should be thinking about."

I never stop thinking about my children. Most of this book is about me admitting I've been selfish - I don't need a psychiatrist to tell me so. I tried to accept how I'd been made. I started relationships, married, and had children. That led to all manner of problems, including heavy financial losses and catastrophic emotional upheaval. I ruined my partner and my children's lives.

A psychiatrist at Charing Cross told me I had to be in a full-time job and pass as a female before surgery was even a remote possibility for me. Convinced I couldn't wait for a full-time job and universal acceptance that I was female, I was close to turning in on myself and ending it all. The suicide rate for untreated transsexuals worldwide is sky-high.

(Gems News no.23 March 1995 cover).

To the psychiatrists it didn't count that I worked part-time as a volunteer for the Citizen's Advice Bureau. They insisted I was in full-time paid employment for at least one year before even being considered for surgery. Voluntary work used to be accepted as employment. There are plenty of people who aren't gender dysphoric who do voluntary work and are seen as who they are, running perfectly balanced lives. For the Charing Cross psychiatrists, voluntary work was only one step to what they called employment. My whole week had to be occupied by what they decided was useful activity, which meant full-time paid employment.

The best I could do at that stage was to work part-time for a voluntary organisation making that first step towards full employment.

Shortly before Christmas 1999, during one of my last Monday training sessions to work as a voluntary adviser for the C.A.B., I was in Norwich walking past the town hall that ran parallel to the market place when my shoulder was grabbed, pulling me round quickly with the force involved. Momentarily losing concentration, the world span for a few seconds before I realised my bag had been snatched by two young males who'd already robbed some old pensioner of her Christmas gas bill money as she was getting off a bus. My emptied bag was lobbed on to one of the coloured awnings of the market stalls. A reasonably fit man had been walking behind me. He gave chase but couldn't catch up with them. Local news reports revealed that a gang was operating in Norwich targeting and mugging vulnerable citizens, so that must have been the first time in my life I looked vulnerable and got mugged!

Following that I remember telling my C.A.B. supervisor at North Walsham: They rob us then they come here for our help. We give them information on how to get legal aid to defend themselves in court from being prosecuted for mugging us.

That takes being non-judgmental to the limit. The thought of my supervisor sitting there sorting out my neighbour's complaint about me complaining about him damaging my health with his lifestyle seemed ridiculous until it came true.

"There's a Mr. Spring in here wanting to know how to sue you," she whispered, like the gentle swish of air in a seashell, just audible.I thought it was a voice in my head at first, me thinking:Oh well, to cap it all I've gone schizophrenic.

Poking her head through the inner door to her interview room she'd opened slightly to stop my dear neighbour seeing me practise my customer service skills, trying to look happy and helpful which was so false because I felt the exact opposite, my supervisor tried to speak to me without him hearing her, her face apologetic.If I'd had to sit there and deal with another person asking me how to get a passport, or demand the post office to refund the cost of a postage stamp that hadn't stuck on an envelope, I would have hit my final nervous breakdown.Virtually everybody I knew who lived on the same estate as me got to know I worked for the C.A.B., so they came to see me at my flat to ask me for advice on a variety of topics and issues.It all helped me decide this wasn't for me. I wanted to help people struggling with the real problems of life who helped themselves without helping themselves to other people's hard earned cash and property."

I was told by the psychiatrists I wasn't sticking to the rules of the real life test, yet quite able and prepared to sit on the opposite side of a desk in the office of a voluntary organisation for no payment to help people. Many of the people who turned up at the C.A.B. seeking guidance were unemployed with no prospects at all, having to look after large families. Were they behaving according to society's rules? At least they functioned. Given my circumstances, was the psychiatrists' definition of 'sticking to the rules' reasonable? What did these psychiatrists expect of me? On a later visit, when I mentioned my voluntary work, a psychiatrist asked me: "What do you want to do that for? That doesn't bring any money in."

In my male role I worked for years supporting a family, paying income tax and national insurance. This was shrugged off by the psychiatrist because that was the past. However, the now, I'd argue, is important because in this working role I was contributing to society as a voluntary helper that in itself was healthy interaction with the wider society as me. It didn't mean that I would not soon return to full-time paid employment that fitted the life skills I have.

The psychiatrists are conditioned to show no compassion. They're trained from a book that shows them there's only one way to treat us poor, pathetic, deluded souls appearing before them, and that's according to Randell's law.

I like to look on these five years as my time out. It's my time to be me. I'm getting some of my family back. It's a slow process though.

In my Carol role I helped set up my Dad's family business in Essex. My role in this could easily become a full-time one in the future. At the moment, given my difficult financial circumstances, it was too expensive for me to commute between Essex and Norfolk on a regular basis.

To be *me*, I needed those who were powerful whether I got on with them or not.

We had covered the same ground over and over again. Wasn't that damaging enough? It ate away at my self-esteem. How could I believe in myself when the vibe I kept getting from them was: "Poor pathetic sod." I didn't look who I said I was I know how unreal I looked to some people because they told me. Powerless, impotent - that's how I felt then. You know, during one appointment one of them told me: "If you want me to do this for you, you'll be here at ten o'clock." A doctor can be late for you but you can't be late for him. He didn't care that I'd had to travel a hundred and eighty miles to see him. He probably only lived a couple of miles from the hospital. I was tired. I'd been up for hours. The traffic was against me all the way, especially that time of the morning. Yet, during the consultation he said: "Why didn't you come down last night and stay in a hotel?"

Of course, all us gender dysphoric people are rich, I threw back at him. My lack of money was a fact I had brought to his attention every time I saw him, which in itself was enough to bring me to breaking point. He dismissed this. Instead, he told me to 'get a job'. I couldn't win. What was right for me wasn't right for them. They insisted: "If you want our help, you do what we say."

By then, I had convinced myself that no amount of counselling would alter my course.

I didn't need counselling anymore. I just wanted my own life.

Why the visit every three months? It was the same with Charing Cross - four visits to the surgery every year. By the time I got back to them it seemed they'd almost forgotten me. They told me: "You need us because you might regret your decision to have gender realignment."

It's a fact that the NHS spends thousands operating

on people who have to be helped after having this surgery because they've made the wrong decision.In my opinion a two year life test does not give enough time for the person to adjust to their new life.

What exactly were the things I said and did that caused them to worry I was going to fall apart afterwards? I was more likely to fall apart then due to the stress of going through all that.I wanted to take responsibility for what I needed. It was my choice. I was mature and responsible enough to make that choice and deal with its consequences, good or bad.

Chapter Twenty

Once I'd moved from the hostel at Cromer to my flat in North Walsham, I thought I'd left behind the non-stop din I used to have to put up with. How wrong I was. Since moving into my flat, over a period of several years I've had to endure worse from one person than I had to put up with from all the boys and girls at the hostel, where sometimes there were eight records playing at once.

Now I live over the top of someone who has no consideration for anyone but himself, my freedom to live a comfortable life here restricted. He's someone who because he can prove he can spread a bit of margarine on a slice of bread and find his mouth to put it in, he's free to impose his selfish lifestyle on me living above him. He's a health risk to everyone. Whoever made the decision to let him loose on society didn't think about the people he lives near and the effect he has on them. Their priority is keeping this person and others like him out of institutionalised care by giving them enough rope to hang both themselves and their neighbours.

Totally dysfunctional, he's the master of designer anti-social behaviour. Since moving in, I've never been able to go to bed when I want, having to wait till he's turned off everything he's using. It doesn't end there. What sounds like a compressor - which for all I know could be inflating a blow-up doll he may have in his possession - replaces the noise from his sound system with a vibration of a different kind, running on and off all night. It is amazing that someone could open and shut a door fifty times in one hour, life becomes reduced to putting-up with some of the most stupid human behaviour going. I don't care what anybody says. He should be in secure accommodation.

At twelve-thirty one morning, through my persistent badgering of the council environmental health department, one of its representatives sat in my bedroom, told me he wouldn't be able to live in my flat, then left. He never came back.

Can you believe this same man poisoned our lawns so they would not be cut by the people who are supposed to cut them? Two years went by with the grass still dead till, after several complaints, it was treated. We all pay a service charge so that the lawns around the property are kept nice. Let loose by the State, this is supposed to be a person who can live in the community. As a person who's pleased that people get better if they've been unwell, and can rejoin society, I'm not insulting those who do this and show at least vague signs of an ability to mix with their neighbours to form a pleasant community. Laws intended to protect citizens with a social conscience appear to me to be so hard to enforce that no one bothers to make the effort to use them when they are most needed. They have nowhere to put him so I have to like it, lump it, or move. I have no choice but to stay.

All I wanted was my operation date. By June 8th 2001 there was still no news. For the last three years I had been told I was near the top of the waiting list. That built up my hopes. Excited by the idea that my completion would be soon, I'd tell all my friends then look as if I'd been lying to them because another year ended and I still hadn't got my date.

Lately, I need company. Although I've been able to cope with being by myself for the last few years, the loneliness has got to me at times. I now noticed things I had never taken the slightest bit of interest in before, like being concerned about the welfare of my friends and my friends' children, my approach to life had become conscientious.

I work out my frustration by blaming the world in general. These outbursts are releases of tension that build-up inside me then come out when there's no room for anymore.

In the spring of 2001, I was fifty years old and stagnating. I became more conscious of the amount of time I had left to live running out, and that made me afraid of not having much time left as 'me'.

The pettiness of my neighbour sparked a ludicrous row that made what was important a thousand times harder to cope with. Cornered by Mr Spring because my cat was allegedly interfering with his, we had a run in by my car which was parked near the entrance to our flats. While our cats were probably playing together on the lawn out the back, chasing each other as they often did being male and female, we were locked in dispute.

Pointing his bony finger at my face with a body odour coming from him that smelt like a bottle of milk that had gone off, my neighbour was asking for real trouble from me. That somebody could stand there arguing about a cat telling me he had his first and I shouldn't have one, spelled out to me the depressing fact that I'd come to the one part of this estate where evolution had stopped.

For a few seconds, I lost it and pushed him up against my car. I got my temper back under control, my mind saying: "Don't hit him. Remember what happened outside Cromer Jobcentre."

Bounding towards us from further down the estate was a male who I put in the same category as Spring shouting "Let him go!"

"Put him down!" he ordered me. That was too tempting, but of course he didn't mean the "Put him down" I was thinking of.

On arriving at the fracas, panting out his words that were not quite audible, he thrust his contorted face into mine, sucking in my space as he breathed.

"If you don't leave him alone I'll punch your balls where you won't find them!"

Staring out this Neanderthal, literally 'in my face', I put him straight.

"You stupid man, they were removed years ago," I said, thinking honesty was the best policy here.

His silence was satisfying, his one brain cell looking for somewhere to rest inside his empty head.

This piece of street theatre drew an audience of neighbours who all came to my defence, even though I didn't need it.

"I'm going to have you done in," threatened the Neanderthal. "It's already been arranged," he promised. This is the kind of statement someone like him would come out with. All he could deliver were empty threats.

Like a little Jack Russell snapping at Norman Spring

and his bodyguard's feet, one of my helpful neighbours, Lorna, failed to listen to my advice to everyone to stay back and leave me to settle this alone. She began shouting at the pair. Thoroughly bored with the situation, I returned to my flat. Curled up in my chair was my cat, who'd started the dispute, purring happily away. I listened to Lorna ranting outside my window till she and the sad ones went home out of boredom. I knew the feeling.

All this leads me to wonder whether I should, if I could, help people now I'm cured. Here I am going on about how everyone should understand me. What if I had to help someone like Norman Spring?

Those of us who've suffered from gender dysphoria know that before our treatment we thought and felt in similar ways. We now see how that sometimes led us to behave badly. I can't comment on the individual differences between us. I can share my experience with other people though in the hope it'll help them.

We knew what we had to do but we had different ways of doing it. We don't all take the same route. Where we share the same route we don't all get off at the same stop. Some of us go on longer journeys than others.

If someone asked people who are, or in my case *were* gender dysphoric what is it like? They could most probably generalise about it but they wouldn't be able to describe the experience right down to the subtlest details of their feelings and thoughts, all of which are difficult to capture in words. You have to feel a person's feelings and think their thoughts the way they feel and think them for you to understand the exact nature of them, which is impossible, so what hope have I got describing mine to other people? Wouldn't it be wonderful if everyone could see who I really am?

You can see how much I cared about what people thought of me when I wrote that around 1997.

Another piece from my journal of the late 1990s shows how frustrated I was by then."

The course of action I continue to take is the right one for me even if I have to struggle at every moment along the way to reach my goal. I've left it late, but I could not have dealt with it until I was ready. Now it's urgent I get it done before I'm too old. I wish they would bloody well get on with it! I'm sick of pretending to be someone else.

That's how I saw it. If I was standing in a room surrounded by all my friends I would have behaved as I believed they all wanted me to behave rather than be me.

Typically, I'd do this to avoid the risk of losing my friends which when I look back was a sad way to think. It's clear to me now that whatever happened, only my true friends would stand by me. The ones who wanted me to look and behave in ways acceptable to them would have rejected me if I hadn't. We all need friends.

Some people abuse their friendships with others by using them for their own ends.

Most of the people I called friends turned out to be false. My true friends are only the people I can really trust.

It wasn't just my judgmental friends who wanted that from me. For me, society was saying: "If you look male how can you be female? - be male or else!

I think of all those years I was conditioned to be

male right from the time I was born, and inwardly not wanting any part of that, and I feel sick. If you can imagine being held down by a small crowd of people, struggling to move with no effect at all, that's what it's like. Barely able to breathe with almost no room to move, I built up a ferocious energy that gave me the strength to break free. I hope my story will help people appreciate that however negatively they see a non-threatening but unusual looking person at first glance, what matters is how careful they are to treat that person with kindness.

Often, people think they know what they're talking about when they don't. This can be dangerous. I would suggest that gender dysphoria is still an issue that is more avoided than faced up to. There are still a lot of people out there who can't get their heads round it.

Most of us accept gay men and women nowadays. They're easier to cope with because they want to stay the biological sex in which they were born.

Accepting people who've crossed the forbidden line to be themselves is difficult.

How do I judge people when I first see them? We form our own ideas about each other that we use to explain what we're like.

Say I meet a man for the first time. He appears to me in a certain way. I make assumptions about him based on my past experiences, information I've gathered through mysenses, and stories I've heard about him from other people.

I would judge him by the way he looks at me; by his body language; and by what he says to me and how he says it. The surroundings and the vibe of the place I meet him in also affect the way I see him.

If I met a man who I knew had the reputation for being violent or shifty, and on first meeting him sensed he fitted either of these descriptions, I'd approach him carefully. He might also be extrovert or introvert, active or passive, but my perception of him would be organised around my idea of the potential danger he was to me. Another person might see him as simply either extrovert or introvert or active or passive without noticing anything unusual or threatening about him. Sometimes, then, what people look like, the verbal/non-verbal signs they show, and what we believe about them already, help us decide if they could be a danger to us. Our implicit personality theories can help us live together safely and productively.

I'm only concerned with what's real in my life. I've often looked at my stereotyping and other people lives by seeing what really lies behind the person or group being labelled or stereotyped. I want to see what people or groups of people are really like, not what I think or have been told they're like. Of course, I'm no Saint. I often get it wrong. When I talk about kindness to others I do mean people who don't interfere with your, anybody else's or *my* well-being, hence my problem with Spring in the flat beneath me.

A typical attitude towards gender dysphoric people is that they're all sexual perverts. People actually start believing that's true, which is dangerous. What can we do about this?

In human psychology, there are three parts to attitudes: the knowledge part; the feeling part; and the behaviour part. The knowledge part needs improving or the person's ability to tell the difference between what's real and what isn't is weakened. The feeling part that results from poor knowledge can be the kind of anger that leads to violence. Those who have difficulty understanding gender dysphoria may fear it. That fear can be reinforced by further negative information. Their dislike of people who have gender dysphoria can be made worse by watching a biased portrayal on television of someone suffering from the condition, strengthening their belief that everyone who's gender dysphoric is weird. This may encourage discrimination against individual transsexuals. The behaviour part of the attitude that follows from a general dislike of transsexuals, might be avoidance, ignoring them in a room while talking to other people, verbal abuse, or even physical violence. If the knowledge part of the person's attitude is weak, the picture they'll get will be distorted. There needs to be a strong knowledge part to it for that person to see what's real. I may not like some people when I first see them, but I hope I'd always get the facts about them first before I made-up my mind.

Prejudice or discrimination within people or groups can be direct or indirect affecting all aspects of life from something as simple as a football match to, more seriously, what sex, race, religion, body shape, and so on, a person is. Throughout my life, I've worried about how people might react to me. Suffice to say that prejudice exists in the human condition as a permanent quality that can be made less severe by improved knowledge leading to greater tolerance of individual differences. Realistically, as far as we know at the time we're writing, prejudice, like the tendency towards violence, particularly in males, may never be completely removed from human thinking, no matter what educational policies and laws are passed and implemented to protect people.

Chapter Twenty-one

What I do when I'm confused is come back to what I know, and that is what I feel and think. Keeping a diary has helped. That has given me a way of putting all my feelings and thoughts in order. Poems along with some of my more philosophical reflections are included, a selection of which follow.

All that I'm about.

I have sorted my life as to what I'm about
I feel at ease and am about to shout
I am who I am - no doubt about that
I feel at ease with all that I'm about.

I can see.

I can see the sea, I can see the sky,
No one can see me, I wonder why,
because I've accepted a completely false life?
Trying to be male and taking a wife?
I see the trees, I see the grass,
I see the people and they just laugh,
I want to be seen as I truly exist,
becoming real so life can be bliss.

I see people and life from a different side,
I now understand feelings I was denied,

If I could have been me, from the day I was born,
The path that I trod would have been the norm.
I see my wife, I see my kids,
And the thoughts I have tear me to bits,
The decision is made as to who I am,
I must carry on so they understand.

Communication breakdown.

I look at you and I see me,
the me that I would like to be,
You radiate life with girlish charm,
I know this life can do you no harm,
The strength you have from deep within,
Will pull you through, and you will win,
You hate me now for what I do,
but the me you see wants to be like you.

From anger to love..

My anger was released through the pen,
Helped me calm the turmoil within then,
I have so much to say and do,
Maybe that will help me get through,
Although the words come out in a mess,
I hope from these you'll be able to guess,
What I say is from my heart,
And I'll do my best before we part.

This dual life I lead.

With this difficulty I find myself in,
Will I ever be released from within,
I hope the day soon will come,

When I can shout I'm just one,
Will I ever be freed
From this dual life I lead?

Can they be who they really are?

As I walk along the busy street,
What of the people I'm bound to meet?
Are they the gay male or lesbian type,
Are they like me feeling life's not right?
Can they cope with the truth so far?
Can they express who they really are?
Or are their lives a total mess
With needs they're trying hard to suppress?

I'll be all right.

I have come through the mist into ninety-six,
The problems I had then still persist,
I will use this year to sort out my life,
So by ninety-seven I'll be all right,
I await the appointment that will change my life,
The appointment that will make everything all right.

Release through verse.

When I feel bad I write a verse,
The verses I write take away the hurt,
Writing to myself almost every day
Because I've no one with whom to stay
Who'll understand what I have to say,
I'll say to you now, please don't turn away,
Just give me a chance, listen to my plea,
You have the resources to help me be me.

You have to be me.

That day turned into a week, then a month,
Help me please get out of this slump.
The month has now become a year,
And I find myself still sitting here.
It seems to me you have to be me,
To understand why there's so much you don't see.

Slipping away.

There goes a minute of my life,
A life I know is not right,
It's now turned into an hour, no a day,
My life really is just slipping away.

You look at me, but I am not,
I am the person that nature forgot,
I lead a life that's so confused,
I truly am not amused.

The people around me get hurt,
Because I've been putting me first,
The doctors are so risk averse,
Life with Jackie and the children worse,
And all of them at work step back,
confused disorientated, off-track.

I have no reason to carry on,
With a life to which I do not belong,
I will strive to do all I possibly can
To be the person I know I am.

I wrote the following to my doctor back in 1995:

Doctor, help me.

Doctor, you've got to help me out,
Let me be me at last without doubt,
Help me show my real inner self,
Bring out that person, restore my health
To walk around with head up high,
Instead of hearing the 'pervert' cry,
The people who shout those words that hurt,
Treat you like you're bloody dirt,

They do not understand or try
and see beyond the continuing lie.
Doctor, doctor help me out fast,
Let me be myself at last,
I'll hold this banner saying who I am,
And try and help you understand,
I'll talk and talk to all about,
Hoping they will hear me shout.
I'd like to be as free as you,
Walk into shops and blend in a queue,
Go out at night, maybe to the pub,
Or dance away in a top city club,
But while there's still this awful divide,
"How can I be myself," I cried.
Doctor, help me lose my past
Let me be myself at last,
I feel very low as time goes by,
Please don't ignore my perpetual cry,
The help I need must come from you,
I know you don't know what to do,

So please refer me to those who do,
All I want is to be free like you.

The following are some of my thoughts during the most difficult phase of my struggle.

I will be known for whom I am, and not for whom I was.
To be oneself must be heaven.I live in hell.
Mistakes are made by everyone. It's just that mine seem worse.

Why does it matter what I am?There are terrible things happening in the world and people are worried about what I'm doing

I can be put right.I will be put right.I just don't know when.

Will those who know me still be my friends when I tell them who I really am?

C is for courage to do what must be done.
A is for anger that festers within me.
R is for remembering any good times there might have been.
O is for only being me from now on.
L is for love for the kind people I have in my life.

R is for remorse for all I have done wrong.
O is for operation that will change my life.
Y is for yesterdays with all their hurt.

C is for completion which is what I strive for.
E is for essence when I am female in mind and body.

May 12th 2001. I've just heard today from Doctor Olive and Barbara Ross that I've got my appointment to discuss my operation at last. I'm walking around as if I've been accepted. Whether I am or not can only be answered by them. I hope they can tell me for sure. I'm scared to pick up the phone to ask one of them outright. It's not like me to be scared of anything. I hope it's my turn.

Everyone who knew me and understood was happy for me. My close friend Gail was particularly supportive, telling me in her level-headed way that she had only ever known me as Carol, and whatever the outcome she would not have been bothered. As far as men go, I think I scare them to death. I don't mean to scare them. My strong-minded approach to life tends to put them off.

Whitsun Bank Holiday weekend 1998, I went to a barbecue with a friend. I knew something was going to go wrong. Somebody called me he. The woman concerned had never called me he or at least I'd never heard her do so before then. It's the fact she did it that got to me. It struck me that she must have been discussing my appearance with somebody else. She and this other person had been talking about me behind my back. Why is it that nearly every time I go out, somebody has to tell someone else I was a bloke; not male, a bloke. I wouldn't mind if I dressed and acted like one. Is it something I'm doing wrong? I keep asking myself this. Once I'm called male by somebody, this information is locked in their brain and I have a terrible job trying to undo that image they have of me. It makes it worse when somebody I've known for a long time, who's aware of my history, takes it upon themselves to tell people about it who don't need to know. If anyone was to ask me discreetly, I wouldn't have a problem telling them. It's when somebody else who feels they need to do the job for me does it without thinking that upsets me. They don't know what they're saying: they don't say it right; it's not explained properly. They say something like: "Oh, by the way, Carol used to be a bloke." I'm the only person who knows what it's like. It's my story, not theirs. If I need to explain myself I begin by telling the person I'm speaking to: "I was gender dysphoric." There's a whole different, appropriate way of explaining it for those who want to listen.

If a man showed interest in me I'd tell him about myself immediately. I'd have to do this both for his benefit and my own. That way complications and all the stress that results from them are taken care of straight away. I would tell him that after surgery, as one might expect eventually some male-to-female gender dysphoric people choose to have relationships with males. That tends to be seen by many in the wider society as a homosexual relationship because they do not acknowledge that the male who has had gender realignment surgery is now female and cannot function as a male. In some cases, the gender dysphoric male who has been realigned to female forms an emotional and sexual relationship with a female, which is also seen by many people in the wider society as homosexual (lesbian) behaviour. I'd make it clear to him that I had always fancied men - having never seen myself as male (despite originally having male body parts) - so I wasn't a homosexual.

The male who has been realigned to female and seeks an intimate relationship with a female rather than a male can't cope with the latter, being now used to living as a resourceful, independent woman having close, high disclosure friendships with other females.Also, this person - now both anatomically and psychologically female - whose sex at birth was deemed to be male and who was conditioned into the male role, has great difficulty relating to males because she is haunted by the memories of playing male with all its baggage.I've spoken to lots of male-to-female gender dysphoric people who have told me they don't want to be with males because it reminds them of their old life.What might be perceived by some as the generally aggressive approach of males is what the post-operative male-to-female gender dysphoric person wants to get away from.

I've learnt that once I tell people who I am they do one of two things.They either go away to think about the situation they've found themselves in, then come back later or they go away and don't come back.If they come back, then we've got to the next stage, giving me hope that the friendship will move forward.

At some point, you have to be honest about your secrets, certainly when they affect other people.The longer being honest is put-off the more you hurt those people.Lie builds upon lie until a mountain of untruths lead to dreadful consequences when social pressures finally challenge them and they explode.Being honest as soon as possible is a wise move that limits any damage that may occur.There's still a fair risk of upsetting people, but there's more hope of forgiveness and healing in the long-term. The result can be the difference between a small firework going off or, if the issue remains hidden, for years sometimes, like with my bombshell, an atom bomb - with fallout.

Whichever way I look at it, the important people in my life have to be told as soon as possible. It'll never be easy to take. The sooner it's done though, probably the less likely the outcome will be tragic.

I once asked Andy who was a close friend of mine at the hostel in Cromer where we both lived whether he thought I was sexy. His answer was: "yes you're sexy - in a masculine sort of way." At the time, this shocked me. I had spent a year trying not to be masculine. Knowing he fancied me and that I definitely fancied him, his telling me that I was 'sexy in a masculine sort of way' took the kick out of the wine we were drinking. The wine's flavour was suddenly more a cheap mouth wash than the exciting taste I was savouring only moments before. What was going on in his head? Was he comparing me with his old girlfriends? I didn't have muscles; I was slim; I dressed nicely: how could he see me as a female shot putter? He later told me he couldn't get across what he wanted to say to me: his words came out wrong. Maybe that's why I'm always seeking reassurance from whoever will give it to me.

The male-to-female gender dysphoric person tends to be large and the female-to-male small. If you're male-to-female you can be twelve stone and six feet tall.

Males tend to have large feet. Thinning hair on the head, killed-off by testosterone - another disadvantage for the male-to-female gender dysphoric person - can be first experienced in their teens. Scientists have come up with a medication that can restore hair growth as long as the root hasn't died. Apparently, even when you have lost hair the actual root can take up to twenty years to die. This medication has to be given under a doctor's supervision. The percentage of people who can be helped is as high as eighty-five. As far as I know, it is not available in England.

I did not believe what I have described above concerning male-to-female gender dysphoric people applied to me so it really did hurt that when Andy looked at me, he saw a man in drag. His comment led me to want to justify my way of being because I was really worried about his perception of me. A woman can add a little masculinity to her feminine dress code and still be accepted as female: she is no less female for wearing a few clothes generally seen as more appropriate for males. By wearing trousers, she may feel less vulnerable in a male dominated work environment.

I only have to walk around the city a short while to spot a number of women who look what I would call 'assertive' or even 'power dressed', for reasons that might include discouraging unwanted male attention, but is probably because it makes them feel comfortable and good about themselves. A male seeing a female dressed in a suit generally would not, I hope, think she's a woman wanting to be a man. I'd like to think he'd accept her as a woman who has decided to express her femininity in an assertive way. Sometimes women dress-up for the day to see what happens. They can be surprised by the reactions they get from men. A woman can alter the power balance of her relationship with a man simply by changing the way she dresses. She'll probably tell you that by wearing a jacket and trousers, she draws out the masculine side of her femininity, and suddenly she has her own space and feels in control.

For the sake of illustration, I want to use a stereotype which I'll call the 'man's man' type of male. Man's man walks around in his own safe space he's created for himself. That is the male's battle-ground. If it's invaded by other males, man's man is prepared to defend it at all costs. Animal instinct kicks in. Some men have no problem walking straight up to a woman and entering her space. Nature is telling this type of male: "Look, there's a female. Your genes can be passed on." If a male invades the space of another male and won't leave it, there may be a confrontation that in our hunter-gatherer days might have meant a fight to the death. I can see you saying to yourselves: "If it is so good in the male-dominated world why would you want to leave it?" The answer is, if I'd been able to accept my male body I would have been able to walk around with greater ease, but I still would not have belonged. If you feel, as I did, that you aren't male, it's pointless trying to be one, whatever social advantages that gives you, yet no-one can deny that I functioned as a male in that the male characteristics I had would often come out in my behaviour, and that had its benefits. For instance, I could create and control my own space; I could be violent if the situation called for it; I could drive like a maniac. All these can be seen as 'things that males tend to do when their adrenalin kicks in' regardless of the fact they're also examples of anti-social behaviour.

There are always exceptions. I've lived as a male. I believe that's the way many males behave, or did.

Make-up can be a problem. Arguably more important than getting my clothes right, if I think I look good in the mirror because the make-up I'm wearing makes my skin look naturally feminine, this has a positive effect on the way I behave, which in turn influences how positively others see me. Appearance and deportment need constant attention to become second nature. A male-to-female transsexual only has what she's picked-up during brief moments of trying to be herself. In my case this was interrupted by large chunks of male role socialisation forced on me.

That would not have been enough for me. I wanted him to see me as an attractive female. I certainly didn't want him to accept how I saw myself simply to make me feel good, when that was not how he saw me.

Am I cured? It's the same person, same life, but now it's growing in the right direction.

The process goes on. When do I actually become everything I'm capable of becoming? I don't know. I see myself as forever becoming. I believe we're never complete. There's always potential for further growth and development. I like to think there's no limit to what can be. It hasn't suddenly become easy.

My time out for adjustment and reflection is coming to an end. I'm ready to live.

Chapter Twenty-two

I asked Damon how he saw his sexuality. At the time I interviewed him about this he was twenty-five. By asking him and a few others to give me details of that most private part of their lives, I thought I would get an idea of how a handful of today's young people felt about sex. Had much changed in this area in the thirty to thirty-five years since I was first struggling with my own need to know where I belonged in the complicated world of human sexuality.

Damon talked openly about his life. He explained that whilst at school, he saw himself as a heterosexual young man who did everything he imagined would be expected of a heterosexual young man. Damon doesn't remember having any gay feelings up to the age of sixteen. He did say that when he reached puberty he started straying from his old path. He explained this by using the term 'metamorphosis' because it was a gradual process that changed hissexuality to what it is today. I asked Damon: "Are you gay?" "No," he insisted. "I see myself as an intellectual bisexual. I like the idea of bisexuality. It is in my head rather than outside it. In other words, I'm a virtual bisexual rather than a practising one. The freedom I have to imagine myself in and sometimes play the bisexual male role without labelling myself or being labelled either 'heterosexual' or 'homosexual' is exciting."

You mean the tents are next door to each other? You

don't have to walk across the field to the other one. You just roll over, I said, laughing.

Damon had no problem being in female company. In fact, he loved it. He felt at ease with the girls. He could relate to female issues in a fun as well as serious way.

"Girls really do have more fun. They don't have the hang-ups men have when it comes to problems 'down-under."' He wasn't talking about Australia here, by the way. "Buying knickers, for instance, is so natural to them, yet I bet there are a lot of men out there who don't feel comfortable buying underwear for themselves. Girls are also able to hold three conversations at once without losing track of the themes and issues those conversations are about. They're more comfortable with gay men because there's no sexual pressure with them and the gay male's feminised world is obviously compatible with theirs because it is so similar.

Damon added that he felt protected when he was in female company and free to talk openly about 'girlie' things. He became part of them: it was as if his identity blended with theirs to form an emotionally supportive whole.

"I don't see myself as relationship material," he confessed, "but when I do meet someone who I believe is right for me it often turns out to be me falling for them."

He said again that he didn't want to give himself a label and he certainly wouldn't label anyone else. "At the end of the day I'm male and to me sexuality is less important than the greater picture of simply being myself. Why should I be labelled? I am what I am and there's no changing that."

Although he admitted that his sexuality had caused him problems, from his point of view these problems were largely down to other people's attitude towards him and little to do with the way he came across. It was their ignorance of his true identity that caused them to misunderstand him, he told me. He was adamant that his sexuality was so personalised that he found it difficult to explain it to anybody who didn't understand things that weren't black and white. He felt as I do. Sexuality is such a private, unique experience, he'd only want to share details of his with close friends like me who could accept as well as appreciate what it is like for him.

Damon is a complicated person and you really need to know him to understand how he sees himself. I've known him for many years and feel that his role in life is to shock.

"I see myself as a chameleon. I like to imagine I can change from one thing to another depending on whose company I'm in. If I'm with a group of straight males, I can blend in with them. It's more like putting on a show. I can also switch the other way round and in a group of homosexual males be more camp - really limp wristed and shocking."

I wanted to say to Damon what follows and said it without expecting him to challenge me. You see what I mean by him shocking people? He shocked me here by showing such a strong objection to this:

So, Damon, you're a person who doesn't seem to mind how long it takes to sort out your sexuality and see this process as a game.

"What do you mean by that? I don't feel I have to sort out my sexuality. Are you saying I'm neither one thing nor the other? If people want to assume I'm gay, let them; if they want to assume I'm bisexual, let them. There's nothing I have to sort out with myself. I'm me. That's all that matters."

This was one of those rare moments when I was brought to silence.

I had to ask him this question though: What if you really fancied a girl who disapproved of your bisexuality?

"I'm afraid I'd either have to accept it or reject it. There are reasons why I said that".

1) If somebody told me my bisexuality was dirty and immoral I'd see that person as narrow-minded and dangerous; if they couldn't accept me as I am, they wouldn't accept many of my friends, so I'd have to finish with them.

2) As I see it, I wouldn't fall for someone who's narrow-minded because I don't believe in love at first sight: I'd have to get to know the person before I fell for her and if I even suspected she was homophobic, or found bisexuality disgusting, I'd dump her. To me love is being compatible in every area of the relationship, which has to be worked at all the time. It's rather like having to change myself to suit another person. This leopard doesn't change its spots to order and a potential partner's need to do this isn't a good foundation on which to build a relationship.

3) I believe in being honest and feel strongly that my sexuality - which as far as I'm concerned has no label but is best described as 'ambivalent' - needs explaining to anybody who I decide to have a close relationship with. I've told you I don't see myself as relationship

material.I usually keep a comfortable distance between myself and people who're interested in me that way.I'd be more at ease in a relationship that's formed and developed in a non-judgmental atmosphere with no strings attached, because if there were strings attached they'd be pulled.I'd feel choked and that would lead me to think that my partner was taking the lead and having control over me.My personality is based on my sexuality.I might even go so far as to say my personality is my sexuality."

Damon's answers to my questions were fascinating. I'd always assumed that we had no control over who we fell in love with, yet here was someone who had, it seemed, control over how he felt and who he got involved with. "Who's he kidding?"I asked myself.

I interviewed a further two of my friends who gave me their views on life and sexuality. The first was a young woman of twenty-two who has an open-minded attitude to life.My conversation with her was full of the emotions you'd expect from someone who's passing through the early stages of womanhood.She's following a straight line with her sexuality, how she sees herself, and where she belongs in life.It's apparently the usual step-by-step pattern of human growth and development that she's following - Young girl grows into a woman, has boyfriends, and eventually a husband or partner, forming a stable relationship, with children -She'd no thoughts of there being any problem with her sexuality while she was 'young', as she put it.

"Nature got it right for me," she said.

That was a little dig at me, I think, I told her. She laughed.

"Although I feel like this today that's not to say I will tomorrow. What will be will be. I've no thoughts about same sex relationships or wanting to be a different sex to what I am."

There you go again, I said.

"Now you're being paranoid," she retorted. I love being female. I love being female and what goes with it even though it has its downside. My periods can be difficult to put up with sometimes. No, bloody painful is what I meant to say."

She said that as if periods really are the curse of womanhood. Liz felt men should go through something like this then maybe they would understand us better. It made me wonder if at the height of the pain and inconvenience of that monthly drag, all women would say something similar should happen to men. I came back with the comment that twenty five million women in this country would agree with her. In defence of men, most have to shave - that is those who don't grow beards - and depending on the sensitivity of their skin, that can be painful. We agreed it still wasn't as much suffering as what women had to put up with. Shaving was more an inconvenience than something that caused pain.

If males had to have babies there would only be one child per family. While that may solve the problem of overcrowding on the planet, it would also bring the human race to an end. That's why God didn't leave the tough side of reproduction to males.

Liz traced her life from her entering puberty to the time of our interview. I was surprised she had trouble talking about herself. She was shy at first, and needed prompting. She admitted later that she found it easier to respond to my questions than struggle to remember her story in chronological order. This is a summary of Liz's views:

At thirteen or fourteen, I reached puberty. I went to a girls' school so I hardly saw any boys. My only contact with them was on the school bus. I was fifteen when I had my first boyfriend. It wasn't really a boyfriend and girlfriend relationship. It was just mucking about. We never got any further than kissing. I was seventeen when I had my first real boyfriend.

That was the full works. I wouldn't say going into that relationship was frightening. Daunting is a better word. That was my first sexual encounter. It turned out to be my nightmare.

Well, it wasn't a nightmare at the beginning. I thought I was in love with him but then he was all I knew about love and sex. I'd nothing to compare him with. It wasn't how I thought it was going to be. I was locked in that relationship for three and a half years and it stopped me growing as a person. Since coming out of it, I've learnt about my sexuality, but more than that, I've learnt a lot about myself. It's as if my eyes are open now whereas before they were closed. I suppose it's like I'd always been going down to the corner shop out of habit because it felt unsafe to do otherwise, but really that was unsafe and the otherwise - if I'd had the courage to explore it – would have given me new, albeit initially daunting but stretching avenues of choice - opening me out to a greater self-confidence and the feeling of being in control of my own life. Yes. It's having known nothing else but the corner shop and then suddenly finding a giant superstore with lots of choice and the freedom to choose.

My former partner had to control every part of my life even down to who I talked to on the phone. He was booking my life in advance.

He arranged for us to go up to Burton (Burton-on-Trent) to see my relatives. Can you believe that? He didn't give me what I wanted but having said that, I would not have known what to ask for then, but I do now. Sex was him on top and no love. Sometimes I told him 'no' but he still went thrusting on. I'd cry half way through. I didn't and still don't see it as rape. It was consensual in the weakest sense of that word. I was hoping he would show some spark of emotion, but I was living in a dream world.

I have gone into a new relationship. My current partner helped me escape the first one when he was just a friend of mine, and we ended up getting involved with each other. We're seven months into it now - nearly eight. We have become too much for each other and now we're cooling off. I like to look on it as a bit of space for us to work out what we both want.

At first it was him cooling off rather than me, but now I realise I want the same: I too want a chance to cool off and have a bit of space to find myself because I don't want another three and a half years - which was the length of time the other one lasted - in a relationship that's going nowhere. I don't know what I'll do when the cooling off has gone as far as it can. I don't know until I get there. In one way I'd like the relationship to carry on and in another I feel like saying, "*Sod it.*"

There are some things we need to change. Most of these are down to me. I want to ask him what's going on for him and then what's going on for us. Where are we? I want to ask him: "*Am I your friend or girlfriend?*"

He says: "We'll be friends. I'll see you when I see you."

He's thirty and a bachelor. He wants to see me when he wants to see me; he fits me into his schedule. That's not good enough for me.

When I went out the other evening I enjoyed myself. I had a girlie night out with my old friend, Jess. I wanted to find out if I could pick-up a bloke but that wasn't my overall intention. I like to flirt. I wanted to feel attractive and prove to myself I still was, and I did by showing myself I could go out and do that. If I'm not with him I can still go out and do something and not be sitting at home watching the telly on my own waiting to book my next appointment with him. I say I enjoy flirting but I wouldn't have a one-night stand. I'd have to trust someone first and that would take time. It took me three months to completely trust him sexually.

I asked him where he saw us in ten years' time. "I don't see us being married and having kids," he said. "I've never seen that with any of my girlfriends." And so it goes on. "When I don't see him I don't think about him but when I do the rush comes back and I feel I want to try and get him round to the idea of us being a couple rather than this 'just friends' crap. I mean, on Tuesday night there was somebody who looked just like him in the pub where I was having a drink with my friend. This bloke's hair was like his and I started to go a bit wobbly. Well, that's it really, Carol. You don't want a label. I do. Since I've understood the meaning of it I've always known that I was a straight female. I'm comfortable in male company and I enjoy sex with my boyfriend. I want to be his girlfriend and by that I mean I want to be his partner, not his friend.I want to commit myself to our relationship and I want him to be committed to it and act the mature, responsible man he should be at thirty."

Liz was interesting in that she wanted a label. She felt that owning the label 'girlfriend' made at least one of her roles clear, giving her life purpose and meaning which led to a more stable sense of self.

My next interviewee surprised me.Helen was just coming up to forty years' old.She had been married with two children both of whom had grown-up and left home.She had a good job and a car.When she was very young she used to like being a girl, not that the difference between being a boy and being a girl bothered her, she told me.

I just simply enjoyed being a girl.

She explained that when she was a teenager doing what teenagers do, life was fantastic.

We spent our time talking about boys; clothes; who we'd marry; mapping out our lives in advance, fantasising.

I asked her how she saw boys when she was young. "As a teenage girl I wasn't what you'd call promiscuous.I never dated anybody until I was seventeen.My first boyfriend was a year older than me and that made me feel good, and the fact he was good looking - or was to me.He must have been good looking to other girls as well because he was the envy of all my girlfriends.I used to fall in love, not like it is today.It was a year before we slept together, not that he didn't try to get me to do it a number of times before that.Today youngsters need sex.They're not interested in what the future holds for them. The problem now is that young people today think if sex with their partner is good they might as well live together. Both my children are separated from their partners and they are in their early twenties. It's sad that so many lives are hurt because the sexual behaviour of young people in our society has become generally promiscuous. One-parent families seem to be the norm.

I met my husband when we were both eighteen. After a short engagement, we got married. We found it hard at first but as most young married couples would say, we were in love. I used to lean on my mum a lot of the time, especially financially. We were really good friends. I was an only child and although people say we get spoilt, I think we also miss out on a lot. I used to ask mum all sorts of questions when I was first married. I decided that if I was going to have children then it would have to be two and as it happened I had a boy and a girl close together. There is only a year between them. Sadly, my husband died in a car crash five years ago and really I've not wanted to meet anybody else, or at least not yet. My daughter has become my friend just like I did with my Mum. I see her most days. She pops round to make sure I'm okay, or we go shopping together."

"Don't you miss male company?" I asked her. Her reply was:

"Are you asking me do I miss sex? If you are then the answer is yes. My husband and I had a good sexual relationship. We had our ups and downs but we always made up with a cuddle and most times this would end in loving sex. That's how we dealt with any turmoil in our relationship.I have not met anybody since my husband died who I've fancied, not that I'm really looking for a partner.I've men friends at work and sometimes I go out with them, but that's it.I'm a woman and proud to be one both emotionally and sexually.

I see things going on around me that I don't like. Most of the time I feel sorry for the people who do them."

What are these things you don't like? I had to ask her.

" Gay people wanting to bring up babies."

"Don't you like gay people, Helen?"

Her reply came in a raised voice.

"I've nothing against gay people in general.I'd like to think I have an open mind when it comes to talking about human sexuality.There's a difference between same sex partners on there own and same sex partners bringing up children."

For Helen, the whole idea of a gay couple being parents was a distortion of human relationships.

"I think children need both a Mum and a Dad. They need to have that balance of a male and female role model while they're growing up.Children need to get used to the idea of the differences between males and females to know how to behave in their roles as sons or daughters."

There was a news item on television about the rights of two gay men to be parents. Had they given any thought to what long-term effects their actions could have on their adopted children?I'd say the same thing if two gay women said they wanted to bring up a child.

There are lots of heterosexual couples who would

love to adopt a child but because they can't buy them like these two gay men can, they stay childless. Something is wrong with our society when it lets this happen."

I decided to end our chat there. For her, some human relationships are so distorted they go against biological facts that are in the interests of human physical and psychological health.

For Helen, children adopted by same sex parents - whatever the kind intentions they have towards those children - are more likely to be confused by having either two male or two female parents, which could make them emotionally unstable and possibly lead to distorted sex-role socialisation causing gender identity problems later in life.

Once they get to school-age, these children may become socially isolated. Awkward questions like: "Why've you got two daddies?" and so on, could result in a child affected this way being isolated and victimised, ending in the boy or girl having psychological problems. Remember the old saying: "Children can be cruel?"

Her view is of course speculative: we don't know what the outcome of homosexual couples bringing up children will be. Frankly, why shouldn't they be trusted to be capable of loving their children the same as a heterosexual couple, and bringing them up to be balanced adults?

I dreaded asking her the question: "How would you feel if I wanted to adopt a child either on my own or with a partner, forgetting for a moment I'm now in my fifties and it's unlikely I'd be allowed to?

I was asked why I thought Helen would ask it?

I knew she would. I've not been a good parent.

Learning from that disaster, if in the future I ever met a man who had children, using that hindsight I'd hope I'd deal with this type of situation responsibly. I would go into the relationship as a female doing her best to be a mum to her partner's children. Although people who know my background may judge me harshly, in this designer children age, we're witnessing some very strange distortions of human relationships that in my view make my situation look relatively mundane.1

Nowadays, I sometimes think of how it might've been had I been born a biological female and been able to have a baby when I was in my twenties or thirties, especially when I see all my girlie friends with their children.

I accept Helen's view, but social norms now seem to be based more on personal choice than common sense to the point where human beings are redefining what it is to be male and female. I believe we'll always need the distinction of male and female in our society, yet as I discussed earlier, there are people who are even challenging the idea of gender identity itself.

A British man had some of his sperm frozen before having gender realignment to become a woman. He now lives with his lesbian girlfriend. The couple want to make a baby girl using the sperm he had frozen before his operation, and her eggs. What makes this case exceptional is that this lesbian couple only want a girl, and if the fertility treatment works the baby will have two mothers one of whom will also be her biological father.

This is the best illustration of Helen's argument. She can accept my transsexuality on its own. She cannot accept these cases where children get caught up in the confusion of the sexual identities of the adults who are responsible for looking after them, because of the possible implications of these adults' behaviour on their children's lives. Is taking lifestyle choice this far an unacceptable distortion of human relationships and, further still, life?

Chapter Twenty-three

I'm not sure it's a good idea to include Damon's thoughts on me. However, I feel I should be up for what I hope will be some constructive criticism which is why I've agreed not to censor his version of our time together. God help me.

"When I met Carol for the first time in May 1997, she came across as extremely domineering. I felt she had a powerful influence over everybody in the hostel. If I am honest, I think people feared her not because of her sexuality but because of her controlling attitude towards them, which seemed extreme and demonstrated that she was more than capable of showing her teeth if need be. Don't get me wrong. Carol is the type of person who would associate with anyone, but upset her and then it would be like entering a lion's cage.

It was clear she needed the company of others in order to blank out the problems she was facing herself. She would still express her thoughts and feelings if they were aroused by questions that people asked, although frequently her answers would be short, sharp and straight to the point. There was certainly no beating about the bush as far as she was concerned. It was clearly understood by me that she was still undergoing the process of shedding her integermentary system to become the person she should have been, which was difficult for her when you consider where she was living at the time. There must have been a great deal of anger inside her. This would explain why she was so short-fused. I can personally recall many incidents where Carol showed aggression. This was terrifying to the person on the receiving end of it. Carol would willingly change roles to show her authority. It was like she had a demon within her.

It probably reads like I'm showing her in a bad light. That, I want to stress her, was not my intention. In all truth, she had a subtle side to her as well that only those she was close to saw. For me, I can only say that once the cat was purring it was wise to leave it alone. Living within a hostel - sometimes hostile if you'll excuse the pun - environment had caused Carol to become the centre of attention; top dog, so to speak. She showed she had a powerful will to achieve whatever she wanted in life. I feel she must have been a very strong-minded person to have coped with all she had been through and I have great admiration for her. She was the kind of person who liked those who fell in with her plans, and disliked those who did not. I think I was particularly drawn to Carol by the way in which she made me and other people like me feel protected. It must be said that we did have some really bizarre people living in the hostel who would take the vulnerable ones for granted.

Carol made sure those who needed protection got it. As I remember, much of her time was spent in the kitchen ironing, cooking and cleaning. I have to say that her popularity was huge. She had a way with people that were almost indescribable; she was magnetic. Residents would flock to her room daily for advice or the odd drop of wine, but mainly for the odd drop of wine. She really did enjoy her wine - as a matter of fact we all did.

They were all beer drinkers before Carol arrived. She was always up for having a laugh and we would all spend hours at the kitchen table or in her room drinking and smoking until God knows what time.

During my nine months at the hostel she had become, I suppose, a sort of agony aunt, although her advice could not always be taken seriously unless you wanted conflict with another resident. I don't think she saw herself as a resident. It was more like she was someone running the place who was seeking a managerial position there. Becoming a house manager was important to her and when she failed to get that position, everything changed. From then on, there probably wasn't much point in her continuing to live in that kind of environment. It got completely up her nostrils because whatever power she had was taken away from her. I was due to move out of the hostel shortly afterwards. Carol remained there for a while, but all was lost for her. It had come to an end. Some weekends she would come and stay with me at North Walsham. However, it was not long after my move that Carol was allocated a flat of her own near me. That move was to change her for the better. I felt she needed a sense of freedom back in her life. Over the last couple of years or so she has certainly mellowed and has shown various interests in the local Citizen's Advice Bureau and Voluntary Services. She has also played a large part in the setting-up of a family aquatics business which is doing very well. She has great support from a good friend she has living on the same estate as she does and they spend a lot of time in each other's company. I think, overall, to become part of her family again has given Carol all that she needs and things can only get better for her.

From my journal, it's clear how in my most depressed moments the seemingly unending wait nearly finished me:

It's July 16th 2001 and I feel really low at the moment.Over the last few months I've had very little sleep.It has started to take its toll on me and I am feeling totally drained.The stupid people that live around me are not letting up with their selfish behaviour, playing their music that I'm getting in shifts, belting through the wall of my flat.

I'm sitting at my computer thinking about what I've achieved since moving to Norfolk.My life is controlled by these morons who live around me.Over the last three years I've been deprived of sleep.Earlier in this book I mentioned how I thought everything had come to a dead stop.I've just had my Mum down for a couple of weeks and things seemed to improve.I think that's because I was occupied.The minute she left life hit dead stop again.I'm a person who needs people and activity.I feel I'm coming to a time in my life when I need to move somewhere that will allow me to grow. The time out I've allowed myself is coming to an end. I've so much still to do.

Deep down I have feelings of kindness and sensitivity, but seem unable to transmit them to the outside world.Why that is I don't know.Is it that I just don't want to appear weak, or is it that I want to hold people emotionally at arm's length to avoid getting hurt?I know I couldn't deal with any baggage at the moment.I still have too much to do to be explaining my life to anybody or trying to make them understand why I'm doing what I'm doing.Maybe this maleness that's followed me around for so many years just doesn't want to leave? I don't go out of my way to act male. It may just be what others pick up from what I transmit to them, and what I transmit to them could include bits of my sub-conscious. How would I know? I'm not aware of giving out these signals, and go out of my way to be careful how I act.

"Asking a friend David", you told me you'd raised the subject of gender dysphoria with a Christian. How do the teachings of the Bible square with the facts of gender dysphoria? There have been suggestions that it's caused by genetic and hormonal irregularities.

You told me that it was this Christian's view that nowadays gender dysphoria could be seen as being caused by a genetic defect, and because of this it's politically correct to say gender dysphoric people can't help it so they aren't responsible for managing the condition themselves. This suggests to me that I should have the willpower to resist my real inner self and over time that'll cure me of the sin of being gender dysphoric and I'll live happily ever after. Several times in this book I've told of how I lived the male role to the full and how it nearly killed me. At that time, I knew nothing much of God and Christianity but I knew a lot of hell and loneliness. A strong faith in God may work for some. Other sufferers however never find God because they are, or at least led to believe they are, rejected by society. By society I mean all secular and religious organisations and institutions. They suffer the anguish of believing they are freaks of nature.

When I lived in Cromer, a Jehovah's witness who'd been told about me came to the house where I stayed to see his two sons.

"You're an abomination," was all he said to me.

I thought one of the most important lessons of the Christian faith is that you shouldn't judge other people? If you do, expect to be judged yourself.

Surely our all-powerful, all-good, all-loving creator doesn't want us to judge our fellow humans?

All through my youth I prayed to be rescued from my torment. Maybe I didn't do it right, but I can tell you I tried. I may find God later. Before I can I need time to come to terms with my recently adjusted body.

Church of England bishops set out strict guidelines published in a 1991 document, "issues in human sexuality", that, for example, gay canons are advised to obey. Celibacy is included in these guidelines. Imagine the torment of that, particularly at times when you feel compelled to satisfy your urge. I'm celibate because I haven't found a person I fancy I can trust who can cope with all my problems. Do my judges want to deny me my sexuality that's an inseparable part of my whole identity?

I now take the approach that people who discriminate against those who are different from others are the ones who need help. There wasn't a cure for seeing my real inner self as painfully at odds with the male body I had. Whatever my faults, I'm just another variation of nature, strange to some people perhaps, but no less human than anyone else.

Chapter Twenty-four

My operation date was set for the 21st February, 2002. I decided that it would be my new birthday. On that day, at the age of fifty-one, I was reborn.

The cost of the gender realignment surgery itself was about twelve thousand pounds. The tablets I take aren't exclusively for patients suffering from gender dysphoria. Zoladex 10.8mg injections, which I have, treat prostate cancer in males and endometriosis in females. I used to take androcur which is an acetate. This was given to me at the Albany. It's another cancer drug and I'd been taking it for a long time. Basically, these drugs are designed for short-term use. The effects of the hormones on my system made me noticeably more feminine, increased the size of my bust, reduced the muscle density in my arms and legs, and so on, and my hips became desirably more rounded. Androcur slowed down my facial hair growth making it lighter. It also stopped the possibility of the hair on my head falling out. Had I had a hair loss problem I would have either gone for hair transplant or the regain treatment: the roots of the hair can take up to twenty years to die so there's a chance that with a particular treatment like a powerful prescribed drug, the degrading hair roots can in about eighty-nine per cent of cases be re-booted into life and grow back to full strength. In other words, there's hope.

Early on in the process, the secretions of the prostate gland become less until there is no ejaculate. Lovemaking had never been easy for me, my libido so far down in my boots that when I took them off I couldn't even find it. Before medication, I didn't have much of a libido, soon after taking it, the erections - or almost but not really erections as I used to have - dropped back to plasticine mode then to permanently limp. This was a welcome development. My penis shrunk to the size of what I have to admit was a rather enlarged clitoris.

Premarim, made from mares' urine, which I was also prescribed, three times a day, was given to women for Hormone Replacement Therapy (HRT). My psychiatrist told me: "Take these (ethinyloestradiol) as they are less harmful (reduced risk of thrombosis) and you'll be kinder to horses."

When I thought about them being made from urine (they extract the hormones from it) I wasn't going to argue. It gives a whole new meaning to the saying: 'taking the piss'. He used to say that I was argumentative. I would argue with him about everything else, but not that.

Electrolysis is something that all male-to-female gender dysphoric people have to face at sometime during their transformation. I was introduced to this at a place in Luton before I left Jackie in 1996, continuing to have it throughout 1997 and early 1998 when I lived at the hostel in Cromer. For most people, electrolysis is a painful treatment that can cost thousands of pounds; it's also time-consuming, and you may have to travel many miles to find an understanding practitioner. Although an important part of the male-to-female on process, electrolysis is one of the areas of ;nment that is not covered by the National ice, which is ridiculous. It can take many ....r the male-to-female's facial beard growth even at the rate of two visits per week, with costs varying, depending on where you live and where you go for treatment. There are still a lot of beauty salons that won't do electrolysis for transsexuals. Basically, it's down to searching the telephone book or the yellow pages, ringing a number, then asking the proprietor of the clinic you have chosen if he or she'll do it. I've found there are a lot of sympathetic, caring professionals out there who know the distress gender dysphoric people can experience. Most times these practitioners agree to do the work at a reduced price. Because of the extensive work I needed the person who treated me offered me a reasonable deal which, needless to say in my financial position, I welcomed.

Now we come to the nasty little hair itself which is the commando of all hair. It can survive nearly everything thrown at it. The hair root buried deep under the skin, living in its follicle, can't wait to stick out. You chop it off and it'll grow even quicker just to get its own back. No matter what medication you take during transformation, facial hair growth cannot be stopped once it has started. This begins at puberty. The only way to get rid of it successfully for a male-to-female gender dysphoric person is to have it removed by electrolysis or laser treatment. I found that when I started the treatment on my face it began to scar due to the regular visits and extensive work I had commissioned someone to do.

This should be done gradually on small areas at a

time. There are electrologists out there who would make sure the procedure was done correctly. Before any gender dysphoric person starts treatment it is wise to make sure the electrologist has the relevant qualification to carry out this type of work.

The procedures which female-to-male gender dysphoric people have to go through are far more complicated and traumatic. From my male-to-female viewpoint the actual gender realignment surgery is usually completed in one operation. The female-to-male circumstance is better from the point of view of physical appearance. Unfortunately, the surgical procedure has to be done in stages. This can be a long-winded, painful experience. What has to be done includes: full double mastectomy as breasts don't disappear with hormone therapy; hysterectomy; and penile, scrotal and testes construction. In a channel four television programme, Doctor Russell Reid did say words to the effect of: "I think that in the diagnosis of female-to-male transsexuals it is much more important to establish firmly than in the male-to-female simply because giving [male] hormones [like testosterone] to a woman produces irreversible effects quickly."

The female-to-male is prescribed androgens which when taken over time result in a gradual masculinisation, the features of which include varying degrees of beard growth; deepening voice; change in physical appearance from softer, sinuous feminine muscular and fatty tissue distribution to solid, sinewy, masculine structures; thicker, more noticeable body hair, and, genitally, an enlarging clitoris that becomes more erectile but cannot pass as a fully-developed penis.

My operation was performed by the surgeon Mr. Michael Royle at The Sussex Nuffield Hospital, Woodingdean, Brighton Sussex.

Mike Royle told me that his work gives those suffering from gender dysphoria quality of life.

I felt honoured because I turned out to be one of his last patients. I've learnt since that he plans to retire soon. That's sad news for all those people who would otherwise have benefited from his skill. A sense of achievement comes with the best jobs: for all the hard work he has done to meet my needs, not to mention all those lives he has saved over the years through his devotion to relieving the misery of gender dysphoria, he should certainly know that Carol Royce wants to thank him for helping her become whole.

To be labelled mentally ill is unjust because I have tried to keep functioning on a practical level for most of my life. If any label should be attached to me it is 'selfish individual'. I deeply regret how I've acted in the past. To all those people who have been unfortunate to enter my world when I wasn't a nice person, I want to thank you. Understandably, some will have regretted doing so. Without them I would've been lost. Even though I was locked inside a world of contradictions that led me to behave impulsively, sometimes aggressively towards them, those people gave me purpose simply by being there: if there is nowhere for you to go and, crucially, no-one for you to meet, then there is no life.

It is my belief that every human being has a purpose: we're all here for a reason. Sometimes that reason for being gets blotted out by the darkness of the human condition descending on us, covering our faces, our minds and our hearts with its thick, black veil. It is at those darkest moments we cannot, literally for the life of us, remember or do not know what our reason for being is. By making provision for my body to be donated to medical research as soon after my death as possible, I hope I can give back something to enable the people who have relieved my suffering, to further research into gender dysphoria. Hopefully this will, in the future, perhaps lead to faster, gentler, more precise treatments and help relieve the similar suffering of those who are still very young, or as yet unborn.

Pre-op day was Wednesday, 20th February, 2002. On arriving at the hospital with my Mum and brother, I thought I'd treat us all to lunch. Disappointed that what I ended up getting was not the ploughman's lunch I ordered but a bowl of clear chicken soup - so clear there wasn't any chicken in it, my stay there didn't begin very encouragingly. In the afternoon I was obliged to take this horrible white fluid. Empty me out it did. Taking two hours to work, this stuff went through me like an attack of dysentery. One false move and there would have been a major clean up on the agenda. Very few people, I'd imagine, would ever pray for constipation. I did that afternoon.

For tea, chicken consommé was on the menu again, with jelly to follow. The next part of the procedure for that day was the removal of my pubic hair. This was followed by a shower to rid myself of any pubes still hanging on to my body for dear life, then a lovely, long relaxing bath. After that, I had TED stockings fitted to control my circulation and stop me having embolisms and thromboses.

A visit from the anaesthetist and Mr. Royle for a last minute chat and to sign the consent forms was a nice way to round off the day.

Ten past seven the following morning, after a virtually sleepless night through the excitement of it all, having had my pre-med I was wheeled along a hospital corridor towards the lift down into the operating theatre.

Without going into morbid detail over the surgical procedure, my shrunken penis was removed. To provide sensation in my future female genitalia, the surgical team avoided cutting the sensory nerves of my penis. Due to my original male external genitalia being so atrophied, it wasn't possible for me to have the usual six to eight inch deep pouch that was the artificial vagina I would have had, otherwise known as a 'cul de sac'. 'Cul de sac' is a term used to indicate that it [the artificial vagina of the constructed female] has no connecting uterus, unlike that of the biological female. The pouch is lined with the preserved sensory nerve endings of the penis to provide sensitivity similar to that of a fully-functioning vagina.

For the deeper pouch, it is possible to have some of the bowel cut away, but if I had wanted this I would have needed to have a second operation. Because of my age, Mister Royle was not prepared to do all that in one operation. Telling me I could go abroad and have it done if I wanted it straight away, he added that the surgeons agreeing to do it would almost certainly not be concerned for my aftercare once I had returned to England, whereas he would. Appreciating Mister Royle's concern that I didn't put my life at risk for the sake of a few more inches of vaginal depth, which would have been nice to have, under the circumstances perhaps it was better to stick with the simpler, safer option. At least then there would be no accusations of vanity on my part - pun intended.

"Do your best," I told him, grateful that I was having the operation at all, and carried out by an eminent surgeon who was concerned for my welfare. Far from being an obligatory part of his role in my gender realignment programme, Mister Royle came to see how I was every morning I was in hospital, a gentleman from the old days whose kindness I'll never forget.

While I was coming round from the operation at about four o' clock in the afternoon, Caroline, with some of the other nurses, tended to my needs, amongst other tasks ensuring I hadn't crimped any of the drainage tubes attached to me. Drifting in and out of a post-operative sleep, I knew little of what was going on. Once back in my ward, nursed flat, because if I pulled myself up I would have damaged the sutures that were in place. I was encouraged to take water orally in the early evening to wash my system through. Intravenous fluids, for which the nurses were always coming in to check, continued throughout to maintain hydration, which is always important. Regular checks were made on my dressings and T-bandage and intravenous/oral antibiotics were prescribed and administered as required. Bed rest was forced on me, not that I could move much on that first day of freedom.

Day one, post-op, I was nursed flat until the afternoon, a ceremonial rolling over from side to side courtesy of the nursing staff on duty, as I understand it painfully necessary for keeping the blood flowing normally, and making it easier for them to do anything else they had to. My fluid intake was increased. I had to drink huge amounts of water. A jug full with ice - that's BUPA for you - would be lovingly placed on my side table with the accompanying order: "I want to see this empty when I come back!" As someone who hates drinking water and having to down about eight jugs a day, was my idea of torture. Antibiotic treatment continued, with 20mg of enoxaparine given eighteen hours after the operation and then on a daily basis. Mercifully, pain killers were readily available, these being the only way of keeping me sane given the degree of physical discomfort post-op, despite my high pain threshold. Being catheterised restricted my movements, to my absolute frustration, the catheter having to be kept in for a while, the nurses in and out at least hourly to check its status.

Treatment and nursing procedure remained the same for day two. The exception was the removal of the drainage tubes after my consuming a whole bottle of gas, taking deep breaths, only coming down from the ceiling having endured considerable discomfort.

"I thought you said this didn't hurt," I said to a nurse. With a smile, she replied: "It depends on the patient."

Lunch consisted of consommé - again! - fruit jelly. The T-bandage was checked to see if it was still in place which it was. If there was one thing that didn't move, that was it: it was well and truly bunged up there.

Day three post-op from the point of view of treatment passed like day two. On day four, a light solids diet was introduced and on day five my vaginal pack was removed personally by Mike Royle and the first dreaded very uncomfortable dilatation through the large amount of tissue swelling and sutures up there, was done.From then on dilatation was three times a day, preceded by a hot bath.

Day six was a repeat of what happened on day five, as was day seven, with the exception of the removal of the catheter and the regular observation of my urine output. When on day seven it was confirmed that I could pass water and stools normally (I was all right with the first two legs but the third one made my eyes water) I was given the all clear to go home.Mid-morning of day eight, I was discharged, with a letter from my doctor, and the usual post-op survival kit for home care: analgesia; KY Jelly; betadine douche kit and betadine pessaries; and dilatation kit that included two glass rods with a rounded taper at one end to save me from injuring myself.Both were 8" (200mm long) one of 1" (25mm) in width and one of 13/16" (30mm) width.Loaded with my two missiles, a reluctant smile on my face given the potential damage these two items could cause, I said farewell to Mister Royle and the wonderful nursing staff there, leaving for our old family home in Essex to be waited on by my Mum for the next couple of weeks.

Lubricated at the rounded tip with a combination of betadine and KY jelly, the smaller dilator is placed at the entrance to the vagina and inserted carefully, avoiding rotating or side to side movements that would damage the sutures or rupture the delicate tissue, such damage difficult to repair.In the vagina of a biological female, the length is approximately four and a half to six inches and ends at the cervix or neck of the womb.

Using the larger dilator, the way made easier by the initial use of the smaller one, the nearer I got to the end the more unpleasant it felt, as if it could take little or no more. The griping sensation in my pelvic area came in breath-robbing spasms until I withdrew the instrument with a gentleness that any woman in a similar situation would appreciate.

It's wise to stick to the recommended frequency of dilatation: three times a day in the first fortnight following surgery, changing down to twice a day at four months, once a day at one year, once or twice a week after one and a half years, and twice a month after two years. Betadine gel isn't needed to lubricate the dilator after one yearFive months after my operation it was with great satisfaction that I reviewed how successful this ritual had been. Even at that stage, my vagina was self-lubricating to some extent. This doesn't happen in every case.

Chapter Twenty-one

In this post-operative phase of my life, I may be a little slower through a combination of the after effects of surgery - which will last for some time - and my age, but I'm coping.

This was how I felt shortly after my gender realignment. The post-operative dilatation ritual, which was unavoidable, got me down though. My new bits would have healed and sealed if that had not been done at least twice a day. By late August 2002, six months after surgery, it was only necessary to dilate once a day, which was far more manageable because I could just do it at night after a relaxing bath before going to bed.

What was I going to do with this time? Did I follow my desires, and like some recently liberated, mature woman seek all the pleasures going to satisfy them, or did I go out there to help other people as I had in small ways before my change? Had I really become a more tolerant person less judgmental of others? I had certainly appreciated people not judging me when I was at my most vulnerable.

The novelty hasn't worn off. Now it is me getting on with life without that inner struggle. It's not easy. I never expected it to be, but it's easier because that inner conflict has gone. I'd been thinking virtually all the time: "Does it show? Can people tell?"

When I came round from the operation my first words were: "Am I cured?" and the nurse with me said sympathetically: "Course you are, dear."

As long as I generally pass in society and I feel comfortable with myself I can probably live with my worst critics telling me I am not real. Now I'm rid of that useless appendage that hung between my legs, I'm cured. Life is to live. There will still be the bad times, but there will be more good ones. I can face new challenges without the distraction of gender dysphoria draining a large amount of my time and energy. I have time and energy now to be myself and to help people who need me.

Many years ago, I looked into the possibility of raising the pitch of my voice, but in those days it was hard to get this done through the National Health Service. I remember reading an article about someone who had to resort to going abroad for surgery on her voice box. She had money. Although she had also found it hard to find somebody who would do it, there were two surgeons who were prepared to carry out the procedure privately. One was in California - Beverly Hills, no less - and very expensive. The other was in Amsterdam. The latter was a cheaper option, but it was still expensive when you considered all the costs. This type of work goes under the frightening name of "cricothyroid approximation".

At that time, in America, cricothyroid approximation cost the equivalent of five thousand pounds. That did, however, include a reduction of the thyroid cartilage, better known as the Adam's apple. In Holland, you could have the job done for about two thousand pounds.

I started with a male voice that was deep and gravelly. To try to correct this, I had to resort to surgery. It was necessary for me to see a specialist in the Audiology Department at Norfolk and Norwich Hospital to have an assessment and tests to find out what could be done to help me. As I've smoked most of my life this was a worrying time for me. My age was also a concern and still is. I am now over fifty and that generally decides the limits of what can be done. In other words, as the speech therapist at our local hospital told me, the older you get, the more difficult it is to change the pitch of your vocal chords. It was still possible to have something done to save my voice.

In 2002 I was still waiting to hear from the NHS about a date for an operation to modify my vocal chords.

Apart from men and women tending to use and emphasise different words, women perhaps use more feeling or emotional words, while men use more cognitive or thinking words. Women also tend to show more subtlety in the way they talk. As well as this, the style and inflection of their speech often give a wider range and greater depth of emotional expression.

Speech therapy, which focuses on raising the vocal pitch or tone, keeping the modulation from dropping too low while at the same time aiming for a gentler, softer, less resonant quality to my voice, didn't work for me. Whatever improvements I made at my ten, hour long classes were lost when they finished, because once separated from my therapist I all too easily reverted to a lower pitch. An hour was hard work for me because I had to think what I was saying all the time, which made the exercise feel unnatural."

This remains a difficulty for me?

Well I won't be singing in a female choir yet. If organisers of a mixed choir wanted bass I'd be the ideal candidate; they'd only need me as I had enough volume and depth to do the bass for the whole choir on my own."

So what was the problem I had with speech therapy?

Holding the modulation was very difficult for me. Although I can do it under certain circumstances I'm still called 'Sir' on the phone. I believe it's something to do with the electronic amplification through a telephone. No matter how hard I tried I couldn't trick technology.

Voice modification and corrective facial surgery are the finishing touches I need to complete my picture of how I see myself, and how I'd like everyone to see and hear me. I don't want people being confused by hearing a deep voice coming from me now I look comfortably female.

The tension, mass, and length of the vocal cord controls vocal pitch. Surgery can adjust its tension and mass by positioning, in most instances, nylon sutures at four key locations in the existing laryngeal framework. This draws close together the cricoid and thyroid cartilages within a range whereby they work in a way that imitates the shortening of the cricothyroid muscle, to raise vocal pitch.[1]

My larynx still has its basic male structure. I have discussed the cricothyroid approximation procedure with my Otolaryngologist, I agree with him that it is necessary for me to have it done, that I am a suitable candidate for it, and that I understands the possible outcomes of this surgery, good and bad.

An important medical study that examined twenty-nine transsexual patients has provided evidence that the greater the cricothyroid distance was reduced in these patients, the more noticeable the rise in their vocal pitch. In the main, only those whose laryngoplastic surgery resulted in a slight reduction of cricothyroid distance found that their vocal pitch went back to a lower level. Suggestively, the greater the reduction of the cricothyroid diameter, the less chance there is of the vocal pitch returning to the lower level it was before the operation. The technique used is relatively simple, no cut, or squeezing or compacting into a smaller space of the cricoid and thyroid cartilages necessary, all these put together making a good case for choosing it.

There are, of course, disadvantages of using the procedure: the cricothyroid cartilage that has been surgically manipulated may not tolerate this adjustment for long; the suture site can become dense with blood vessels or ducts (a condition called vascularisation); parasthaesia - or loss of sensation in the area of the operation - can happen sometimes, but not often; and the patient's vocal pitch may drop to a lower level, making it sound more male than female again.

Spiral Computed Tomography or Computed Tomography (CT) is a method of scanning the structure of the male-to-female transsexual larynx to examine its existing male framework.[2] CT has the ability to accurately determine the distance between the cricoid and thyroid cartilages affecting the vocal pitch elevation of a person both before and after phoniatric surgery. Due to its high degree of accuracy, CT is a recommended method of following-up patients who have found that after surgery their vocal pitch has sadly gone back to a lower level. CT gives details of the person's laryngeal framework. These details are of a standard of precision that best informs the Otolaryngologist treating the male-to-female transsexual how much and where as exactly as possible work needs to be done to raise her vocal pitch to a level with which she is happy.

Notes

1.
Speech pathology considerations in the management of transsexualism - a review. Oates Jennifer M., Dacakis Georgia., School of Communication Disorders, Lincoln Institute of Health Sciences. British Journal of Disorders of Communication 1983 vol.18 no.3. pp 139-151.

2.
Spiral computed tomography before and after cricothyroid approximation, Pickuth D.,Brandt S., Neumann K., Berghaus A., Spielmann R.P. and Heywang-Kobrunner, S.H. Department of Diagnostic Radiology, Martin-Luther-University, Faculty of Medicine, Halle/Saale, Germany. Clinical Otolaryngologist 2000. 25. pp 311-314.

Chapter Twenty-six

If the cause of gender dysphoria is genetic and it could be genomed out in the future, think of the suffering that would prevent?

I know nothing of the science involved, but if stem cells could be used to reduce or even cure disabilities caused by strokes or impacts; or correct impaired motor function through diseases of the nervous system - such as multiple sclerosis and Parkinson's - then the future looks bright. Imagine this treatment working for Gail, giving her back her life.

Could humans' potential to develop diseases of the nervous system be genomed out in the future? If so, the disabilities that restrict the lives of the sufferers of these diseases would never happen. In the real world, I guess that class of treatment would only be available to the rich? Whatever your postcode, I don't see that up for grabs at the local hospital.

"What about shyness? This could be seen as a possible barrier to a person achieving his or her full potential in life? What if scientists could tamper with genes in order to correct so-called genetic weaknesses? Yet without genetic manipulation, some individuals might develop shyness and struggle with it, but come out the other side with qualities such as humility, self-discipline, generosity of spirit, compassion, and empathy.

If the cause of my gender dysphoria was genetic, what if that gene had been all right and I never experienced the struggle that led me to be who I am? Who else would I have been?"

"We come back to: is it right to stop from happening or change what some people might see as handicaps, imperfections, and so on?

I'd've been a different person because my gender dysphoria is the root of who I am now: however much it made me suffer, I feel sick just thinking about what might've been if I hadn't gone through it.

The way I see it, we're continuously trying to adapt to an increasingly complex world. In their mad rush for knowledge in order to cope with this, are scientists in danger of not just tampering with some of the essential qualities that make-up the unique identity of a human being, but also what it is to be human? This tampering with nature is happening in other ways as well, and it's affecting our environment, which in turn affects us.

Are we playing God through what I think is our desperate search for perfection?"

"I'm grateful to medical science though for bringing your appearance into line with my inner self."

"That's the understatement of my life, It's realigned my identity to make me a more balanced, healthier person."

"According to my psychiatrists - at least to start with – but I'm sure if I hadn't've had my operation in 2002, I wouldn't've been any good to anyone. Time moves on. They'd probably never have agreed to it if I'd got to fifty-five and still hadn't had it done.

Some cosmetic adjustments to the body are more necessary than others. Who decides what goes to the top of the list and what goes to the bottom? Is this another opportunity for some of us to play God?

A few of my female friends have told me they'd like some of their bits altered: smaller boobs; a few layers around the midriff removed; skinnier legs, and so on. That's normal for most of the women I know.

Breast enlargement and reduction surgery is available on the NHS. While in some cases it could be argued that people who want these procedures done don't really need them, in their own minds they're convinced they do. Is their cause as important as a male-to-female transsexual's need of electrolysis to remove unwanted hair?

Botox injections to reduce sweating - one of the latest body-modification treatments - aren't available on the NHS. If you want them, you have to pay for them. How necessary they are depends, I suppose, on how much you sweat, and if it's a lot, how much is the treatment's likely to improve your quality of life.

People rely on recent advances in medicine to help them adjust their minds and bodies to achieve a sharper, more attractive image: they want to delay the ageing process or reverse or reduce the physical and psychological discomfort of their differences from others which limit their life chances and overall happiness. Most of us, I argue, want to live as long as we can providing we have what we call 'quality of life'."

We can think of the human life course as having roughly three stages: youth, middle-age, and old age, ending in death. Generally, going through each of these stages provides people with experiences that give their lives purpose, and therefore meaning. In middle-age, Carol has found her true identity. She is looking ahead to new possibilities of happiness and fulfilment.

What if scientists could find a way of extending the human lifespan? How would we keep life interesting and meaningful if we were to live up to a hundred years longer than what's considered to be the norm, with all the social and economic difficulties that would entail? The way we live, from the cradle to the grave, would need seriously rethinking.

It's something in the water I keep telling myself? Is gender identity and sexuality being influenced by exposure in the womb to slightly higher than average levels of gender-bending chemicals found in our food and the environment? Could these gender-bending chemicals be leading to changes in the play patterns of both male and female children? Evidence suggests a link between this exposure in the womb and boys being more likely to enjoy feminine play during the first seven years of their lives - preferring dolls to toy racing cars - and girls being more likely to enjoy masculine play, even to the point of favouring a rough and tumble to dressing up.

As I have mentioned, a theory that a hormonal surge in the womb - either from the mother or from the foetus itself at a very important stage in the development of the foetal brain - has been considered possible.

An interesting article appeared in the Daily Telegraph of Monday, the 4th of June, 2001. Called "Mothers' hormones turn girls to tomboys", its author, David Derbyshire, refers to the Avon Longitudinal Study of Parents and Children, led by Professor Melissa Hines.[5] The study, funded by the Wellcome Trust, which is a medical charity, looked at two hundred children aged three and a half, and found a clear link between the presence of high levels of the male hormone testosterone in a mother's womb and subsequent masculine behaviour in girls.

By contrast, no link was found between mothers' testosterone levels and the later behaviour of boys. Testosterone levels are already high in unborn boys so the researchers believe small differences in the mother's womb would have little effect on later behaviour.

Another suggestion the study makes is that sexuality may be affected by testosterone levels. If, as some psychologists and psychiatrists appear to believe, the womb environment and not genes or how one is raised as a child can determine that some people will become homosexual, is it not reasonable to suggest the possibility that a particular environment in the womb can also determine that a developing human foetus will become a person who is gender dysphoric?

A statement by Professor Hines that is of interest to us - bearing in mind our discussions recorded in this book about the likelihood of such a thing happening - said that the foetus's exposure to testosterone in the womb during a critical period of brain development, we believe, for example, such as that of the hormone surge Professor Reid has suggested is possible, could have lasting influences on the development of the individual's sexuality.

If I like, the transsexual's equivalent of the Big Bang,

We don't need the transsexual's guide to the galaxy, but it would help. A surge of female hormone while I was in the womb in the way Russell Reid suggests could explain why from an early age I felt and thought like a female in spite of the fact I had a male body with male hormones whizzing round it. The little boy's body didn't have the little girl's hormones to match 'the feeling like a little girl inside', so, without ever having had naturally what other little girls have, how could I be naturally female for the real life test? I wasn't pretending. I can understand psychiatrists refusing transsexuals surgery before they've taken the real life test, but they should be receiving hormone therapy throughout the period they're living in their chosen gender role. How could I be a woman with a body that doesn't match in general anatomical and biochemical detail those of other women I know, respect, and identify with, without the support of hormone therapy?"

I suppose I'm saying that the fact others like me hadn't wavered from my belief that I'm female entitled me to hormone therapy to support me throughout my time on the 'real life test'?"

"I believe that if you'd said to consultant psychiatrist John Randill: I believe I'm a woman inside he'd've replied, as he did to Julia Grant: feeling like a woman doesn't make you a woman. Nobody knows how anybody else feels inside. You have to live like a woman to be one.

Speaking from my experience, the real life test is more humane with the support of hormone therapy as early as possible because then sufferers are helped to look and feel more balanced in the role of their desired gender."

On or about the 3rd of June, 2001, Professor Hines described how historically gender role had been thought of as completely determined by social behaviour.

However, this study in which she was involved shed light on the importance of the role the environment of the womb played in determining the future gender identity of a developing human foetus.

She added: "Boys are socialised much more strongly to conform to sex-typical behaviour" - a fact supported by my experience of growing-up with my parents and male siblings in Harlow in the late 1950s.

Although there were no girls' toys in my family home when I was young, I knew that if there had been and I had been caught playing with them, my dad would have stopped me and got the boxing gloves out immediately, taking over the back garden as an emergency rough and tumble boys only play area to stop any of his lads turning into poofs. There would be no girlie boys in his house - or garden, for that matter. By contrast, my mum's friend had three girls and one boy. The girls always played with his toys without being told off for it, and Carol's daughter, Sophie, by her second partner, Jackie, rode a bike like a boy, climbed trees, and preferred playing football to girls' traditional competitive sports: Sophie was arsenal's number one fan, which I recalled, again with laughter in my voice.

Is there an increase in the number of people suffering from gender identity disorders? If there is, how much of what causes it is biological, how much of it is environmental, and how much of it is cultural?

Are males becoming more feminine and females becoming more masculine?

"There are so many young men around now who express their masculinity in very feminine ways, putting being in a steady relationship, getting married, or living with a partner first, even though in their own minds they're unquestionably male and pass as male in their overall appearance and behaviour. The same goes for females. I see a lot of young women looking and behaving in ways that are more masculine than feminine, putting independence, learning new skills, and adventure first, even though in their own minds they're unquestionably female and pass as female in their overall appearance and behaviour.

It's also been suggested that female shapes are becoming androgynous compared with the curvaceousness of earlier generations.

As a general picture, the roles of women and men in our society have become blurred and in some cases reversed, the successful working woman and her male partner or spouse/housekeeper - a role that includes part-time childcare - being a strong example of the latter.

I believe it's true that women are becoming more independent; more likely to want to learn new skills, and travel, sometimes to dangerous, challenging places, while men are tending to look for steady relationships because they need someone to rely on who they can settle down with?

I've even heard that some career women are using testosterone implants which release the male sex hormone into their bloodstream, increasing their energy levels, self-confidence, self-esteem and performance in the workplace. This is so they can compete with the tougher, competitive type of male. Skin patches that also release the hormone into the bloodstream can, apparently, improve a woman's sex drive."

"What you might call an extreme lifestyle choice," these days, we're encouraged to 'be ourselves', within reason. The range of appearances and behaviours that are acceptable to many of us is increasing. This, in turn, has widened the range of gender and sexual identity permutations in our society. Some of these are real examples of how blurred the traditional male and female role boundaries have become. In fact, in the last couple of decades, the boundaries of what's morally acceptable to many of us have been pushed back a lot further.

If there is a gradual feminisation of men and masculinisation of women, surely this has serious implications for the future of humanity? Along with the rise in sexually transmitted diseases - particularly in young people - notably chlamydia, which threatens fertility in both sexes, and AIDS, which threatens everyone's lives, and other causative factors reducing the fertility of young men and women, there may come a time when humanity is struggling to survive."

Notes

1 Chromosomes are thread-like structures that play a vital part in transmitting the characteristics we inherit from our parents. The genome is all of the heritable genetic material in the chromosomes, taken as a whole. The human genome contains around 24,000 genes, each one having a fixed position on a chromosome. The term 'genome out', which was used on a television programme, we take to mean removing particular unwanted inherited characteristics from the human genome: in other words - as we see it without any scientific knowledge in this area - an advanced form of genetic engineering.

2 As an embryo is forming, stem cells are life-giving cells that develop into body parts such as skin cells, blood cells, heart muscle cells, and so on. These can be stored and used later in life to treat strokes, cancer, diabetes, spinal cord injuries, Parkinson's, Hodgkin's, and Alzheimer's disease, and other illnesses and conditions.

3 At Erasmus University in Rotterdam, scientists measured levels of polychlorinated biphenyls, and dioxins, in the blood of 207 mothers in their final month of pregnancy. Levels of PCBs were also measured in the umbilical blood at the time of birth, and in breast milk two weeks after birth, to find out the amount each developing foetus was exposed to in the womb. The researchers asked parents to record the details of their children's play patterns up to the age of seven years.

The behaviour described is the result of this research. It was also found that dioxins produced more feminine play in both the boys and the girls of the mothers tested. 'New gender-bending poison fear for young'. Daily Mail, Monday, October 21, 2002.

4 Pre-natal hormonal function as an indication of pre-natal hormonal gender looks at how oestrogen and progesterone is working in females and testosterone is working in males before birth. You will remember our earlier reference to Doctor Russell Reid suggesting a surge of progesterone or testosterone in the womb being, in the case of the progesterone surge, the possible trigger of a male foetus becoming a little boy who from

a very early age feels and thinks like a little girl, and in the case of the testosterone surge the female foetus becoming a little girl who from a very early age feels and thinks like a little girl.

5 See also "Mothers' hormones turn girls to tomboys", by David Derbyshire, The Daily Telegraph of Monday, 4 June, 2001, which refers to the Avon Longitudinal Study of Parents and Children, led by Professor Melissa Hines.

Chapter Twenty-seven

This book traces the unique life of "Carol Royce" me as I am now. It tells a story that has serious implications for all of us.

At between four and six years old, a little boy began to feel and think like a little girl. From everyone else's point of view, what this little boy felt and thought like was wrong; by all appearances, I was a boy. Could this inner conflict have been caused by either a chromosomal irregularity, a freak surge of the female hormone progesterone whilst I was still a foetus in my mother's womb - or both? Then, after I was born, I might have learned bits of feminine behaviour from my mother and other females around me, and internalised these so they became part of my growing sense of self.

I was actually she. Whichever way we look at this conundrum, there is no definite answer as to what caused my gender dysphoria. My way of being something I`m not. The often complex and paradoxical nature of humanity today.

Has human life got too complicated? It seems to me that we are searching constantly for new pleasures and new ways of being, sometimes to escape boredom, sometimes pain, and sometimes just general unhappiness.

Will we eventually have to redefine what it is to be human? Before I wrote this book, I had assumed that an important condition of being human was to have some form of sexual identity, be it male, female, or 'intersex'. Yet some people do not even want to be recognised as male, female, or any sex?

Professor Oliver Sacks, an American neuropsychiatrist, wrote the following passage, which is a short extract from his book, 'Awakenings'4:

For all of us have a basic, intuitive feeling that once we were whole and well; at ease, at peace, at home in the world; totally united with the grounds of our being; and that then we lost this primal, happy, innocent state, and fell into our present sickness and suffering. We had something of infinite beauty and preciousness - and we lost it; we spend our lives searching for what we have lost; and one day, perhaps, we will suddenly find it.

When I think back about what l have been through, I am thankful for the love I have from my family and friends, and my appreciation of the natural world.

My critics told me I should have been stronger and put up with my condition. To them it seems I have no interest in achieving a higher spiritual state to earn myself a place in heaven or in some long-awaited paradise on earth. But I am not looking for sympathy. My inner conflict often led me to do selfish things, and I accept responsibility for that.

I hope this book is written in a way that makes a difficult subject less mysterious and threatening. To try to make the concept of gender dysphoria clearer and seen as one of many variations of human existence has been a real challenge.

It is also about life and the human condition in a post-modern, technological world of increasing and accelerating human activity, bringing into focus our need to consider very carefully the repercussions of what is happening to our environment, and, indeed, what is happening to us.

Maybe the globalised economy, and the self-absorbed, consumerised individual - for whom the acquisition of money, status, and power seems to be the main purpose in life - dominating our culture, turning our minds away from the important issues of protecting our environment and our humanity which we need to do to survive?

For me and others' struggling to overcome their challenging individual differences, we hold the view that human nature does exist and that its essence is an innate need for survival that in those who function adequately drives a desire for social cooperation, justice, altruism, inner peace, and so on.

By accepting my way of being - encountering me as an individual rather than a patient who has been diagnosed with gender dysphoria - a friend of mine was able to empathise with my need to realign my body so that it was in harmony with my inner self. He went on, "Here was a person struggling to adapt and survive. I got a sense of what it felt like to be her. As I shared in her pain, I became aware that what we were experiencing was the quality of being human."

"Perhaps this is where to stop,?"

"Through writing this book I've come to realise how complicated we humans are."

There has been a real change in me since I first began writing "The reality of my life".

I'm so laid back, I'm dangerous,

This book is a selfish note on my life covering 58yrs and I could not see any other way to write how I was.

I have shortened this book taking out a lot of medical information but have left the bibliography at the end of the book for anyone who is interested in reading material on the subject.

Chapter twenty - eight

Just a few lines to bring my life up to date.

May 2008. I had a brain bleed which has made life quite a struggle over the last year. I have found that my way of life has been turned upside down, and have been relying on other people to do shopping and housework for me. Being someone who needs to control everything it has not been easy for the last 6 months. It should be easy having people doing everything for you but I`m afraid in my mind this is not the case. Living with two bombs left in my head makes everything uncertain knowing they could leak anytime, makes you think. Its funny really knowing your life is over, when I remember what I used to do, I am now ready for a nervous breakdown.

("Just joking.") Trying hard to keep everything as normal as possible is taking its toll on me. I'm good for about one hour in the morning then it goes down hill and I can sleep for England.

The people that helped me were the best, I ended up at three hospitals and I was the worst patient anybody could have to look after, I did not intend to be but I thought everyone was trying to harm me. If that's not being a little bit paranoid, well what can I say. The best place for me was The Colman Hospital in Norwich at least they let me do things that helped me. I used to do a lot of exercise to try and get my legs working again, (

mostly doing exercise bike work) for me being able to get up was good. It was the worst thing to have to stay in bed all the time like I did at the Norfolk and Norwich hospital and at Attenbrooks hospital. It's all me me again I'm very predictable really I seem to always swing life on itself instead of being great full.I have decided to do a home course probably a course on psychology, this I find fascinating and believe this might get my brain working again. Its funny how things that don`t mean much to me goes straight out my brain, I have no concentration at all at this point in my life. I still do my befriending when I can as this gets me out and stops me being lazy. I have started a web page to help others who feel they have gender troubles like I found myself in. My help comes free and hopefully we can help one person not to have to go through life's course the same way as myself.

I will leave it here as I can ramble on for England.

Notes

1.From my understanding of what I have read on the subject of gender dysphoria, at some point between conception and birth an irregularity may occur which causes a sexual differentiation that is vague. Such ambiguity can result in strange variations in the plotting of the shape the sex chromosomes will take: variations such as X, XXX, XXY, XYY, XXXY, X/XY, X/XX, XY/XYY, and so on, instead of XX 'female' or XY 'male'.

1.. I note that it is known that in general, these irregularities cause visible physical changes or effects following birth, or when the individual reaches sexual maturity.

2.. We refer again to Doctor Russell Reid's suggestion of a pre-natal endocrinal stimulus influencing the developing thalamus of the foetal brain possibly creating the permanent effect of an inner sex differentiation, which might have happened to Carol and so many others who suffer and have suffered from gender dysphoria.

3.. I See again The Daily Telegraph of Monday, 4 June, 2001 "Mothers' hormones turn girls to tomboys", by David Derbyshire, which refers to the Avon Longitudinal Study of Parents and Children, led by Professor Melissa Hines.

4.. Sacks, Oliver, 'Awakenings'.

Bibliography

Allen, Clifford, A textbook of psychosexual disorders, Oxford, 1986

Allgeier, Elizabeth R., and McCormick, Naomi B., Changing boundaries:Gender roles and sexual behaviour., Palo Alto: Mayfield, 1983

Archer and Lloyd, Sex and gender, Cambridge University Press (Penguin Books), 1985

Benjamin, Harry, The Transsexual phenomenon, Julian Press, New York, 1966

Bonhoeffer, D, Ethics, SCM, 1955

Christie, Elan Cane, 1999 (Gender neutrality)

Cook, C, The moral maze, SPCK, 1983

Cossey, Caroline, My story, Faber

Cossey, Caroline, Tula, I am a woman

Cowell, Roberta, Roberta Cowell's story, Heinemann, 1954

Crawley, E, The mystic rose, Spring books, 1965

Derbyshire, David, "Mothers' hormones turn girls to tomboys",. The Daily Telegraph, Monday, 4 June, 2001.

De Savitch, E. Homosexuality and transsexuality, Heinemann, 1958

Douce, Pasteur J., La question transexuelle, Lumiere et Justice, 1986

Doyle, James A., The male experience, Dubuque, Iowa, William C. Brown, 1983

Fallowell, Duncan, and Ashley, April, April Ashley's odyssey, Jonathan Cape, London, 1982

Fienbloom, D. Transvestites and transsexuals, Delta

Foster, Jeanette, Sex variant women in literature, Muller, 1958

Frazer, J.G., The golden bough, Macmillan, 1907

Getsul, Imji, An English Buddhist in a Tibetan monastery, Lobzang Jivaka, Routledge, 1962

Goffman, Erving, Stigma. Notes on the management of spoiled identity, Pelican

Gooren, L.J.G. and Eklund P., Sexual dimorphism and Transsexuality, clinical observations. In: De Vries, G.J. et al (Eds): Progress in brain research, 61, 399-401, Amsterdam, Elsevier

Green, Richard, Sexual identity conflict, Duckworth, 1974

Green, Richard, Transsexualism and sex reassignment, John Hopkins Press, USA, 1969

Gross, Alan E., "The male role and heterosexual behaviour", in Journal of social issues, 34(1), 87-107

Hall, Radclyffe, The well of loneliness, Corgi, 1974

Harrington, John, Male and female identity, Wiley, New York, 1972

Hodgkinson, Liz, Bodyshock, Columbus

Holden, Ethics in the new testament, T & R Clarke, 1992

Holt, Lunde et al, Fundamentals of human sexuality

Hyde, Janet S., Half the human experience: The psychology of women (3rd ed.), Lexington, Mass.: Heath, 1985

Hyde, Janet S., Understanding human sexuality, fourth edition, McGraw-Hill, 1990

Issues in human sexuality, Church House Publications,

1997

Jay, Monica, For the love of a transvestite, Caliban Books, 1986

Keane, Dillie (mostly), Fascinating who? Fascinating Aida: The Anatomy of a group on the crest of a ripple, Elm Tree, 1986

Laub, Donald, MD, "Gender dysphoria syndrome: proceeding of the second interdisciplinary symposium", and Gandy, Patrick, MS, eds, Sanford University, 1977

Law and sexuality, Various authors, Grassroots

Lloyd, Stephenie Anne, Stephenie's a girl in a million, Ebury Press

Lodge, David, "Sense and Sensibility", The Guardian, 2 November 2002.

Lundstrom, Bengdt, Gender dysphoria, Gothenberg press, 1981

Macquarrie et al (ed), New dictionary of Christian ethics, SCM, 1986

Money, J. and Ehrhardt, Anke, Man and woman, boy and girl, Baltimore, USA John Hopkins Press, USA, 1972

Money, J. Sexual signatures, Harrup, 1967

Morris, Jan, Conundrum, Penguin

Oates, Jennifer M., Dacakis, Georgia., "Speech pathology considerations in themanagement of transsexualism - a review." School of Communication Disorders, Lincoln Institute of Health Sciences. British Journal of Disorders of Communication 1983 vol.18 no.3. pp 139-151.

Personal origins, Church House Publications, 1996

Pickuth D., Brandt S., Neumann K., Berghaus A.,

Raymond, Janice, The transsexual empire, Woman's Press

Sacks, Oliver, Awakening, Picador, 1991

Scheper-Hughes, Nancy and Lovell., "Breaking the circuit of social control: lessons in public psychiatry from Italy and Franco Basagia", in Soc.

Sci. Med. Vol.23. No2, pp. 159-178, Pergamon Journals Ltd. 1986

1 Department of Anthropology, University of California, Berkely, CA 94720,U.S.A.

2 New York State Psychiatric Institute, 722 west 168th Street, New York, NY10032, U.S.A.

Somerset, Georgina, A girl called Georgina, The Book Guild Limited

Spielmann R.P. and Heywang-Kobrunner, "Spiral computed tomography before and after cricothyroid approximation", S.H. Department of Diagnostic Radiology, Martin-Luther-University, Faculty of Medicine, Halle/Saale, Germany. Clinical Otolaryngologist 2000. 25. pp 311-314.

Stoller, R. Sex and gender, Hogarth

Stoller, R. The transsexual experiment, Hogarth

Stuart, Kim, The universal dilemma, Metamorphosis Press, 1983

Utton, Tim, "New gender-bending poison fear for young", The Daily Mail, Monday October 21, 2002, p.29.

Vardy & Grosch, The puzzle of ethics, Fortress, 1994

Vasey, M, Strangers and friends, Hodder, 1995

Wallinder, Jan, Transsexualism, Gothenberg University Press, 1967

Wilson, Colin, "Are some people born criminal?" The Daily Mail, Friday 2nd August, 2002.

Wilson, Glenn, ed, Variant sexuality - Research and Theory, Croom Helm, 1987

Woodhouse, Annie, Fantastic women: Sex, gender and transvestism, Macmillan, London, 1989

About the Author

My name is Carol Royce age 59yrs and retired. I spent a large part of my life in the wrong Gender, known as a sufferer of Gender disorder or Gender Dysphoria. I hate both terms but that is what people like me are called by the medical Doctors which help. Having now undergone realignment surgery to correct myself I thought I would share my life.

01263 515229
17-19 WATT ST.